Ex Libris

Leslie Miscampbell Frost

CASES IN COURT

By the same Author

THE AUTOBIOGRAPHY OF SIR PATRICK HASTINGS

SIR PATRICK HASTINGS, K.C.

CASES IN COURT

BY

PATRICK HASTINGS, K.C.

WILLIAM HEINEMANN LTD
MELBOURNE :: LONDON :: TORONTO

PR6015 .A775.C3

FIRST PUBLISHED NOVEMBER 1949
REPRINTED JANUARY, MAY 1950

PRINTED IN GREAT BRITAIN
AT THE WINDMILL PRESS
KINGSWOOD, SURREY

Dedicated
to the Middle Temple,
and to the memory of the late
Theobald Mathew, Esq.

Author's Note

A FEW of these reminiscences, in a slightly different form, have been published elsewhere. Inasmuch as this volume is intended to be a record of my more memorable cases, they cannot very well be omitted.

Contents

	Memories	ix
I	The End of a Long Road	1
II	Libel and Slander	22
	A Princess's Libel Action	26
	The End of Robert Sievier	40
	The Laski Case	55
	The Trainer and the Jockey Club	72
	The Case of the Talking Mongoose	84
	The Stockbroker and the Yo-Yo	100
III	Miscellaneous	107
	The Case of the English Member of Parliament	114
	The Case of the Diamond Syndicate	129
	The Princess from St. Petersburg	145
	The Tragedy of the Kentish Farmer	154
	The Case of the Illuminating Dot	166
	The Case of the Three Sisters	181
	The Courtauld Arbitration	195
IV	The Central Criminal Court	208
	The Case of the Royal Mail	213
	The Gambler's Story	229
	The Lost Pearls	236
V	Murder	244
	The Case of the Blazing Car	249
	The Trial of Mrs. Barney	263
	The Case of the Polish Officer	279
	The Case of the Hooded Man	292
	The Vaquier Case	305
VI	Ave atque Vale	326
	Index	339

Illustrations

Sir Patrick Hastings, K.C.   *frontispiece*

The Prince and Princess Youssupoff at the Time of the Trial
The Prince and Princess Youssupoff Study "Stills" of the Film
A Scene from the Film "Rasputin the Mad Monk"   *at pages* 32–33

Mr. "Bob" Sievier on Newmarket Race-course   *facing page* 42

Sir Patrick Hastings Walks to the Law Courts   *facing page* 160

Lord Kylsant with the Earl of Coventry Leaves for the Summing up   *facing page* 224

Alfred Rouse   *facing page* 256

Mrs. Barney in Her Earlier Days
Mr. Scott Stephens who was Found Shot in Mrs. Barney's House
Mrs. Barney after her Acquittal   *at pages* 272–273

Jean Pierre Vaquier Leaving the Court   *facing page* 320

Memories

LIFE takes a very long time, but there is no possible excuse for anyone who finds it dull. To be a bore may be a misfortune for which others will be compelled to suffer, but to confess to boredom should be made a criminal offence. To anyone who is fortunate enough to be obliged to earn his own living and who is wise enough to select an occupation that he enjoys, there will be no time for boredom; such a state of mind can exist only in a person who is engaged, either in doing nothing, or else in doing something which is not and never was worth doing at all. None but a fool tries to advise another in his choice of a profession; each must decide for himself, and the decision is far from easy. It may have to last him all his life. It may even be better to starve at work you love rather than to earn all the money in the world at work you hate.

I have been very fortunate. Nearly half a century ago I chose to be a member of what is perhaps the greatest profession in the world, and during all that time I cannot look back upon one moment when I was bored. I cannot remember one day which was not tinged with some element of adventure, either of hope or disappointment, of failure or achievement. I entered the Middle Temple filled with the most glorious anticipation; I was not disappointed. It would be indeed an ungrateful spirit that could find no word of gratitude for the memories that he has left behind, and no word of encouragement for all who will come after him.

So long as civilisation continues, English justice will remain the admiration of the world, and English justice could never have reached the position which it now enjoys without the independence and above all the inflexible honesty of the English Bar. No statute controls its activities; it knows no master but itself; it knows no rules except those handed down by centuries of tradition, and those rules are very simple: to the client whom he represents an advocate owes a duty to act with fearless independence; to the Court before whom he appears he owes the duty of complete and absolute honesty in all that he says and does. If he fails in either of those duties he will sink into well-deserved oblivion; if he maintains the tradition which he has inherited he will have earned his place upon an honoured roll.

In years to come will the Bar still occupy the rich position that it now enjoys? Will it still offer to young men of limitless enthusiasm an opportunity to fulfil their high hopes and ambitions? Personally I think it will. In a world temporarily torn by new ideals and great uncertainties, it is only natural that people should grope blindly for some change in their conditions, but there is one thing that will never change, and that is the English sense of justice. With all its possible defects, English justice is the best thing that is left to us. If I could give one word of advice to the great minds who will be chosen to control our destinies, I would suggest to them that, with all the changes they will be called to make, they should leave our Law alone.

Minor improvements and reforms will develop automatically and if they do not do much good, at any rate they will not do much harm. But fundamentally our Law is built on a sound foundation. Let it remain there.

A little more than 100 years ago men were hanged for stealing sheep, and lesser felons were transported beyond the seas. These unpleasant happenings called for great reforms, it was a period of great reforms; everybody decided to reform something; novelists declaimed passionately against injustice; legal anachronisms were exposed, and the whole practice of the law was overhauled. Most of the changes were for the public good and some of them were long overdue; it is only within the last century that a prisoner has been permitted to give evidence upon his own behalf, in consequence of which permission many a murderer has stepped joyfully into the witness box and by his own eloquence has promptly hanged himself. No doubt he is among the first to appreciate the improvement in our legal system.

For my part, the greatest change that I have noticed during the past forty years lies amongst members of my own profession. Ponderous oratory, once so popular, and based undoubtedly upon Cicero's orations, has completely disappeared. Just as Gerald du Maurier sounded the death knell of the old-time school of thunderous declamation from the stage, so Edward Carson put an end to forensic platitudes and passionate but irrelevant perorations from the Bar. That such a change is an improvement no wearied juryman would deny. Yet there is one change that has been forced upon us, and it comes not from within the legal system but from without: the public are beginning to lose interest in the Law. Important as it is that justice should be done, and still more so that justice should appear plainly to be done, the most important element of all is that the Law should appear to everyone as their one protector against most if not all their social ills. And how can that be made apparent unless a true picture of its working can be brought before their eyes!

Not very long ago, every trial of the slightest interest was reported in the public Press. Morning papers had a page devoted to Law reports; evening papers displayed posters announcing every detail of so-called important trials and possibly even of the persons mainly concerned; there were murder cases, libel cases, cases about old ladies disputing over garden walls, even breach of promise cases. Every tribulation known to human life was brought before us and its appropriate remedy displayed. When the Courts were closed, the papers were half empty, and people knew that the silly season had arrived; something was missing from their daily lives. And how right they were. There are few things more enthralling than a trial in the Law Courts. However trivial or unimportant may be the issues, to the parties immediately concerned they are vital, and, above all the human troubles that are brought to light, give, perhaps if only for posterity, a real picture of the times at which the trials took place. After all, the libel action of to-day would probably have been a duel a hundred years ago. Now there is a world shortage of all those things to which we have grown accustomed: newsprint is in short supply; newspapers have been cut down, and law reports have practically disappeared. The public hears no longer of the working of its Courts, so its interest in Law has gone. The pictures of a justice working continually to remedy human wrongs and to sustain human endeavour are no longer placed before them; all that is left behind are memories. That must be my excuse for attempting to record some memories of my own.

It should be so easy for a lawyer to call upon his own recollection, and to select at will those incidents and cases which have most appealed to him; but it is not. Time has blurred the picture; even the great figures of his own profession seem to have become merged into one comprehensive whole, and all that he remembers of them is a great friendship and a real affection. The most unlikely faces may stand out most clearly; great reputations tend to disappear, while a well-timed jest may last for ever. A bishop in his endeavours to persuade a friend of mine to cross-examine a half-witted curate, urged that the case was unimportant and that the remuneration should be correspondingly low. "My dear

Bishop," was the reply, "you do not appreciate the deadly risk that you're asking me to run in cross-examining this Reverend gentleman. He says that he is the Almighty. Now you don't believe him and nor do I. But supposing he is right?" Frivolity towards a bishop may not be the attribute of a great lawyer, but what is lost in learning may well be balanced by a twinkling eye.

If from the many figures that I know so well there is one who stands out among them all, it is one who was known to few people outside his own profession, but loved by everyone within it; "a fellow of infinite jest" with a mind that saw humour in everything, and a heart that held sympathy for everyone. I can see him now strolling through his beloved Temple, where he loved to saunter, perhaps arm-in-arm with a distinguished judge, commiserating with him upon the stupidity of the junior Bar, or else sympathising with a member of the selfsame Bar upon the stupidity of judges. No one was too highly placed to be safe from criticism, no one was too lowly for his friendship and encouragement; many a pompous silk has been chastened and subdued by his caustic comments; many a quivering junior has been uplifted by his kindly smile. He knew when sorrow was so real that it could best be shared in silence; when troubles were so imaginary that they could best be laughed away. He had done both to me. "My dear Pat," he once greeted me, "you look harassed and depressed. Doubtless you must have heard of the conflagration in the chambers of Spitting Joe." Spitting Joe was a member of the Bar gifted with great enthusiasm but defective teeth, so much so that his opponents were invariably bespattered with moisture when he addressed them. "But be of good cheer. This danger is past. Spitting Joe himself was quickly on the scene, and with a few well-chosen words rapidly extinguished the flames." Perhaps Theo Mathew did not achieve the great success of others I could name, but then he did not want success; he was a glorious companion, and will be remembered long after many of his more famous contemporaries are forgotten.

To me he will remain for ever as a living picture of all I have loved best at the Bar.

If it is not the greatest advocates who recur most clearly to my mind, it is not necessarily the most important cases that can be brought back to light. Many are too secret or too intimate; many are too sad and might cause pain if they were revived. All these must remain for ever locked away. Moreover, purely forensic cases are too dreary and long legal arguments too dull. What is left? Just pictures. In the following pages I have tried to reproduce some trials as I remember them; not photographic pictures—indeed some remembered cross-examinations are merely an attempt to reconvey the scenes, and not the actual words employed—but pictures of the litigants themselves, just ordinary human beings seeking redress against their wrongs, real or imaginary; men and women struggling to protect their reputations and perhaps their lives. As memories have they been written; as such may they be judged.

CHAPTER I

The End of a Long Road

I SAT back in my seat in the Lord Chief Justice's Court and I knew that I should never see that Court again. Nobody except myself was aware that this had been my last appearance in any Court. Why should they? Everyone has to make his own decision, and those decisions are far better made alone. I could not very well complain. I had enjoyed a long innings, and it was quite time to make way for younger men. Fortune had not been unkind to me. I had climbed up a long steep road, and had managed to achieve a fair measure of success, and now was the time to go. After all, it is better to leave from the top of the hill than to wait until you begin to slip down the other side.

I looked round the Court that I had loved so well. It seemed precisely the same as it had seemed upon the day I entered it for the first time so many years ago. The faces were different, that was the only change; all the old ones had gone. I suppose I ought to have seen the ghosts of old friends, but I did not; the years had been too happy to leave ghosts behind, but I permitted myself the luxury of memories. The Court was full of memories. I had seen well-known men and women fighting out their life stories within those walls; I had taken part in stories of all kinds—tragic stories, pathetic stories, foolish stories, I had known them all. If only I could bring them back to life. And there were other stories of no interest to anyone except myself, but to me of the greatest interest of all, stories of very small and unimportant cases which are the only ones a young man should ever know. Memories of those little cases began to crowd back upon me, memories of the time when each case was so vitally important and left a footmark on the road which I had chosen, when each victory was perhaps a further step in my long climb up the hill. Their details may be forgotten but their memory will last with me for ever.

The associate had just discharged the jury, the last jury who would ever be compelled to suffer from my oratory, and he was calling the next case. A very young barrister rose timorously in his place; he was almost a boy. He was shaking in every limb; his hands were scarcely able to untie the tape which bound his brief; his voice was cracked with nervousness; it was obviously his first case. He was starting off for himself upon the long and winding road that I had left behind. But he was in the wrong place. I could have warned him that the Lord Chief Justice's Court is not the place in which to learn his work. Probably some kind friend or relation had hoped to give the boy a chance; but the kindness had been misconceived. He would have to begin at the very bottom, probably by devilling for someone else, in a case that did not matter, in a Court he could not find; no friends could help him, the patronage of kind relations is merely transitory, his future must depend upon strangers who will have heard him floundering through the morass of his ignorance and indecision until at last they come to the conclusion that the boy begins to look as though he is going to be some good.

I had begun my legal life by devilling, that wonderful system by which a young man works for someone else at someone else's expense. The first brief entrusted to me was not very important; I remember that it was marked with the magnificent fee of one guinea, and consisted of two sheets of foolscap. The learned lawyer who had been retained upon this epoch-making litigation and who was too busy to attend to it must have been more industrious than I could ever hope to be, because he had prepared himself with a series of monumental notes: there were notes for opening his case, and notes for cross-examining the plaintiff. I read them with amazement. To this day I can remember the first line of his notes for cross-examination written in his own handwriting. "Now witness, let me see if I can understand your case." Why he should have thought it necessary to record so early in the proceedings that he did not know what the case was about, I could not understand, but I am sure it must have betokened great legal learning, because not very many years later this very gentleman was appointed a County Court Judge. For a long time I devilled without ceasing, struggling to overcome my ignorance, and hoping against hope that some unknown but misguided solicitor's clerk might imagine that I was going to be some good. And then at last the moment came. A stranger spoke to me as I left the Court. "Young man," he said, "you managed to put up a damned good fight." That night he left at my chambers a small brief of my own.

At that time motor-cars were not so universal as they are to-day, and there were at least some horse-drawn vans upon the streets; there were also tram-lines in the southern parts of London, many of which, after years of service, were projecting slightly above depressions in the roadway. As the period of usefulness of vans diminished, so the occasions increased in which aged and decrepit vans managed to catch their wheels in projecting tram-lines, as a result of which the wheels came off and the van suffered partial or even total collapse. Even the van horses suffered surprisingly from these occurrences, and inasmuch as van horses at that time were somewhat at a premium, insurance companies began to feel the strain. These accidents were too frequent to be ignored, the claims must be disputed, and that meant a trial in Court. My first days as an advocate were passed in an atmosphere of decrepit vans, and still more decrepit horses.

The opportunities for advocacy in its highest sense were surprisingly small. To cross-examine a van driver whose van has collapsed in the street, in the hope of establishing that his wheel did not come off, is a somewhat hopeless task for a beginner. I decided to concentrate upon the vans themselves. I learned a great deal about vans, and also about the ingenuity of people who desired to make claims upon insurance companies. I heard of vans, obviously upon their last legs, which were driven through the highways of southern London, apparently looking for an accommodating projection in a tram-line; I even came across vans which were let out for that purpose, although when the accident occurred and the case came into Court, the value of the relic seemed out of all proportion to its decrepitude. The horses themselves were also a useful object of enquiry, and there I was greatly helped by a very clever veterinary surgeon whose name was John Coleman, and who was amongst other things the veterinary surgeon to Sandown Park Race Course. He owned a racehorse of his own named Submit, a horse that had won a famous race, and had then broken down and become useless. Coleman patched him up, and although as a result his bandaged legs looked like something in a pantomime, he won many races on them. Generally the old horse would amble along, a hundred yards behind his field, and then on his next outing would surprise everyone by winning with the greatest ease; it was all a question of how he happened to be feeling. Coleman once asked me if I ever backed horses, and when I told him that I did not, he said: "Quite right. It's a mug's game. Never back a horse unless I tell you to". He told me to back Submit twice and each time it won. I once backed it without awaiting Coleman's good advice, and the old horse was still plodding round the course when the next race had started. Coleman was a past master at persuading a judge as to the true value of a decrepit horse. There was also a gentleman whose name I forget, who was equally expert in the matter of obsolete vans, and between the three of us we managed to reduce the claims until there came a time when the game was hardly worth the candle. I felt I was rapidly becoming a past master in defective tram-lines. And then out of the blue came good news. I was promoted to the more important task of dealing with old ladies who fell off omnibuses.

At that time omnibuses were not so perfect as they are to-day. Sometimes they would not start; sometimes they started with such enthusiasm that old ladies fell off the platform at the back. Sometimes no doubt the accident was genuine, and the passenger was genuinely injured, but there came a time when it began to be appreciated that such misfortunes could be extremely profitable. Omnibus companies would far rather pay than fight and unscrupulous individuals began to take advantage of that tendency. What had once been a misfortune became a habit. Old ladies began to fall off omnibuses with surprising regularity; in fact some old ladies made a profession of so doing. The procedure in those cases became almost standardised. At the very moment that the conductor rang his bell an old lady would have her foot up on the step; the omnibus would start upon its way, either with or without a jerk, causing the old lady to subside into the gutter. There she would lie, moaning with pain, until the arrival of an ambulance, in which she would be removed to hospital. A careful medical examination would discover no possible reason for her detention and she would be advised to go home. Thereafter followed a most curious sequence of events. Upon leaving the hospital she would be accosted by an extremely sympathetic bystander, who would place her tenderly in a cab and accompany her, not to her home, but to the office of an even more sympathetic solicitor. What happened between them could of course only be a matter for surmise, but when next heard of the old lady was found to be under the care of an eminent medical man who had discovered that the accident had caused her to be suffering from a serious complaint which he diagnosed as "traumatic neurasthenia". This remarkable form of illness had sprung into notoriety very much at the same time as motor omnibuses had appeared upon the streets. It possessed certain curious features. There were no outward and visible signs of its existence, indeed its symptoms were both undiscoverable and indisputable, and consisted of headache, nervousness, sleeplessness, and above all inability to do any work. The treatment was equally mysterious, requiring as it did repeated visits to a specialist, undertaken in the most expensive manner, large expenditure upon chemists, and a curious form of diet known as "extra nourishment", which consisted of enormous quantities of eggs, butter, beef tea, with occasional doses of the best brandy, all of which tended very largely to increase the bill presented to the omnibus company. It is scarcely surprising that there came a time when the companies decided that these bills must be disputed, and there arose a flood of litigation, in which the central figures were these unhappy ladies and their traumatic neurasthenia. It was into this branch of legal activities that I had been promoted.

It very soon became apparent to me that, just as in the case of the decrepit vans, these cases were mainly bare-faced frauds; indeed I began to fear that my future life would consist in fighting frauds. There was another similarity between the old ladies and the vans; it was practically impossible to prove, either by cross-examination or otherwise, that the accident had not happened. When an old lady is seen by a sympathetic crowd to be lying groaning in a gutter, it is a hopeless task to suggest that she had placed herself there of own accord, unless—and here was the one spark of hope—unless there were such gross exaggeration in her claim that her whole conduct became suspect, and a jury might be persuaded to disbelieve every word she said. That was the course it was decided to adopt. The best case available was to be chosen and a concerted attack was to be made upon every item of the plaintiff's claim, and even upon the persons who had assisted her to make it, in the hope that the whole fraud might be exposed. I was delighted. It was the very chance I had been waiting for; I could only hope that a good case might be brought to me to fight; and a good case came along.

It was the usual story. The old lady; the visit to the solicitor; the appearance of the specialist with his traumatic neurasthenia and the extra nourishment, and all the usual features, only in this case they were particularly pronounced; the specialist himself was a trifle open to suspicion. He was a somewhat peculiar specialist; he had frequently been known to attend old ladies in precisely similar circumstances, and that no doubt was the reason why he was able to diagnose traumatic neurasthenia when no other medical man was able to find anything wrong with her whatever. He undoubtedly possessed an address in Harley Street, although he seldom occupied his room, which was apparently in the basement, and he was generally to be found at the address where he carried on his general practice in a back street in Walworth. As the injured lady herself lived in the neighbourhood of Walworth, it was thought to be surprising that she should have preferred to pay two guineas apiece for her many visits to Harley Street, rather than the more modest fee presumably charged by the same medical gentleman when occupying his surgery off the Walworth Road. It was decided to make some slight experiments into the habits of the specialist. The office boy employed by my solicitor paid him a visit in his house at Walworth. Being an intelligent young man, he knew all the symptoms of traumatic neurasthenia, having learned them from a perusal of the plaintiff's claim, and he informed the specialist that he was suffering from all of them. The doctor gave him a cursory examination, for which he charged one shilling, and a bottle of medicine, for which he charged an extra threepence, and foretold a quick recovery. In case it should be thought that the extremely moderate charge was due to the obvious youth of the patient, it was decided to send an older visitor on a similar errand, and accordingly an older clerk paid a visit to the Walworth Road. He too was suffering from traumatic neurasthenia and so he not unnaturally received the same attention and strangely enough at the same charge of one shilling together with an extra threepence for the medicine. A still more important patient was thought desirable, and so the managing clerk himself called at the surgery. He was attired in a splendour surpassing that usually enjoyed by managing clerks. He wore a frock coat of surprising elegance, shiny boots, and in his hand he bore a new top hat. In his case the maximum fee would obviously be demanded. It was. For precisely the same treatment, for precisely the same complaint, he was charged two shillings and the medicine cost him sixpence. Armed with this information I awaited the appearance of the specialist with joyful anticipation.

In due course the case came into Court, and the plaintiff was constrained to tell her story. Her faltering progress towards the witness box was somewhat out of keeping with her extremely robust appearance, but once firmly established in the box she displayed every symptom of advanced traumatic neurasthenia; her nerves were shattered, and her memory had gone. Upon that point she was quite determined. She remembered the omnibus starting with a jerk, and after that she remembered no more. She could not remember the name of the friend who took her to the solicitor, or whether that friend had met her for the first time upon the steps of the hospital. Her sufferings had been terrific and were not improving; before the accident she had earned immense sums as a charwoman, but now, alas, she could work no more. It must have been her husband who had paid the large sums charged for medicines, but he had been far too worried to obtain receipts, and as for the extra nourishment, it had been forced upon her.

I thought I observed a tinge of suspicion creeping into the jury's mind, and even the specialist seemed a trifle worried as he stepped into the box. He looked extremely grave; he took a very serious view of the stout lady's condition; traumatic neurasthenia was most difficult to cure, and even more difficult to diagnose. He was not in the least surprised that no other doctor could find any touch of it. I was obliged to screw my courage to its highest point to cross-examine such a distinguished witness. I asked him if he was not accustomed to treat and cure such cases at a shilling a time and threepence for the medicine. The doctor smiled contemptuously; the question was ridiculous. I invited Mr. Thompson to step forward. With a bound the office boy appeared in the well of the Court; in his hand he clasped a bottle of medicine. I asked if Mr. Thompson was a patient suffering from this very serious complaint. The doctor was quite sure that he was not. I am afraid I stated, quite improperly, that as Mr. Thompson had learned his own symptoms from those set out in the Statement of Claim in the present action, he was not likely to be mistaken as to the illness from which he suffered; I asked if he had been cured at the price of one shilling for attendance and threepence for the medicine, and the bottle of medicine was handed up with a request that the doctor should tell us if the medicine was a good cure for traumatic neurasthenia. The doctor was quite unable to say without analysis, and as to the charge of a shilling, he did a great deal of work for charity. That answer seemed to call for the appearance of the clerk. Mr. Smith stepped into the well of the Court, and he too clasped a bottle of medicine in his hand. Had he suffered from precisely the same symptoms and been cured at precisely the same cost, and been presented with precisely the same medicine? The doctor felt affronted by the question and appealed to the judge for protection, but the learned judge was beginning to enjoy himself; he could not stop the cross-examination. The witness was becoming flustered, he could only explain that his patients were sometimes of the poorer class. That was the moment we had been waiting for. He was asked, if he were visited by a wealthy patient, would that patient be charged a proper fee? Of course. The managing clerk rose gravely to his feet. He was a resplendent figure, displaying every evidence of wealth; his frock coat must have been the envy of every onlooker, his boots were immaculate, and in his hand was clasped a glorious top hat. Slowly and almost sadly, he drew from his tail pocket a bottle of the medicine, with which by this time we were all familiar. Here was a wealthy patient who had been cured at the maximum fee of two shillings for the attention and sixpence for the medicine. By this time the Court was hilarious, and when it was pointed out that if the unhappy plaintiff had only been charged at Walworth instead of Harley Street rates, she would have been able to attend the specialist every night and morning for about three years, the onlookers rocked with laughter. Only one more simple calculation was required. If the medicine for which we were being asked to pay had been dispensed by the specialist himself on his usual terms, the plaintiff would have enjoyed enough medicine to have cured the whole of Walworth of traumatic neurasthenia. This obvious exaggeration was sufficient to discredit the whole case, and the jury found in favour of the defendants; the action was dismissed and the plaintiff got nothing. I began to think that my education was approaching completion.

It required one more good experience before I was able to feel that I was justified in daring to take my place in the Court of the Lord Chief Justice, and that experience was not very long delayed. It was a remarkable case, perhaps one of the most remarkable cases of fraud that I have ever known. It arose out of very small beginnings. A workman was engaged in unloading boxes of oranges by means of a crane when a rope broke, and one of the boxes fell on to the pavement. When the workman descended from his crane he was amazed to find a man lying groaning on the kerb. His amazement was the greater because he had not observed any passer-by at the time the accident occurred, indeed he was quite satisfied that there had been no one present. However, the man was found to be suffering from a serious injury to his leg, and in due course he made a claim for damages against the owners of the crane. A careful medical examination seemed to establish that the injury to his leg might well be of long standing and liable to recur, and not only liable but capable of being made to recur by careful and knowledgeable manipulation. It so happened that the insurance company who were called upon to deal with the alleged accident had some previous experience of the claimant. Upon other occasions he had made claims in respect of accidents, one of which had apparently resulted in precisely the same injury to precisely the same leg, and amongst other misfortunes which had befallen him, one in particular had aroused considerable suspicion. He had alleged that while walking along a railway platform, the guard of a train had so negligently waved his flag as to cause an injury to his face, which had apparently resulted in a septic nose. Although the guard in question had indignantly denied the happening of any such occurrence, and no trace of any injury could be discovered at the time the claim was made, it was considered to be more economical to settle a comparative small claim by payment, rather than incur the expense of litigation. Now that a much larger claim was being made, particularly as it related to the same old leg, suspicion was again aroused that the applicant might be engaged upon a regular course of making fraudulent claims with the object of getting money out of underwriters, and it was decided that some enquiries might usefully be made from other insurance companies in order to ascertain if they too were fellow sufferers from the same source. The answers to those enquiries were certainly surprising. The first company approached replied that, shortly before, they had been required to meet a claim, not from the present applicant himself, but from his family. It appeared that his father had suffered a grave misfortune. He was a property owner who had recently acquired some derelict premises in the north of London. He had employed a firm of builders and a firm of decorators to renovate the building; the applicant was proprietor of the decorating firm, and his brother was the builder. Immediately the building and the decorating had been completed, the whole structure was burned to the ground, and the insurance company had been compelled to pay a heavy claim. But that was only a beginning. Information began to pour in from every different insurance company approached. In every case the story was exactly the same. A claim for loss by fire; the father had bought derelict property, the eldest son rebuilt it, and the present applicant did the decorations. Immediately the work was completed the premises were burnt to the ground. There had been a dozen such cases, and in one particular instance the same property had been burnt upon no less than three different occasions. How in the world the family had managed to continue successfully for so long without being found out it was difficult to understand; the only possible explanation could be that they never upon any occasion insured their premises more than once with the same insurance company.

It was unanimously decided that something must be done to curb the activities of this enterprising family, but the question arose as to what steps could possibly be taken. The fire claims had all been paid and there had not been the slightest evidence that any of the fires had been deliberate. To re-open each particular claim would cause enormous expense, and in the end might have resulted in nothing more than very grave suspicion. If only some means could be devised of forcing one member of the family into the witness box so that he could be cross-examined as to his share in what was now believed to have been a wholesale conspiracy! Might not the unexpected incident of a box of oranges falling from a crane be a heaven-sent opportunity? It was not easy to correlate the two events; the fall of oranges in Pimlico might well seem far removed from mysterious fires in distant parts of London, and it might well be difficult to persuade a judge and jury that an enquiry into the former was materially assisted by a prolonged cross-examination into the details of the latter; the cross-examiner would be forced to take some risks. To my great surprise, and to my even greater joy, I was asked to take the risk. The same solicitor who had helped me to cross-examine the peculiar specialist with complete success invited me to try my luck once more, this time in the High Court.

To say that I was overjoyed was to put the matter mildly. At last I had been entrusted with a case which might well end my period of education; no risk would be too great to bring about that much desired result, and I entered upon a study of these fire-raising activities with an enthusiasm which knew no bounds. I learned every detail of every fire until I knew them all by heart; mentally I cross-examined the only witness I should see until I knew every question I should ask, and every answer he must give; I awaited the morning of the trial as eagerly as a youthful bridegroom awaits his wedding day. As the Court assembled I even forgot my nervousness.

I remember that Mr. J. B. Matthews, K.C., a most excellent lawyer, appeared for the plaintiff, and as he told the story of the falling oranges, the whole case appeared a trifling matter; he even expressed a mild surprise that the defendants appeared to dispute that the accident had ever happened, but he said whether or not the defendants intended to persist in that defence no doubt the Court would know when the plaintiff was cross-examined. This trial would always be memorable to me if only for the reason that I learnt for the first time that if you are going to charge a witness with fraud, it is wise that your first question should make that clear. If the witness is dishonest, a violent blow at the outset will very often knock him completely off his carefully prepared pedestal of integrity. I well remember the plaintiff's change of countenance at the opening of his cross-examination.

"I am going to suggest to you that this case is a deliberate fraud, and that for years past you and your family have lived by making fraudulent claims upon insurance companies."

The whole atmosphere in Court changed in a second; the jury seemed to awaken, Mr. J. B. Matthews looked amazed, and the witness glanced miserably round the Court. We had taken the precaution of subpœnaing his father and his brother to attend the trial, and it was quite obvious to me that he was suddenly terrified lest we had discovered something of the family activities. Indeed we had. I began with the first case of which we had detailed knowledge.

"Five years ago, did your father buy a derelict house at this address?" I gave him the address. The witness did not know.

"Did your brother repair that house?"

"I don't know."

"Did you yourself redecorate that house?"

The witness seemed to hesitate.

"Please don't say you don't know, because I hold in my hand your actual bill that was sent in to the insurance company." I handed it up to him. "Is that your bill?"

"It seems to be."

"Is that bill grossly excessive?"

"Certainly not."

"Did any living person ever see what work you had done upon those premises, except your father, your brother, and yourself?"

"I don't know."

"Within two days of your work being completed, was that house burnt to the ground?"

"There was a fire."

"And were your family responsible for those premises being set alight?"

The whole Court was almost in an uproar. The plaintiff's solicitor rose in protest. Mr. Matthews sprang passionately to his feet, trembling with indignation. What possible relevance could there be in such a question? How dare counsel make such an attack upon his client. It was an outrage. The dangerous moment that we knew must come had now arrived. Would the judge allow the questions to continue? If he did not, my great attempt would end in ridicule, but if he did, the chance of a lifetime had arrived. I well remember his hesitation, and the grave warning that he gave me.

"I understand," he said, "that you are alleging that the claim in the present action is a fraud." I bowed assent.

"And you are proposing to attack the plaintiff's character by alleging that he has been a party to earlier frauds?"

"I am, my Lord."

"Very well. I shall not disallow the questions. But I must point out to you that you are incurring a grave responsibility and may be running considerable risk. You understand that to charge a man with being a party to a fraud of this nature is a matter of the utmost gravity." I had come to the Rubicon, and it was as well to go in up to the neck.

"I do, my Lord, and I am going to suggest that this witness and his family have been parties to the same fraud on no less than thirteen previous occasions, in precisely the same manner, and for precisely the same purpose, namely to swindle insurance companies."

After that there was no drawing back. For hours I cross-examined the plaintiff. I put to him house after house—always the same story; the father bought dilapidated premises, the sons restored them, and immediately they were burnt to the ground. What actual share the plaintiff took in the transactions, it is impossible to say. What view a jury takes of any cross-examination it is always impossible to know, but in this case there seemed little doubt. By the time we had arrived at the last case in which the same premises had been burned to the ground on no less than three separate occasions they had heard enough. It only required the evidence of the crane driver to deny that the plaintiff had ever been injured by a falling crate of oranges to enable them to find a verdict in favour of the defendants. The plaintiff left the Court with a suggestion ringing in his ears that the papers in the case might well deserve the consideration of the Director of Public Prosecutions.

That case was heard a good deal more than a quarter of a century ago, but the memory of the trial will remain with me for ever. Before then I was a beginner, floundering through a morass of ignorance and pitfalls, surrounded by all the anxieties and terrors which are born of inexperience; I had not even reached the beginning of the road up which I longed so passionately to climb. In a day, all that changed; I had found my feet. To every professional man, sooner or later, such a moment is certain to occur. For a long time he is in the ranks of those who want; the doctor wants patients; the lawyer wants clients; they all want someone to discover that they are worth consideration for employment. Then, perhaps suddenly, perhaps imperceptibly, the position is reversed; patients or clients begin to want them;

the doctor and the lawyer have left the ranks of those who want, begin to find themselves among the fortunate few who are themselves wanted in their turn. When that happy moment comes they have crossed the Rubicon in their profession, and they can begin to climb the heights which their ambition pointed out to them.

Can it be a matter for surprise that the memory of that case of oranges came back to me as I sat for the last time in the Lord Chief Justice's Court and watched the young beginner floundering through his first attempt to be an advocate? Perhaps some day he will take part in cases that will bring him happy memories. I have had so many. It will amuse me to recall them. Perhaps if my young friend should care to read them, they may amuse him.

CHAPTER II

Libel and Slander

THE joy of reckless driving in motor vehicles is probably responsible for most of the litigation in the Royal Courts of Justice; reckless writing and talking unpleasantly about other people would seem to come next in the order of popularity. Anyone who writes or speaks words of another person calculated to bring that person into "hatred, ridicule or contempt" may find him or herself as a defendant in action for defamation. Undoubtedly the Law applicable to libel and slander was intended primarily to protect character and reputation, and as such was of immense importance in public life; unfortunately the breadth of definition given to legal defamation has resulted in the possibility of actions being brought without any real desire to protect anything. Sometimes, but very rarely, a libel action is of great, indeed vital, importance; more often it is of very little importance; generally it is of no importance at all. A person learns that some other person has said or written something unflattering about him; in a fit of temper he rushes off to a lawyer and asks if the words are capable of defamatory meaning. He is told that they are. He asks if it is necessary to prove that those words have caused him any damage, because he knows quite well they have not; he is told it is not necessary to prove damage; so he decides to bring an action. In the result immense expense is incurred and much time is wasted. The plaintiff gets a few pounds damages, the defendant has to pay the costs, and everybody is dissatisfied. It is scarcely a matter for surprise that in the generality of cases the ordinary public are left under the impression that no one gets any profit out of libel actions except lawyers.

But there is another side to the picture, a side in which, a reputation having been greatly injured, justice is able to give redress for a very grievous wrong. No one who was in Court will ever forget the picture of Princess Youssupoff standing in the witness box forced to tell a story of tragedy and sorrow as the only means of freeing herself from an imputation, the publication of which she had done her utmost to prevent. If ever vindication were required for the righteousness of an action for libel it could be found in her case.

But it is not always the protection of a reputation that results from an action; sometimes it is the reverse. The canvas may be turned around to read the picture of a man fighting almost for his life to maintain a nation-wide popularity against a libel deliberately published in order to drag that popularity into the mud. When Robert Sievier drove gaily down the Strand towards the Royal Courts of Justice he was a hero; when he emerged once more, socially he was a dead man. The law of libel which he had invoked so lightheartedly had proved a boomerang which had almost brought about his ruin.

Actions such as these must leave behind an indelible memory, not only upon the parties themselves but also upon anyone who took any part in them; the exposure of an undeserving public idol may be only a cause for satisfaction; while the privilege of fighting for a most deserving cause may well give rise to pride in being a member of a very great profession.

Some cases which develop into trials of the greatest interest may arise from comparatively small beginnings. When Mr. Laski made a speech upon a cart in the market place at Newark, few people could have anticipated that the result would be a libel action tending to rouse political controversy to a pitch of extreme rancour, and possible synthetic indignation. If a General Election had not been taking place when Mr. Laski made that speech, and if one side or the other had not been anxious to make party capital out of a comparatively unimportant incident, the action might never have been fought, and the public would have lost a great deal of interest and amusement; but fought it was. And the Laski case must always remain as an outstanding example of much being made out of very little. If Sir Cecil Levita had been wise enough to apologise to Mr. Lambert for the observations which he made at lunch to Mr. Murray, the "Talking Mongoose" would never have raised his head in Court, and Sir Cecil would have been saved a great deal of pain and a great deal of money. If there is any moral to be derived from actions such as these, it may perhaps be found in the suggestion that a little common-sense is the best antidote for tactless speech; but that is a lesson which seems never to be learned and perhaps it never will.

One class of libel action stands alone, and that is a case in which an action in the Courts is the only means of clearing the plaintiff's name from a grave stigma totally undeserved, and yet the Law may be such as to render the chances of success extremely problematical. What advice could best have been given to Mr. Chapman in his action against the Stewards of the Jockey Club? In a sense both sides were right, and only one had to suffer. Mr. Chapman himself must have listened to the legal arguments of which he was the centre with great interest, if not with satisfaction, but at any rate he left the Royal Courts of Justice, after having been warned off Newmarket Heath, with everybody's sympathy. That may perhaps have been some consolation to him.

And last of all, why did the stockbroker think he had been libelled by the advertisement for Yo-Yo? Anyone who cares to read of it can form an opinion for himself, but it is true to say that hundreds of actions, at least as serious as his, have served to while away the tediousness of the Law Courts.

Anyone who has derived some portion of his livelihood from the law of libel must at least look back on his cases with some degree of satisfaction; anyone who has watched those cases as an onlooker must have learned a great deal about human nature. I have known them from both aspects, and the memory they have left behind is very clear.

A PRINCESS'S LIBEL ACTION

The Princess Irena Alexandrovna Youssupoff was a royal Princess of the Imperial Court of Russia. She was the niece of the Czar and had lived her early life amid Royal surroundings. Just before the First World War she had married Prince Youssupoff and her home was the Moika Palace in St. Petersburg. When she stood in the witness box of the Court of the Lord Chief Justice in her action against the Metro-Goldwyn-Mayer Pictures Corporation the story she told contained more elements of human tragedy than any other civil action I have ever known. It unfolded the life history of a young Prince and Princess driven into exile by the Russian Revolution, and it told the awful story of the assassination of Rasputin, the man who did so much to bring about the downfall of the Imperial House.

The family and fortunes of Prince Youssupoff seem to have sprung from the most romantic beginning. It is said that he was directly descended from the last Emperor of Tartary. When that country was overrun by Russian hordes, Ivan the Terrible adopted the heir of the defeated ruler as his son, and upon his death bestowed upon the young Prince, who then took the name and title of Prince Youssupoff, tracts of lands so enormous as to be almost incapable of measurement. In 1915 Prince Felix Youssupoff was the survivor of the family, and possessed of their vast inheritance.

The Prince was a young man of great charm alike

in manner and personal appearance; there is a portrait of him, painted by a well-known Russian artist, which is remarkable in its beauty. His wealth was unbelievable even for a Russian Prince; money meant nothing to him; whatever he desired was always at his disposal; fabulous would be the only word which could convey the immensity of his possessions. In 1914 he married the Princess Irena. The beauty of the Princess must have been outstanding even in the Russian Court, and the young couple may well have been envied in their lives and in their home, the Moika Palace. The tragedy, which was so soon to blast all the nobility of Russia, fell with unexampled cruelty upon the young Prince and Princess Youssupoff.

By now the strange figure of Rasputin is well-known in history. He was said to have been a monk, although there appears to be no evidence to support such a contention, and his origin remains wrapped in mystery. He suddenly appeared in the Russian capital and was presented at Court in 1907, and almost immediately became the centre of controversy; there were some who regarded him almost as a god, while others looked upon him merely as a dangerous and disgusting rascal. In appearance he was dirty and unkempt, while in his personal habits he was revolting, a drunken libertine without, as far as I have been able to discover, a single redeeming merit. He, however, claimed for himself a unique gift, in that he possessed the power of magnetic healing, and such was his peculiar personality that he undoubtedly succeeded in persuading many people that his claim was justified.

His visit to St. Petersburg was singularly well timed. The young Czarevitch lay dying. Doctors from all over Europe had been summoned to his bedside without avail; no one could effect a cure; no one could even diagnose his illness, and all hope of recovery was practically abandoned. It was in those tragic circumstances that a lady of the Court related to the Empress the strange reputation of Rasputin, who was openly claiming throughout the city that no cure was beyond his power. Tortured by an agony of misery and despair, the Empress was prepared to clutch at any straw, and consequently Rasputin was summoned to the palace and taken to the sick room of the dying Czarevitch.

In all probability no one will ever know what steps, if any, Rasputin took to achieve the results which were certainly remarkable. From the day of his arrival at the palace, the health of the young Prince improved; his pain left him and his illness seemed to disappear; outwardly, at any rate, the monk had made good his claim, and the heir to the Russian throne was saved.

The gratitude of the Czar and Czarina knew no bounds; no gifts could be too great, and no position could be too high, for the saviour of their son; in a day Rasputin sprang from being a charlatan in the city streets to becoming the favourite of the Imperial Court. If he had been content with mere financial recognition no great harm would have been done, but he was not; power and still more power was his ambition, and with an Emperor distraught with trouble, and an Empress hysterical with gratitude, he found instruments ready to his hand. Within a few months he became the virtual ruler of all the Russias; suggestions to his Imperial master became commands; he caused generals to be degraded, and high statesmen to be removed; no one in Russia felt safe in the face of his devilish machinations, and through all the changes Rasputin remained the same: drunken, dirty and debauched.

That he should be hated outside the Court was of course inevitable, but so great was the terror he inspired that even his unpopularity might not have brought about his downfall but for a rumour that began to spread throughout the city that he was not a loyal Russian but a German spy. Men began to whisper that he was in the pay of Germany, and that the betrayal of Russia was his aim; the Czar was to be deposed, and Rasputin was to be ruler in his place. So long as personal hatred and even fear was the main feeling inspired by the charlatan monk, no one could be found to raise a hand against him, but once their country was in danger the situation changed; while Rasputin lived Russia was in peril, so Rasputin must die. Even then no one could be found with sufficient courage to bring about his death, and it was in those circumstances that Prince Youssupoff undertook the task himself; to him it was not assassination but a duty to his country.

To kill Rasputin would not be easy. Superstition claimed that he was impervious to poison, and by no means the least remarkable incident in his subsequent assassination was the apparent support afforded to this contention; bullets, it was said, could not harm him; in fact Rasputin could not die. In the plan which he formed the Prince obtained the willing co-operation of a number of young men of the highest position in Court circles, and the death of Rasputin was prepared with the utmost care. Prince Youssupoff in his own book has described how he performed his self-imposed task. Rasputin was to be invited to the Moika Palace, under the pretence of enjoying one of those drunken orgies in which he revelled, where the food for his consumption was saturated with poison, and revolvers were held in readiness in case the poison failed. No loophole was left unstopped.

On the appointed night Rasputin arrived, and was received with every evidence of luxurious enjoyment; music was provided for his apparent entertainment, but in reality to prevent the noise from any struggle reaching the outside world. He was conducted by his host alone to one of the lower rooms of the palace, and there regaled with a surfeit of the sweet cakes in which he revelled. The cakes themselves were saturated with enough poison to kill a dozen men, and Prince Youssupoff stood by and watched him wolf them one by one. To his horror and amazement the poison appeared to have no effect, and the Prince rushed from the room and obtained from his companions a revolver with which to complete his awful task. On his return Rasputin was still at the table, and the Prince fired shot after shot into his body, while his victim charged about the room roaring like a bull. At last he fell to the ground and Youssupoff, in a frenzy of horror, beat him to death with a loaded stick; his colleagues came to his assistance, and with their aid the body was thrown into the ice-bound river.

It was of course inevitable that the death of Rasputin would become public knowledge, and suspicion almost immediately fell upon Prince Youssupoff. He was arrested, and possibly because of the universal hatred felt towards his victim, the only sentence passed upon him by the Czar was one of banishment. He was exiled from St. Petersburg to a remote portion of his estate in provincial Russia, and he never returned. Thereafter came the Russian Revolution, and Prince and Princess Youssupoff escaped from Russia, bereft of all their great possessions, to live their lives in comparative poverty and obscurity in some foreign capital. With the exception of themselves all the principle characters in the tragedy were dead; Rasputin at the hand of Prince Youssupoff, and the Czar and all his family foully murdered.

Some years later the Metro-Goldwyn-Mayer Corporation of America decided to produce a film portraying the tragic death of Rasputin. In order, no doubt, to stimulate public interest, the production was to be as near the truth as possible; real characters were to be portrayed upon the screen, the Czar, the Czarina, the Czarevitch, and, of course, Rasputin himself. They were all dead, and there was in consequence no danger of any complaint being raised by any of them to the representation, but the case of Prince Youssupoff was more difficult; without a killer there could be no assassination, and Prince

Youssupoff was alive. So two purely imaginary characters were introduced into the story, a Prince Chekodieff, who was portrayed as having slain Rasputin, and a Princess who was described as his fiancée, and was afterwards to become his wife. Unfortunately for the film company there was further deviation from accuracy in fact. Possibly with a view to affording a more sympathetic explanation of the Prince's action, a purely imaginary incident was introduced into the story, namely that Rasputin had seduced or raped the Princess, and that incident formed one of the important incidents in the plot.

When the film was publicly produced the Princess was horrified. She saw herself degraded in the eyes of all who knew her, and she tried her utmost to prevent the production, or at least to have deleted those portions which represented her in such revolting conditions, but her efforts were unsuccessful. The film company stoutly denied that she was in any way portrayed in their production; Prince Chekodieff and the Princess were both, they said, purely fictitious characters bearing no possible resemblance either to Prince or Princess Youssupoff, and they declined both of her requests. In consequence the Princess instituted proceedings against the company for libel, and the case was brought to me.

The difficulties in the plaintiff's path were obvious. The characters of the fictitious Prince and Princess were entirely different from those of Princess Youssupoff and her husband, and the jury

THE PRINCE AND PRINCESS YOUSSUPOFF
AT THE TIME OF THE TRIAL
(*Photo Planet News Ltd*)

THE PRINCE AND PRINCESS YOUSSUPOFF STUDY "STILLS" OF THE FILM
"RASPUTIN THE MAD MONK"

(Photo: London News Agency Ltd.)

A SCENE FROM THE FILM "RASPUTIN THE MAD MONK".

would no doubt be invited to see a performance of the film, when those differences would be called to their attention; moreover the Princess on the screen was merely a fiancée and not even married to the Prince. But the real difficulty arose from quite a different consideration. The main ground upon which the plaintiff must rely was based upon the fact that in real life Rasputin had been killed by Prince Youssupoff, and consequently if the film was, as it purported to be, a true picture of the story it portrayed, the fictitious Prince Chekodieff must have been intended to represent Prince Youssupoff, and consequently the Princess of the film must have been intended for his wife. But in a Court of Law facts have to be proved; if the defendants would admit that Rasputin had in truth been killed by Prince Youssupoff, many of the difficulties would disappear, but if on the other hand they denied it, the only witness who could prove the fact was Prince Youssupoff himself, and it was a terrible responsibility to put a witness into the box to give evidence that he had been guilty of such an act as the assassination of Rasputin. I am bound to confess that I entered upon this case with feelings of considerable anxiety.

The action was tried before Mr. Justice Avory and a special jury. The court was crammed to suffocation with well-known men and women, many of whom must have known the Youssupoffs in happier days, and all of them eagerly listening to hear at last the true account of events which had rocked an empire. Of them all, the Prince and

Princess alone appeared unmoved as they took their places in the well of the Court, where they sat throughout the long trial motionless and silent. It was not necessary to open the case with any rhetorical embellishment, the story was sufficiently dramatic in itself, and I was anxious that the Princess should go into the box as soon as possible. It is always impossible to foretell in advance what impression a witness will make upon the Court; the most intelligent may appear nervous and uncertain; the most truthful, in their desire for accuracy, give the appearance of prevarication; no one but an advocate can ever know the anxiety with which he calls his client, and particularly in a libel action the demeanour of the plaintiff is all-important.

Princess Youssupoff was the realisation of an advocate's dream. Throughout a long and somewhat painful ordeal, her demeanour never changed; she displayed neither indignation nor distress, and she answered every question without hesitation and with unfailing courtesy, although some of the suggestions made to her might well have provoked an outburst. Every dissimilarity in character between herself and the Princess in the film she accepted without question, she neither argued nor explained, but merely told her story. No doubt in part owing to the impression she was creating, the defendants were driven to a form of cross-examination which personally I thought to be unwise; no doubt with the object of minimising any possible damages. It was suggested to her that she had been induced to bring the action with the unworthy or at least undignified object of obtaining money from the defendants. Such a line of cross-examination may succeed in some cases, but in others it may well prove a boomerang, ultimately to be reflected in the jury's verdict. The Princess treated any such suggestion with calm contempt, and when she left the box there was no doubt that at least she carried with her the sympathy of all who had heard her. But even then we had not reached the real substance of the case. Who had killed Rasputin? I rose in my place, and asked counsel who was appearing for the defendants if it was disputed that the death had been caused by Prince Youssupoff. That was the moment for which everyone had been waiting, and the defendants' counsel at once replied that he disputed it completely. No doubt the defendants fully realised the difficulty in which such a denial would place me, but it had to be faced; I called Prince Youssupoff into the box.

If the Princess had been a most impressive witness, the Prince was no less remarkable. It was an awful story that he had to tell, but he told it without passion, and indeed without emotion of any kind; the invitation to the Moika Palace, the poisoned cakes, the revolver shots, the loaded stick, he told it all.

"I killed Rasputin," he said. "It was my duty to kill him. So I killed him."

As the defendants had denied that Prince Youssupoff was in fact the real assassin of Rasputin, they were constrained to challenge every statement that he made, and to endeavour, if it were possible, to discredit the evidence he had given, even to the extent of suggesting that it was not he, but one of his friends, more closely resembling the fictitious Prince Chekodieff of the film, who was in fact responsible for the assassination. Ordinary Englishmen and women do not like such tales of horror, and the defendants may well have thought that the longer Prince Youssupoff were required to tell his story, the greater was the chance that the jury might be prejudiced against him. He was cross-examined for a period that must have seemed to him interminable. Every detail was disputed; every statement that he made was challenged.

"Are you really suggesting that you gave Rasputin cakes soaked in poison—and that he ate them?"

"I gave him poisoned cakes. He ate them. He would not die, so I had to shoot him."

It was suggested that it was not he, but one of his companions, who fired the shots.

"As he would not die I left the room. I took a revolver from my friend. I shot Rasputin. Many times I shot him. Still he would not die. He roared like a bull. I beat him to death with a heavy stick. Then we threw him into the river."

Well may all who heard him have been appalled by such an awful story, but to question the truth of anything that he was telling us was quite impossible. Throughout his long ordeal the Prince stood like a figure carved in stone.

"I have not killed a man before, but it was my duty to kill Rasputin. So I killed him."

The defendants' main defence of course remained.

The total dissimilarity between Youssupoff and the fictitious Prince Chekodieff was again accentuated, and just as in the case of the Princess, the Prince agreed without the slightest attempt at argument to every suggestion that was made to him; in character the two people were in no way the same. Once again I thought the defendants had been unwise. Well may they have thought that we should hesitate a long time before calling Prince Youssupoff as a witness, but once we had been forced into doing so, the real importance of dissimilarity between the characters tended to fade into the background. Whatever else had been established, Prince Youssupoff had told the truth.

At the conclusion of the plaintiff's case the jury were invited to see the film so that they might observe the dissimilarities themselves, and special arrangements were made to enable them to do so. It might perhaps have been in the best interest of the defendants to have left the matter there, but upon the jury's return to Court, the defendants adopted a course which played into my hands. They decided to call evidence in order to accentuate the differences upon which they so strongly relied, and that was exactly what I hoped would happen. They called many witnesses, many of whom had known the Youssupoffs in happier days and were well acquainted with the Russian Imperial Court, and they were all unanimous that the characters of the imaginary Prince and Princess of the film bore no resemblance to those of the Prince and Princess who were in Court. But unfortunately for them, every witness called had to face the same inevitable question: "Who is the person popularly believed to have killed Rasputin?" However much they tried to avoid it the answer had to come in the end: "Prince Youssupoff." The rest seemed to follow. "In that case, the ordinary person seeing on the film that which purported to be a true picture of the killing of Rasputin would think he was watching the action of Prince Youssupoff? And the only lady engaged or married to Prince Youssupoff was the plaintiff?" There was no escape from it.

Again the jury asked to see the film, and again their request was granted. On their return the judge summed up, and the jury retired to consider their verdict. During all my years at the Bar I never lost my feeling of anxiety during that period of waiting. However little the result may matter to an advocate, to the parties themselves it may well be the most important moment of their lives, and it is impossible to avoid sharing in some degree their feelings. In this particular case my anxiety was accentuated. It meant so much to the Princess. She had been compelled to lay bare the most tragic episode of her whole life, and to lose her case would be intolerable; moreover small or contemptuous damages might have meant that the cross-examination as to her unworthy motives had been justified. The usual whispering and speculation was passing round the Court amongst the spectators who were merely there to be amused, and I could not help wondering what the Princess was remembering in her mind as she sat in her place in silence. In the days of which she had been telling us she had been living in a palace in St. Petersburg, the envied of a capital, the favoured of fortune; now she was an exile in a foreign land, without her fortune and without hope of returning to her home.

Then the jury returned, and the judge came back to Court. The chattering ceased and every eye was turned upon them, except that of the Princess and her husband who still sat as they had sat throughout, immovable and apparently unmoved. The jury were agreed; they returned a verdict for the Princess, and awarded her as damages the enormous sum of twenty-five thousand pounds. For the first time the Princess showed any feeling as she turned to thank me for what I had been able to do to help her.

As usual, I think the jury was right. It had been a cruel libel, with every element which might tend to aggravate the damage, and I have little doubt that the defendants had intended to portray the story of Prince Youssupoff under a fictitious name. At a later date the Court of Appeal were asked to order a new trial upon the ground that the damages were excessive, but the application was refused, and the Princess was allowed to keep the sum awarded to her. I only hope that it did something to alleviate her most unhappy lot.

THE END OF ROBERT SIEVIER

Robert Standish Sievier was an Edwardian sportsman. He was well known upon every race-course and at every sporting gathering, from Hurst Park to the National Sporting Club. He would gamble upon anything and drink with anyone; in doing which he was not unnaturally known among his sporting friends as "Good old Bob Sievier."

In appearance he was a shade flamboyant; his clothes were rather louder than was customary; and his language rather more forceful than was necessary, but that was all part of his Edwardian character. Sievier's social position was never very clearly defined. He had been good enough to present to his admiring sycophants a short volume containing some details of his boisterous career. He had married a lady of fortune; he had even received an invitation to a Royal Function, and he had been a member of well-known sporting clubs, as far afield as Melbourne in Australia. He had owned the best known racehorse of his time, a mare named Sceptre who had proved herself just as popular with the public as was her jovial owner. For a short time he had been a bookmaker. He was a great patriot. To a Company of Imperial Yeomanry departing for service in South Africa he had promised insurance against death or injury, so that each might face the risks of war without anxiety for his dependants. But it was in his gambling exploits that lay his greatest pride. There was not a game of skill or chance upon which he was not prepared to risk a fortune; even at billiards he had played for stakes of many hundreds of pounds, particularly in the case of a man named Horne, with whom he played one night at Monte Carlo.

Sievier had other occupations beside that of a gambler. He was a journalist. He owned and conducted a periodical known as *The Winning Post*. *The Winning Post* was a peculiar paper. It included in its issues a series of short biographies entitled "In Glass Houses", which contained details of the life history of well-known personalities. If the details were entirely laudatory, of course no reasonable objection could be taken, but if they were not, other considerations might arise. Among the subjects chosen for inclusion in the paper was an article concerning the history of a certain Mr. Jack Joel.

Mr. Joel was a gentleman who had made a fortune in South Africa, and in whose life there was apparently some incident which he was not particularly anxious to revive. In consequence he requested that the publication should not take place, and in reply he received an assurance that his wishes would be carried out provided that Mr. Sievier received £5,000. Not unnaturally Mr. Joel came to the conclusion that such a demand savoured of blackmail, and his view was considerably reinforced when he was informed that if the article in question did appear a portrait of Mr. Joel would also be included with a photograph of a well-known criminal upon either side of him. Mr. Joel decided to prosecute Sievier as a blackmailer. The subsequent proceedings had most amazing results. So far from disparaging Sievier, his popularity increased a thousandfold. His friends rallied to his assistance; one friend alone, a Mr. Topping, subscribed a thousand pounds towards the cost of his defence. In answer to the charge Sievier indignantly denied that he had ever demanded £5,000 or any sum, and that the whole story was invented by Joel and was nothing but a trick to bring about his ruin. The trial of Sievier took place at the Central Criminal Court. Brilliantly defended by Rufus Isaacs, Sievier was triumphantly acquitted. The chief witness for the prosecution, a friend of Sievier's by the name of Mills, was more than half-hearted in his evidence, and the case practically collapsed. Sievier received an ovation. From the mere position of a popular sportsman, he became almost a national hero. His appearance was greeted with frenzied cries of "Good old Bob", and even his counsel was acclaimed in the universal approbation. When Sievier left the Court, he was once again acknowledged as the most popular member of the sporting world.

Unfortunately he was not content to rest upon his laurels. Feeling, no doubt, that his position as a critic of rival sportsmen was now assured he proceeded to launch a new series of attacks, and for his victim he selected one Richard Wootten, the trainer.

Wootten was an Australian who had come to this country, where his success upon the Turf had been remarkable. In company with his two sons Frank and Stanley, who became the leading jockeys of the day, he practically swept the board, and it was no doubt in consequence of the position all three enjoyed

MR. "BOB" SIEVIER ON NEWMARKET RACE-COURSE
(Photo: Graphic Photo Union)

that Robert Sievier thought they would prove likely subjects for attack. The possibility of an action at law had no terrors for him. No jury could possibly give a verdict otherwise than in his favour. But Wootten was not the kind of man to submit tamely to attack. Although not possessed of Sievier's gay demeanour, he was a determined person quite likely to prove a dangerous enemy; moreover he had known Sievier in Australia and was aware of many details of his hectic life. He determined to carry the war into his adversary's camp, and moreover to do so in a manner selected by himself. With great care, and after much investigation, he prepared a short account of Sievier's achievements in the world of sport, and caused the story to be circulated on every race-course in the country in the form of a small pamphlet, in which in the plainest terms he described Sievier as a thorough scoundrel, calling him a blackmailer, a cardsharper, and a common thief. Such a document, if untrue, was too scurrilous to be ignored; every racing man knew of its contents; even Sievier's most staunch supporters urged that some reply was necessary if he was to retain the great reputation he had earned. Sievier knew it too. There was not room on the English Turf for both Wootten and Sievier. One of them had to go. Sievier would decide which one that should be. He issued a writ for libel, determined to prove once more that an English jury would vindicate an English sportsman. Once before Sievier had been charged with blackmail by Mr. Joel and the charge had been ignominiously dismissed. No one should dare to say the same of him again. Unfortunately Mr. Wootten took a different view. He put a defence upon the record, in which he pleaded that every allegation in his pamphlet was true. Sievier was all things he had been called, and more.

The action was the sensation of the day. The Court of the Lord Chief Justice was thronged with an excited crowd of racing men an hour before Lord Reading took his seat. Sievier must have thought himself to be more than fortunate that the man who, as Rufus Isaacs, had been his counsel was now his judge. He would be the first to know that anyone who accused Robert Sievier of blackmail must be himself a liar. Moreover there were considerable grounds for Sievier's optimism. Wootten had used plain words, every one of which would have to be proved to be true. Indiscretions and peccadillos in Sievier's sporting adventures would be quite insufficient to justify the libels. Cardsharper, thief and blackmailer were strong words, particularly blackmailer. Would it be possible to satisfy any jury that the verdict given at the Central Criminal Court in the Joel case had been wrong? Even the jury seemed impressed with the importance of their task.

Sievier's appearance at the Royal Courts of Justice was almost a repetition of his earlier triumph. As he drove gaily to the Courts he was escorted by a cheering crowd; cries of "Good old Bob" greeted him both outside and inside the Court, and the police had the greatest difficulty in keeping the vociferous enthusiasm within the bounds of decency. With a bright smile on his face and a gorgeous carnation in his button-hole, "Good old Bob" looked the beau ideal of an English sportsman against whom any allegation of dishonesty was unthinkable. He needed no counsel to represent him this time. Completely confident in his own integrity he had decided to conduct his case himself; a simple-hearted sportsman would be able to appeal to a jury as no advocate could hope to do. Moreover his vanity was such that he considered himself mentally superior to any member of the Bar.

His appearance in the witness box was everything that his most enthusiastic supporters could have wished. Gay, debonair, he was disarming in his frankness. "I do not profess to be a saint," he said, "I am a gambler. I have been a gambler all my life. Like all good sportsmen I have had my ups and downs. I have owned the best horses in the world. Also the worst. I am known on every race-course, and I gladly offer my character to the investigation of anyone who dares to question it. First and last I am an English sportsman, and so I would be judged." One could almost hear the jury answer: "Good old Bob." Robert Sievier was not going to be an easy man to cross-examine; finesse would be a waste of time; good humour would be an error. Direct methods would be required to deal with such a sportsman. He faced me with a smile of good-natured amusement: "What questions would you like to ask?"

"You know that Mr. Wootten has said you are a blackmailer and a thief."

"Oh yes."

"I am going to suggest that you are in every way a scoundrel and that your racing career should be ended once and for all."

For a moment Mr. Sievier seemed slightly disconcerted. So it was going to be hard fighting!

"For any particular reason?"

"Many. Let us take one. Supposing an English sportsman played a game of billiards with a friend at a time when that friend was so drunk that he could not hold a cue, would it be a gross fraud to win large sums of money on such a game?" There could only be one answer to such a question.

"Do you know a man named Horne?"

Once again Sievier was his jovial self.

"I knew him well," he said. "There were two of them; two brothers. One was known as Hunting Horne, and one as Drinking Horne. When Hunting Horne went hunting he generally fell off."

Sievier's friends in Court laughed loudly, and he joined in their laughter, but it was the last time he was to laugh that day. The description of "Drinking Horne" was perhaps unfortunate. It was in "Drinking Horne" that I was interested. He was the man who lost large sums at billiards when he played with Robert Sievier one night in Monte Carlo.

"Did Horne pay his loss that night by cheque?"

"He did."

"If Horne was in fact so drunk as not to know what he was doing, it would be essential that he should pay his debt that night before he became sober?"

"Ridiculous."

"Who signed the cheque?"

"Horne."

"Who wrote out the body of the cheque?"

"I did."

"Was that because Horne was so drunk that he could not write it out himself?"

This Sievier indignantly denied. He also denied that at the conclusion of the evening the floor was found to be littered with uncompleted cheques, all in Sievier's handwriting, and with attempted signatures by Horne so undecipherable as to be worthless. It was so easy to make denials in the absence of Horne himself. But there were some final questions which required a good deal more explanation.

"The next morning did Horne repudiate the cheque?"

"He did."

"Was that upon the ground that he had been too drunk to know what he had signed?"

"It may have been."

"And in consequence of what had occurred that night did the British Consul at Monte Carlo direct you to leave the Principality and not come back?"

For that there could be no very satisfactory explanation. Insensibly the whole atmosphere in Court began to change. Was Sievier quite the honest sportsman he had seemed? Perhaps even he may have regretted the playful jest of "Drinking Horne". It is difficult to over-estimate the effect of atmosphere at any trial at which a man's character is the matter of chief moment. It is electric and seems to come from the back benches in the Court and to grow in volume until it can be read on the faces of the jury. It was so in Sievier's case. Even the carnation in his button-hole appeared to droop, and the sweat began to glisten on his face.

But that was only the beginning. There were so many things to ask him; so many episodes throughout his life that seemed amusing when recorded by himself, but became less favourable when produced in Court. One by one he was taken through them all. When he married, his wife was a rich woman. When she separated from him some time later, she was penniless. Where had the money gone? Apparently he had used his wife's fortune for the purpose of his business as a bookmaker which he had started under the name of a cousin, Punch Sievier. The money had all gone and Sievier owed even more. He had tried to avoid liability by alleging that he was a mere manager for his cousin, and when that failed, he had escaped by pleading the Gaming Act; the one course of conduct which racing men do not forgive. He had been more than once bankrupt. His proud boast that he was once a member of the Melbourne Club became less impressive when it was learned that he had been expelled. His invitation to appear at Court lost most of its social value when the jury were informed that the invitation had been withdrawn. And even outside his racing world, his conduct had been contemptible. He had proudly boasted of his generosity to the Company of Yeomanry who were sailing to the South African War. He was asked about that. It was quite true that he had promised an insurance to anyone who did not return, and some did not return.

"It is possible that in some cases their dependants may have asked me to redeem my promise."

"Did anyone of them ever receive a penny?"

"Not that I remember."

"Did you ever insure one single soldier for a penny piece?"

"No."

By this time any claim that Sievier may have had to be regarded as a good sportsman or indeed an honourable member of society had almost disappeared. But he was quite clever enough to know that the strongest ground upon which he could take his stand had not yet been touched. "I have been acquitted at the Central Criminal Court," he said. "Compared with that fact, there is nothing else that matters. You have called me a blackmailer. And that you can never prove."

I told him we were going to try.

In vain Sievier appealed to the Lord Chief Justice for protection; in vain he raised the plea that as he had been acquitted at the Central Criminal Court, no one should be allowed again to maintain the truth of a charge upon which he had been found Not Guilty. Sternly he was reminded that this time the issue was being tried in a libel case before a Civil Court, and if the defendants desired to take upon themselves the risk of re-opening the matter they were entitled so to do, whatever might be the chance of success or failure. And no one knew better than the Lord Chief Justice how difficult that task would be. The whole issue must depend on the story to be told by the man Mills. In the past undoubtedly he had proved to be Sievier's greatest asset at his trial. No one had ever questioned his integrity, and he was undoubtedly Sievier's friend. What would be the result of his evidence to-day?

I had not been present at the hearing of the criminal trial and was therefore untrammelled by a recollection of the sentiments that then prevailed. But on this occasion the atmosphere was very different. At the Central Criminal Court the crowded building was with Sievier to a man. No enquiry had been made into his past adventures, and throughout the trial he remained, as he had been before it started, the object of popular admiration and regard. This time there was a change. The jury had learned something of Sievier's past; they had heard the story of "Drinking Horne", and they knew a little more about his sporting character. When they should come to hear the story of his dealings with Jack Joel, they could at least approach the question with an open mind.

Sievier finally admitted under cross-examination that he had made some attacks upon Jack Joel, and that he had received £5,000 from his friend Mills, but he indignantly denied that the money had been paid as blackmail. It had been nothing but a friendly loan between two friends. Mills had stated that before and would again, and Sievier challenged us to put his old friend into the witness box to deny it. In his indignation at finding his innocence being questioned once again, Robert Sievier seemed to regain that air of confidence, indeed of arrogance, which for the past few hours had slightly languished.

It was under these conditions that Mills entered the witness box. From the outset it was obvious that he was a most unwilling witness, and above all was anxious to say no word to injure his old friend Robert Sievier. With difficulty I obtained the information that he knew of the attacks by Sievier against Joel, and further that he himself had handed to Sievier a cheque for £5,000; but beyond that he would not go. And as it was not within my rights to cross-examine him, indeed I should not have been allowed to do so, I was obliged to leave the matter there. But to Sievier, when his turn came to ask the questions, Mills was far more accommodating; indeed he was prepared to accept any suggestion that was made to him; it was true, he said, that no question or thought of blackmail ever arose; indeed Sievier had flatly refused to take any money whatever from Jack Joel; as for the £5,000, it was nothing but a friendly loan to Sievier from himself.

If Mills had been a wholly unbiased witness that story might have been accepted, but his partiality was too apparent to be easily dismissed. The necessity for a few further questions by way of re-examination appeared to be indicated. They had to be framed with some care, as there is a limit to the latitude allowed to counsel re-examining his own witness, but Mr. Mills was asked to give some further details of this strange transaction, which he did with obvious regret.

"Had Sievier shown you any photographs to be incorporated with the proposed article on Joel?"

"He had."

"Who did the photographs represent?"
"Two well-known criminals."
"Where were they to be placed?"
"One on each side of a picture of Joel himself."
"What for?"
Mr. Mills began to be confused. "I do not know."
"How could the publication be prevented?"
"If Mr. Joel paid £5,000."
"Did Mr. Joel hand you £5,000?"
"Yes."
"What did you do with the money?"
"I handed it to Mr. Sievier."
"And was the publication stopped?"
"It was."

Once again Sievier raised his protest, but it was of no avail. The story had come out at last.

In no case is it possible to know the points in a protracted trial which to the jury appear to be of most importance. It may have been the evidence of Mr. Mills. I do not know. But there was one particular admission made by Robert Sievier which was so disgraceful that it may well have turned the scale against him and disclosed him to the jury as a man without a shred of decent feeling.

When his friend Mr. Topping came to the rescue of Robert Sievier by the loan of £1,000 towards the expenses of defending the criminal charge against him, Mr. Topping might well have expected never-ending gratitude, but his expectations would have been disappointed. Before he could request repayment of his loan, Mr. Topping died, and it fell to his dependants to make the claim on his behalf. Sievier repudiated any liability, and a writ had to be issued against him to enforce repayment of the debt, and thereupon Sievier adopted a course which stamped him once for all as a man beneath contempt. He swore in an affidavit that the £1,000 had never been a debt; that it was money which was owing to Mr. Topping as the result of a bet made by Mr. Sievier on the race-course, and that as such it was a wagering transaction to which the Gaming Acts applied, and that Sievier could and would rely upon these Acts to avoid the necessity for payment. Faced by that affidavit, Sievier had no possible reply. And it may well have been the end. Could any words of Mr. Wootten have been too strong in which to describe a man who could be guilty of such conduct towards his dead friend?

In vain Sievier appealed passionately to an impassive jury; in vain he sought to remind them that he had been already acquitted of the gravest charge now made against him; in vain he sought to brush aside the less important incidents in his career. The jury had heard enough to satisfy them that the allegations made by Mr. Wootten were true. They found by their verdict that Robert Sievier was a blackmailer, a liar, and a rogue.

Even the onlookers who had listened so attentatively throughout the trial appeared to know it too. The same crowd who had cheered Sievier so enthusiastically two days before with cries of "Good old Bob" now carried Wootten shoulder-high into the Strand.

The glory of Robert Sievier had departed, and he

left the precincts of the Court by the back door, never again to be allowed upon an English race-course.

Many an honest sportsman was overjoyed at the complete exposure of Sievier, sportsmen who did not regard sport merely as another name for winning money. A well-known racing man was congratulating me upon the result of the trial. "You seem to have known a good deal about Bob Sievier," he said. "But there was one thing you did not know. Sievier is the only man in England who has ever been black-balled for the Zoo."

THE LASKI CASE

VERY few people have ever embarked upon a libel action without bitterly regretting their adventure before the case comes on for trial. Tempers have died down, bitterness has evaporated and the delay caused by the necessary legal preliminaries seems interminable. All that remains to whip up enthusiasm, already nearly dead, is the prospect of ever-increasing liability for costs. The defamation which had appeared to be so grievious at the outset has dwindled with the passing of the months, until it has almost disappeared. I always felt that Mr. Harold Laski must have regarded the termination of his own action against the daily Press very much from that point of view.

Mr. Laski was a man of great intellectual attainments. For many years he had been a Professor of Political Science at the London School of Economics and at the University of London; he had occupied high and important positions in the Labour Party; and had written a large number of very learned books and other publications upon most aspects of Political Economy. In those circumstances it was not unnatural that he was considered an eminently desirable speaker upon socialistic platforms.

In the 1945 Election Mr. Laski took an active part in the campaign. Although not a candidate himself, he made speeches throughout the country in support of the Labour cause, and upon a night in June of that year about a fortnight before polling day he found himself upon a lorry in the Market Square at Newark addressing a political meeting. At the conclusion of Mr. Laski's speech he was heckled by a Mr. Wentworth Day, who was presumably a Conservative opponent, and the exchanges between them were somewhat heated and acrimonious, as no doubt frequently occurs when hecklers take part in political controversy. In the issue of the *Newark Advertiser* of June 20th an article appeared which contained the following among other references to what transpired.

REVOLUTION BY VIOLENCE

Professor Laski Questioned

"There were some lively exchanges between Mr. Wentworth Day and Professor Laski following the latter's speech in Newark market place on Saturday night.

"Mr. Day asked the Professor why he had openly advocated 'revolution by violence' in speaking at Bishops Stortford and Bournemouth during the war, whilst most Englishmen were either fighting or being 'bombed at home' . . . .

"Professor Laski replied that he was twice rejected in this country during the 1914–18 war. . . .

Reference to Violence

"As for violence, he (Mr. Laski) continued, "if Labour could not obtain what it needed by general *consent, 'we shall have to use violence, even if it means Revolution.' When people felt it was the moment for great experiment, for innovation, because when war is over people so easily forgot—especially those who had the power in their hands—that was the time for experiment. Great changes were so urgent in this country, and if they were not made by consent they would be made by violence, and judging by the temper his questioner had displayed he would be perfectly naturally one of the objects of violence when it came. . . .*

Not An Asset

"*Mr. Day: 'You are precisely the sort of bloodthirsty little man, full of words, who has never smelt a bullet, but is always the first to stir up violence in peace.'*

Mr. Day continued, and ended:

" '*I suggest that you are not an asset to the Labour Party but a liability.*' "

There were some further references to Mr. Laski's own conduct during the war, which were apparently quite unjustified and are not material for the purpose of the subsequent action.

It is not unusual for speakers and hecklers to exchange mutual courtesies during an election meeting and by the next morning they are generally forgotten, but the position enjoyed by Mr. Laski was too important to permit of any observation made by him being ignored. Newspapers throughout the country published reports of these alleged statements. Mr. Laski gave his version of what he had said at the meeting in the *Nottingham Guardian*. "My answer at the meeting was entirely different. What I said was 'it was very much better to make changes in time of war when men were ready for great changes and were willing to make them by consent through the urgency of war, than to wait for the urgency to disappear through victory, and then to find that there was no consent to change what the workers felt was an intolerable burden. That was a way that a society drifted to violence. We had it in our power to do so by consent, that which in other nations has been done by violence'."

No doubt Conservative associations regarded Mr. Laski's statements as set out in the *Newark Advertiser* as affording valuable material upon which to base criticism of Labour views. It is equally possible that Labour organisations considered the same paragraphs to be too dangerous to be ignored in view of the imminent election. By whatsoever motives Mr. Laski was actuated, he decided to take immediate action. He issued a writ for libel against the *Newark Advertiser* and further writs against other offending newspapers.

It is impossible to believe that the paragraphs complained of had the slightest effect upon the result of the forthcoming election; it is equally difficult to think that Mr. Laski's many friends and admirers were in any way prejudiced against him by anything stated in the Press; indeed it might almost have been expected that after electoral fever had died down the whole matter might have been regarded as a storm in a tea-cup. But it was not to be. The action once started had to go on. Mr. Laski put in his claim, stating amongst other things that the *Newark Advertiser* by their false account of his remarks had accused him of sedition and treason felony. The defendants said that, whatever they had written, their words were true and constituted a fair and accurate report of the statements Mr. Laski himself had made. Thereafter thousands of pounds were spent by both sides, and endless ingenuity employed, in preparing for what was apparently developing into a state of trial. The whole matter in dispute between the Parties was a very simple one, namely, had Mr. Laski in fact said: "If Labour could not get what it wanted by general consent, we shall have to use violence even if it means Revolution".

From the outset it was apparent that the ultimate issue would depend upon the one question as to whether or not the words of which Mr. Laski complained had in fact been said by him; but inasmuch as the evidence upon both sides was likely to be extremely controversial, the defendants determined to make exhaustive enquiries into any previous speeches and wordings to find out if Mr. Laski had ever previously made statements to the same effect. Now Mr. Laski had written a great deal and his books upon political subjects bore such titles as *Reflections on the Revolution of our Times*. By the word revolution Mr. Laski meant a change in social conditions, and was at great pains to point out his hopes that such change would be brought about by peaceful means while at the same time pointing out to his readers the dangers and disaster of a revolution by force. But "revolution" is a nasty word, and sometimes an author writing with the highest motives may lead his readers to believe that the object in view is not precisely what he intends. It was with that possibility in mind that Mr. Laski's many publications were scanned from end to end. Mr. Laski had also made broadcasts upon the wireless, and there also it was thought that enquiries might usefully be made. By the time the case was ripe for trial there was hardly a word that Mr. Laski had ever spoken or written which had not been carefully examined.

The action came to trial before the Lord Chief Justice and a special jury, and aroused a great deal of political and general interest. On the one hand the view was held that Mr. Laski was a harmless political economist who had been made the victim of misrepresentation by persons actuated by unworthy political motives; on the other that he was the author of very dangerous pronouncements which ought to be stigmatised in public. The tea-cup storm had indeed swollen to a tempest. No words could be too strong, according to the opening speech of the Plaintiff's Counsel, in which to characterise the attacks made against Mr. Laski. Russell on Crimes was quoted to define the nature of treason felony and the Court was reminded that the offence had once been punishable by transportation beyond the seas. Even Mr. Laski must have felt that his visit to the lorry in the market place at Newmark had been a more hazardous enterprise than he would ever have imagined possible.

In the witness box Mr. Laski did not bear the appearance of a treasonable felon; he much more resembled a Professor of Economics. He gave a list of various distinguished qualifications and appointments calmly and dispassionately. He gave his account on the meeting in Newark and the heckling by Mr. Wentworth Day. He stated quite definitely that he had never preached revolution and gave his explanations of what he had in fact said, very much in accordance with his version as previously published in the *Nottingham Guardian*.

The cross-examination of Mr. Laski by me was both long and difficult. Having regard to the multiplicity of books and documents to which reference had to be made, it was necessary to try and bring before the jury's mind with some degree of simplicity the principles which we sought to establish from his writings. The first few questions were directed to that task.

"Mr. Laski, do you believe that the use of violence to achieve your political ends is practically inevitable?"

"No."

"Have you ever believed that which I put to you?"

"No."

"Do you believe that if achievement of political aims cannot be arrived at without the use of violence, then violence is justifiable?"

"Not in all circumstances. In circumstances where a burden is intolerable, violence may be inevitable, because the burden is intolerable, but not otherwise."

"In the circumstances which existed on the date

you made your speech at Newark, did you then believe that if the aims of the proletariat could not be achieved without the use of violence, then violence was justifiable?"

"No."

"Do you agree that anyone who preached that doctrine would be a public danger?"

"Yes."

After those questions and answers it became necessary to show, if possible, that the two suggestions could fairly be extracted from Mr. Laski's own writings. In fairness to Mr. Laski it must be stated that throughout the cross-examination he maintained that isolated passages could not be taken to represent his whole thesis, and that such passages taken alone might often be misleading, but it was pointed out to him that it was only words actually used by him which we were able to produce, and which he would be asked to explain.

The next questions were directed to finding out the precise meaning to the word Revolution.

Q.: "Have you for years past preached the doctrine that the time is ripe for revolution."

A.: "Revolution in the sense of great transformation always."

Q.: "Have you preached the doctrine that this revolution may be brought about in one of two ways, either by consent, you call it a revolution by consent, or else a revolution by violence?"

A.: "That is so."

Q.: "And by revolution by consent do you mean that the enemy, the capitalists must consent, to their own elimination, that is to say they have to consent to go?"

A.: "They have to consent to great changes."

The following passage was read to him.

Q.: " 'If a change is to be built up on consent,' here we have revolution by consent, 'it assumes the possibility of co-operation by capitalists in their own erosion. That is an immense hypothesis of which for the moment it is only necessary to say that it envisages something entirely new in historic experience. It may be right but there is little in the past to justify the expectation that it is right.' There you have told us what you mean by revolution by consent?"

A.: "Yes."

Then it became necessary to consider the consequences of the consent not being obtained. Passages from one of his books were put to him.

Q.: "Up to this point does not the passage mean that unless the capitalists will consent to their own erosion, revolution by violence is inevitable. Does it not mean that? Could it mean anything else?"

A.: "It means that when the working class in a community like our own are tired of sacrifices and bad conditions which they believe to be unjustified, a period will come when they will no longer consent to the sacrifice, and at that point there is the inevitability of violent revolution unless there is acquiescence in the changes which they demand."

Q.: "I thought you said that the present conditions are intolerable."

A.: "I think that many of the present conditions are intolerable."

Q.: "Do you think that any fair-minded man would doubt that in that book you have indicated over and over again that unless the Conservatives are prepared to consent to their own erosion and to undertake never to seek to upset what the Socialist Government may have done, revolution is inevitable."

A.: "I do not think that is wholly fair. I accept the view that it states that unless, when a Socialist Government has introduced large-scale changes, those large-scale changes are accepted by the Conservative Party, the likelihood is very great indeed of revolutionary change."

Further passages were read to Mr. Laski which were summarised in a final paragraph:

Q.: "Men may abdicate positions they do not deem fundamental. So far in history at any rate they, that is the Conservatives, have not abdicated peacefully as a class from any positions they deemed vital to their well-being.

"That is why Revolution by violence is inevitable?"

A.: "That is why Revolution by violence is inevitable in a continuing contracting economic society. That is the whole point."

Q.: "Does that apply to our country?"

A.: "At the time I wrote, it was a contracting economic system."

Q.: "There are two lines which seem to put it in a nut-shell: 'I have therefore urged that at this stage of economic development the difference between classes can only be settled by force.' Let's face it. Does that mean what it says?"

A.: "Yes, certainly, at the time it was written."

Q.: "What year was that?"

A.: "1934."

Q.: "At that time your view was: The only thing is force, violence?"

A.: "At that time my view was that the relationship between classes, the decline in the well-being of the worker, was such as to make it inevitable that if the condition continued, the relationship between classes would be resolved by force."

Q.: "Inevitable Revolution by violence?"

A.: "Yes."

Q.: "You believe that honestly?"

A.: "Certainly."

Q.: "What was the date on which you changed your mind?"

A.: "The date when I changed my mind was at the beginning of the war."

Q.: "Now I am going to my second postulate, that you took the view that if achievement of your political ends cannot be achieved without violence, then violence is legitimate?"

A.: "Yes."

Q.: "Does this sentence summarise your views: 'To achieve power peacefully and peacefully to consolidate its possibilities must be the desire of every Socialist who has thought at all seriously of the alternative, but to say this is not to say that all Socialist policy must be constructed upon the assumption that the constitutional road to power is the one to pursue in any eventuality'?"

A.: "I accept that."

Q.: " 'If the change in Great Britain from Capitalism to Socialism could be accomplished by constitutional means, no one would be happier at that result than I, but I fear that on the record of history such a change is unlikely. When the ultimate rights of property are in question reason becomes the slave of passions.' Doesn't that mean this?"

A.: "It means precisely what it says."

Q.: "And that is still your view?"

A.: "Yes."

Q.: "Tell me this: If Revolution in this country cannot be achieved by consent—you follow what I mean, if the Capitalists will not give way—?"

A.: "Yes."

Q.: "Do you think violence would be justified?"

A.: "That is one of your questions that it is impossible for a professional historian like myself to answer by Yes or No."

Of course, this is only a short attempt to summarise the questions put to Mr. Laski and his answers. It is only right to say that throughout his cross-examination Mr. Laski argued that his writings, if fairly considered as a whole, merely pointed out his fear of possible violence and his methods of preventing such a result; but the questions put to him were directed to show him that, whatever his intentions, there were main passages in his books which might very easily be misunderstood.

I then referred him to a broadcast which he had given on the B.B.C. in company with Sir Malcolm Darling and Lord Hinchingbrooke in which the following passages occurred:

Sir Malcolm Darling: "As a Socialist, Laski, do you think that Democracy and Socialism are compatible?"

Professor Laski: "Yes, but I don't for one moment say that it's certain you can arrive at Socialism through the processes solely of discussion."

"Let us just pause there. What did you mean, that you mean violence would have to be necessary?"

"Yes. But, you know, I must make a comment on this. It's important. There is the case of Ulster. We nearly came to blows over that."

Lord Hinchingbrooke: "Laski says that he doubts whether Socialism in this country can be established in the final stages through the process of discussion. Now that seems to me to be an out-and-out anti-democratic point of view. It envisages the whip being applied in the penultimate stages."

"You have no doubt at all that what Lord Hinchingbrooke meant was: Laski, you are threatening force by the Labour Party!"

Sir Malcolm Darling: "Or even the gun!"
"That meant fighting by the Labour Party?"
"Yes."

Lord Hinchingbrooke: "Yes, but does Laski

seriously envisage force being used to introduce Socialism into Britain?"

Professor Laski: "Let's be realists. I have never known a case in which a governing class has surrendered ultimate possession of powers without fighting for it. Charles I fought for his privileges, so did the French aristocracy, so did the Russian nobility."

Lord Hinchingbrooke: "You have not answered my question except by implication, but let's leave it at that."

What Mr. Laski really intended to convey by his observations on the B.B.C. was never quite clear to me, but just as in the case of his writings, so in the case of his broadcast Mr. Laski's words may very well have created an unfortunate impression.

Finally, the whole case upon both sides was summed up in the last few questions, in which Mr. Laski was faced with the whole libel of which he complained. The actual words were put to him: "When people felt that was the moment for great experiment, for innovation, because when war is over people so easily forget, especially those who had the power in their hands, that was the time for experiment. Great changes were so urgent in this country and if they were not made by consent, they would be made by violence."

"By whose violence?"

"By the drift of events in the country."

Lord Chief Justice interposes:

"Just read the whole passage. Mr. Laski, what you are being asked in view of that when you say:

'and if they are not made by consent, they will be made by violence' you mean, it would be made by violence by the people who would make the experiment?"

"Certainly."

I then asked him:

"Now, let us see what that means, Mr. Laski. Is this what you admit you are saying: 'If these Socialist changes are not made by consent, they will be made by the violence of those who believe in Socialism'?"

"Yes."

"But where in the world does that differ from the one passage in the libel of which you complain. I cannot follow it. Isn't it exactly the same?"

"No."

That was substantially the last answer by Mr. Laski. What he was really saying was in effect: You are accusing me of having advocated violence. There is all the difference in the world between doing that and between pointing out the possible danger of violence and the best method of avoiding it. Our answer was: We maintain that you spoke the actual words set out in the article, whether you meant them or not.

After Mr. Laski left the box, many witnesses were called upon both sides, their evidence being directed to the one question which was really in dispute, namely as to whether or not the paragraph fairly represented what Mr. Laski had said at Newark. As was only to be expected, people who were listening to a heated debate between a public speaker and a somewhat irritating heckler had very different recollections of the words actually used; some of them did not hear anything, some of them heard too much and some did not remember what they had heard. A very good example of this was one of Mr. Laski's own witnesses who was asked whether he had heard Mr. Laski use the only disputed words "as for violence, if Labour could not obtain what it needed by general consent, we shall have to use violence, even if it means revolution". The answer was No, but unfortunately for Mr. Laski the next question did not get quite such a satisfactory reply.

"Or any words like that?"

Then came an answer somewhat disappointing to Mr. Laski.

"Similar, but the words 'Labour Party' were never used in it at all."

Naturally, in cross-examination the witness was asked:

"So in substance the words were used, but there was no reference to any political party—is that right?"

"As I just said, yes."

For the defendants there were several witnesses who took a contrary view. One in particular was a gentleman in the Consular Service whose evidence was considered so important that it had to be taken on commission in Turkey. He was quite definite that Mr. Laski had in fact used the words, and when he was cross-examined he gave one answer which was very helpful to the defendants. It was suggested to him that in fact the libellous words had been spoken by the heckler and not by Mr. Laski at all. This was the witness's answer:

"It is not my actual recollection of it, and the reason I am fairly confident about it is that that evening after I went back to the hotel I made a note of what had happened actually and it bears me out."

The case lasted five days and at the end of it the jury found that the report in the *Newark Advertiser* was fair and accurate, and so Mr. Laski lost his case.

And what was it all about?

The only lesson taught to anybody was the unwisdom of making heated observations at a public meeting. It was quite obvious that Mr. Laski was, not unreasonably, annoyed by the rudeness of some of the observations made to him. Whether he lost his temper and said more than he meant or whether he did not quite know what he did say or whether he was half right and half wrong in his recollection, no one will ever know, but if ever there was a battle of huge importance fought about nothing at all, in my opinion, it was waged during those five days in the Court of the Lord Chief Justice of England.

THE TRAINER AND THE JOCKEY CLUB

The case of Mr. Chapman against the Jockey Club was, in my opinion, one of those few cases which it was quite right to bring, although the chances of ultimate success were very small. It was the only method by which Mr. Chapman could free his character from the imputation placed upon it, and establish once for all that he was completely innocent. At the same time the action may have done good in the racing world by establishing, even more firmly than before, the absolute authority of the Jockey Club.

The affairs of the Jockey Club are conducted by their elected stewards, who are gentlemen of the highest and most respected position in racing circles, and their jurisdiction is conferred upon them by their rules. Amongst other powers they have an absolute discretion to grant licences to trainers and jockeys, and in the same way to withdraw those licences if they think fit, without giving any reason for their decision; they can warn any trainer or jockey off Newmarket Heath, and also publish the warning-off notices in the *Racing Calendar*, again without assigning a reason. Having regard to the absolute ruin caused to a trainer by a warning-off notice, it may seem that the rules are both strict and severe, but the proper conduct of the racing world no doubt requires strictness and, if necessary, severity, and experience has shown that the interests of the turf are best served by being left in the stewards' hands. Possibly there are some trainers who would wish to be less regimented in the exercise of their profession, but they have no option in the matter; if they wish to obtain a licence to train horses, they must consent to be bound by the rules of the Jockey Club.

One very important duty of the stewards is in connection with the doping of race-horses. This may be done in many ways and either with the object of stimulating the animal in order to develop an unnatural speed in a particular race, or else possibly to prevent it from showing its normal form. In either event, while it is usually not difficult to establish the fact that the horse has been doped, it may be almost impossible to discover who is the actual person who has administered the drug: some fraudulent person may slip unobserved into the stables, or the travelling horse-box, or any of the places surrounding the racecourse, and there seize an opportunity to use the syringe, spray or other device well known to the so-called "clever division". It may always be possible to prove that any particular person is not and could not have been responsible for what has been done, but it is quite another thing to fix responsibility upon someone else. Consequently the stewards decided to adopt the course of holding the trainer himself absolutely responsible for the continued safety of his horse; once any horse is found to have been doped the blame for such a happening must rest upon the trainer.

Mr. Chapman was a trainer who had his stables at Lavant near Chichester, where he trained a horse called 'Don Pat'. This horse was due to run in the

Bedfont Plate High Weight Handicap at Kempton Park. The horse travelled safely from its stable in a horse-box, and in due course arrived at the racecourse where it took part in a race, which it won. Unfortunately for Mr. Chapman, the unusual running of the horse attracted the attention of the stewards of the meeting and upon the return of the horse to the weighing enclosure they directed that it should at once be examined by a veterinary surgeon. Upon examination the surgeon reported that both the saliva and the sweat showed clear evidence that the horse had been doped with a stimulant known as caffein and that a fairly large dose had been given. Caffein is a drug which is not uncommonly given to a horse by rubbing the substance upon its teeth. The local stewards of the meeting thereupon reported the matter to the stewards of the Jockey Club, who in due course called Mr. Chapman before them and embarked upon a detailed and thorough investigation of the whole incident. The hearing of the case took place in private on September 29th, 1936 and, as was only to be expected, was completely fair and impartial. The stewards at Kempton Park gave evidence both as to the running of the horse and as to its excited appearance after the race. In their opinion the horse showed distinct signs of being under the influence of drugs. The veterinary surgeon who had immediately conducted an examination stated that the horse had been doped and that the drug employed was caffein: in all probability it had been rubbed upon the horse's teeth. There was no evidence and indeed it was not even suggested that Mr. Chapman personally was a party to, or had any knowledge, of the administration of the drug. He gave evidence himself that the horse appeared to him in perfect health before the race and none of the stable boys who were called, including the boy who travelled in the horse-box, noticed anything wrong or could throw any light upon the matter. The actual source of the doping remained wrapped in mystery. The probability would seem to be that some person had been waiting his time around the stables before the race and had managed to slip the caffein, which is a drug with a very rapid action, into the horse's mouth just before it went out for the parade.

Upon the conclusion of the evidence the stewards retired to consider their findings and decision, which they finally gave to Mr. Chapman in the following words: "We have given most careful thought to this case. We have come to the conclusion that 'Don Pat' was doped and he is disqualified for life. We consider you, as trainer, were directly responsible for the care of the horse. Your licence to train is revoked and you are warned off Newmarket Heath."

There is no doubt that these findings and this decision were alike fully within the powers of the stewards conferred upon them by the Racing Rules, and inasmuch as Mr. Chapman was bound by these rules he could have no redress against a sentence which spelt his ruin upon the turf. Moreover, the words of the decision itself would seem to make it quite clear that the stewards had found nothing against him except a breach of the absolute duty imposed upon a trainer to use such care as would ensure the continued safety of any horse under his charge. There was no breath of suspicion upon his honesty or integrity. Unfortunately, when the stewards came to publish their decision, which, again under the rules, they were quite entitled to do, the wording was altered; it then read as follows:

"The stewards of the Jockey Club after further investigation satisfied themselves that a drug had been administered to the horse for the purpose of the race in question. They disqualified the horse for this race and for all future races under their rules and warned Mr. Chapman, the trainer of the horse, off Newmarket Heath." It will be observed that the words "you as trainer were directly responsible for the care of the horse" have been omitted. Why this was done was never quite clear to me. The stewards, during the course of the subsequent trials, stated that it was done in Mr. Chapman's interest as the omitted words might have been taken to indicate a closer responsibility upon Mr. Chapman than the mere word "trainer" implied. It is possible that other minds might have formed a different opinion. The statement in the *Racing Calendar* was subsequently repeated in the *Times* under a caption: "Racing. Another Trainer Warned Off. The Doping of 'Don Pat'."

The effect of these publications was immediate. The Press seized upon the incident as a racing scandal of first-class importance and the reports and comments which appeared in the evening papers made it clear beyond all doubt that many, if not most, people were under the impression that the trainer had himself been found guilty of fraudulent practices. Mr. Chapman woke up in the morning to find himself not only warned off the Turf and ruined financially, but also obliged to face the world with his reputation for honesty completely destroyed. To a young man at the beginning of his life, who had hitherto enjoyed an absolutely unblemished character, the position could not be allowed to remain unchallenged. There could be no appeal from the decision of the stewards; all that remained was recourse to the Law Courts; Mr. Chapman decided to bring an action for libel against the stewards themselves for their publication in the *Racing Calendar*, and against the *Times* for their repetition of the libellous statement.

From the outset the difficulties in his way were enormous. As the stewards had acted entirely within their powers under the rules, there was no possible means of questioning the correctness of their decision, and moreover the words they had published taken in their strict phraseology were true; his only possible cause of action could arise if he was able to satisfy a judge that the words were reasonably capable of meaning that he had himself been guilty of doping 'Don Pat', and then of satisfying a jury that in fact that is what they meant. In spite of all the difficulties that existed Mr. Chapman was determined to bring the matter before the Court, and accordingly he issued a writ.

During the months which elapsed between the issue of the writ and the date of the hearing there was one fact which assumed great importance in the minds of Mr. Chapman's legal advisers. As the whole importance of the case lay in the complete vindication of Mr. Chapman's personal honour, it was essential that, if ever the case was allowed by the judge to reach the jury, a verdict should be given for substantial damages. By that means alone could his vindication be complete. Whatever the ultimate decision might be on points of Law, I was determined that if Mr. Chapman's character came up for valuation, it should be valued highly; small damages would be worse than no damages at all. There was one incident which might help in that direction. It was perhaps not unnaturally assumed that the stewards must have been aware, if only from the paragraphs in the evening Press, that an interpretation most harmful to Mr. Chapman had been placed upon their decision, and yet from first to last they had made not the slightest attempt to remedy that false impression. Of course they were not obliged to do so, but a jury might possibly take that fact into account at arriving at any decision they might give. Some attempt had been made to induce the stewards to take that course. Mr. Chapman had many friends and many sympathisers. The Duke of Richmond and Gordon had written to one of the stewards on Mr. Chapman's behalf, saying that all Mr. Chapman asked from the stewards was an intimation to the Press that he had only been warned off for negligence and not for actual doping, and asking that Mr. Chapman might be allowed to have an interview with the stewards to see if that result could not be achieved. The steward in question felt that course to be impossible, as he was a defendant in the pending action. He did not consider it would be proper for him to have any personal interview with the plaintiff, and in consequence no such interview took place. It always seemed to me unfortunate that the very moderate request of Mr. Chapman, namely a public acknowledgment that the stewards' decision was only based upon negligence, could not have been granted, but however nothing further was done and the action pursued its course.

The trial took place before Mr. Justice Horridge and a special jury, and it aroused the greatest interest in the racing world. It was certainly an important case. On the one hand nobody could doubt that it was in the interest of everyone interested in racing that the complete authority of the stewards of the Jockey Club should be preserved. On the other hand it seemed that in this particular case Mr. Chapman had suffered an injustice by reason of the actual words employed against him. The stewards relied upon the Law; Mr. Chapman relied upon the facts. Mr. Chapman, who was the first witness on his own behalf, was a good-looking young man, and he gave evidence with great moderation and self-restraint. He accepted without question the fact that the horse must have been doped, although he had not the faintest idea how or by whom the doping had been done. Although he had taken, as he thought, every possible precaution, he accepted full responsibility for his horse's safety. As for the hearing before the stewards, he acknowledged that he had been treated with every courtesy and consideration, and that the enquiry had been conducted with absolute fairness. His only complaint was as to the misleading words in which, as he maintained, the actual decision was wrongly conveyed to the public. From first to last no one suggested for one moment that he personally was in any way responsible for the horse having been doped. At the conclusion of his evidence there was no doubt that Mr. Chapman had made a very good impression upon the Court, and that the jury would help him if they could.

The stewards all gave evidence in their turn in order to establish a fact, which nobody challenged, that they had acted throughout the enquiry in perfect good faith and strict impartiality. The only fact upon which they were cross-examined was as to the reason for not contradicting the erroneous impression which had been apparently created by the words they had employed in their decision. The hardship upon Mr. Chapman was pointed out to them; the ease with which that hardship could have been removed was emphasised; they were asked if they had not appreciated the possible injustice caused by the publications in the evening Press. Unfortunately not one of them had ever read any one of the copies of the papers in question.

That was the end of the evidence. The defendants asked the judge to withdraw the case from the jury upon the legal grounds (a) that the words in the stewards' decision were literally true, (b) that by the rules of racing the plaintiff must be taken to have consented to their publication in the *Racing Calendar*, and (c) that they were therefore privileged. The judge declined: he said that he would hold the words to be capable, in Law, of a defamatory meaning and that he would ask the jury to decide one important question of fact:

"Do the words complained of mean that the plaintiff was a party to the doping of 'Don Pat'?"

This one question was of course vital to the whole case, and inasmuch as it was subsequently reconsidered by the Court of Appeal, it is only fair to the learned judge to state that at that date the Law upon the subject was not established, and that there had been no previous decision upon the point. The jury returned a verdict in favour of Mr. Chapman, and gave him enormous damages. They awarded against the stewards and Messrs. Weatherby in respect of publication in the *Racing Calendar* the sum of £13,000, and against the *Times* newspaper the sum of £3,000.

It is of course impossible to know what matters the jury take into their consideration in the assessment of damages, and inasmuch as the matter was subsequently reconsidered by the Court of Appeal, it is idle to speculate, but there can be little doubt that they were considerably impressed by the complete absence of any attempt to rectify the unfortunate misapprehension which had arisen. Having regard to the immense importance to the Jockey Club of the decision and also to the very heavy damages awarded, it was obvious that the defendants would appeal, and the appeal was immediate. There were two distinct grounds upon which the opinion of the Court of Appeal was invited: (*a*) Having regard to the fact that the wording of the notice in the *Racing Calendar* was in the strict sense actually true, and that the stewards had admittedly acted in perfect good faith, it was contended that they were completely protected by privilege; and (b) that the damages were too high.

Perhaps unfortunately for Mr. Chapman, between the date of the jury's award in his favour and the hearing in the Court of Appeal, another case had been determined, also in the Court of Appeal. In that latter case, by a curious coincidence, I had been acting for some of the very stewards who were the defendants in Mr. Chapman's action, and had been constrained to argue on their behalf the direct opposite of that which I would have to argue on behalf of Mr. Chapman. The facts were very different, but the point of Law was very much the same, and the Court of Appeal had on that occasion given their decision in favour of the stewards.

Mr. Chapman's appeal was argued for four days and the Court reserved their judgment, but eventually they adhered to their previous decision, and decided that under the circumstances both the stewards and Messrs. Weatherby were protected, and that the verdict against them could not be maintained; on the other hand they held that there was no privilege in the case of the *Times*. But they further took the view that the damages awarded by the jury against all the defendants were too high, and in the result the action against the stewards and Messrs. Weatherby was dismissed, and as against the *Times* an order was made for a new trial.

What, if any, steps were taken about a new trial I never knew; and perhaps from Mr. Chapman's point of view it did not much matter. The only thing that he had really derived in bringing his action was a complete and final vindication of his character, and that object he had abundantly achieved. The public attention drawn to his unfortunate position by the overwhelming verdict of a jury must have gone a long way to wipe away the stigma of his warning-off notice. Was the price he had to pay too high? I hope not. But the case of Chapman and the stewards of the Jockey Club has always left in my mind a strong feeling that there is somewhere a defect in our legal system when a completely innocent person may have to suffer from the public belief that he is guilty and there exists no means of proving his innocence except by bringing an action which he cannot win.

THE CASE OF THE TALKING MONGOOSE

It became known as the case of the talking mongoose, although the mongoose had nothing to do with it beyond being a central figure in the sensational slander action brought by Mr. Lambert against Sir Cecil Levita.

Like so many other slander actions it began as an absurdity, but once it got out of hand it developed almost into a tragedy, partly, no doubt, by reason of the fact that it need never have been fought. A little generosity, perhaps even a little common-sense, might have put an end to the whole controversy, but neither was forthcoming and so the action was fought to the bitter end, with the result that Sir Cecil Levita must have suffered great mental distress as well as enormous financial loss, and the Prime Minister of England found it necessary to appoint a Parliamentary Commission to enquire into the circumstances which came to light during the trial.

Mr. Lambert was the editor of *The Listener*, the official publication of the B.B.C., and he was also a member of the Council of the British Film Institute. This institute was financed by the Government for the purpose of producing educational films, and was closely associated with the B.B.C., so much so that Mr. Lambert could only sit upon the council with the B.B.C.'s knowledge and consent. Lady Levita, the wife of Sir Cecil, also sat upon the council and was well acquainted with Mr. Lambert, with whom she was on excellent terms. For some reason which was not material to the action, Mr. Lambert had incurred the animosity of some people in the Film Trade, who requested the B.B.C. to withdraw their consent to his continued presence on the council, in consequence of which objection Lady Levita suggested that he should consult her husband on the difficulty which had arisen. Sir Cecil Levita was a gentleman of considerable influence, having been chairman of the London County Council, and he warmly supported Mr. Lambert's cause. He arranged a luncheon appointment with a Mr. Gladstone Murray, Mr. Lambert's immediate superior, at which he urged the view that it would be nothing short of a calamity if the B.B.C. withdrew their consent to Mr. Lambert's remaining upon the Film Council. In a letter of thanks to Sir Cecil, Mr. Lambert expressed his gratitude by stating: "But for your weighty intervention I should have had to send in my resignation."

Not very long afterwards two incidents occurred which played a very important part in the subsequent trial. Mr. Lambert was acquainted with a Mr. Harry Price, who was the secretary of the London Council for Psychical Research, and there had been brought to Mr. Price's notice the strange story of a farmer in the Isle of Man who claimed to be the recipient of visit from a remarkable mongoose. According to the farmer this mongoose was possessed of the power of speech; it not only spoke English but many foreign tongues varying from Flemish to Hindustani, and not content with these accomplishments, upon its visits to the farmer it was accustomed to beguile the time by singing nursery rhymes, and occasionally bursting into dance; it also possessed the power of changing itself at will into a cat. From further information supplied it appeared that this versatile mongoose was eighty-six years old, and answered to the name of "Jeff". Not unnaturally these peculiarities aroused the interest of the Institute of Psychical Research and Mr. Price decided to make a personal investigation, and for that purpose to pay a visit to the Isle of Man taking with him his friend Mr. Lambert as an independent witness. Needless to state, the visit was unsatisfactory; no mongoose presented itself, and such manifestations as occurred were related by Mr. Price in a book which he called *The Haunting of Cashens' Gap*, to which Mr. Lambert added three chapters of speculation as to how the trick was done. And there, but for the subsequent slander action, the matter might well have passed into oblivion. The only other incident of importance was connected with a subscription of £100 paid by Mr. Price into the funds of the British Film Institute, and a holiday visit to Germany taken by Mr. Price and Mr. Lambert together.

The next step in the unfortunate story was the estrangement between Mr. Lambert and the Levitas. The cause of the change in their mutual relations was never made quite clear, but undoubtedly a serious difference of opinion arose between Lambert and Lady Levita as to the desirability of retaining in the service of the institute a gentleman about whom they held decided and opposing views, and it may well be that the dispute caused Sir Cecil to change his previous high opinion of Mr. Lambert. Whatever the reason, Sir Cecil decided to withdraw the sponsorship which he had expressed to Gladstone Murray, and with that object again invited Mr. Murray to lunch.

At that luncheon Sir Cecil displayed such a remarkable change of view with regard to Mr. Lambert, and expressed that view in such extreme terms, that Mr. Murray felt it his duty to convey these terms to Mr. Lambert himself. According to Murray, Sir Cecil had stated that Lambert was mentally unbalanced, and that the B.B.C. ought to withdraw their consent to his continuing to act on the Council of the Film Institute. He stated that Lambert was a believer in the occult and he instanced the fact that Lambert had expressed belief in the existence of the talking mongoose. While speaking Sir Cecil was said to have tapped his forehead significantly in order to emphasise Mr. Lambert's mental condition. He also told Murray that Lambert had given up his home on more than one occasion in fear of "The Evil Eye". Sir Cecil had also criticised Mr. Lambert's use of money belonging to the institute, even suggesting that some part of the £100 subscribed by Price had been used by Lambert on his own holiday. He ended up by saying that probably the only way to get Lambert off the council was to get the B.B.C. to withdraw their consent to his acting, and that he (Levita) would have to inform Mr. Norman, the head of the B.B.C.

Not unnaturally Mr. Lambert was incensed by these suggestions and immediately wrote to Sir Cecil stating the substance of what Mr. Murray had told him and demanding an apology and nothing more. It was an eminently reasonable request. If Mr. Murray had accurately reported the conversation, an apology was the least Sir Cecil could have done to make amends; if the report was caused by some misunderstanding, why in the world was not the mistake corrected! The judge himself asked that very question himself at the trial. "Why" he asked Levita, "didn't you ask these two gentleman to meet you at another lunch and say 'I never said these things and of course I never meant them'?"

But nothing of the sort occurred. Instead Mr. Lambert received a letter from a firm of solicitors which, so far from easing the position, made it infinitely worse and became the subject of very serious comment at the trial. They wrote, "We understand that the matters to which you refer are being discussed to-morrow by high officials of the British Broadcasting Corporation, and we suggest that the whole matter should wait over until after the discussion has taken place." What in the world could such a letter mean! How could Sir Cecil Levita's solicitors know that high officials of the B.B.C. were discussing the matter unless Sir Cecil himself had told his solicitors? And how could the officials know anything about it unless Sir Cecil had told them. Having regard to the grave importance subsequently attached to the letter the date is of special interest. It was dated March 2nd, 1936.

A few days later Sir Cecil himself wrote to Mr. Lambert disputing the accuracy of Mr. Murray's statements but saying that if he had repeated gossip about Mr. Lambert he was quite prepared to apologise. As an expression either of regret or withdrawal this letter was considered quite unsatisfactory, and a writ for slander was issued.

Sir Cecil's formal defence to the claim made against him was astounding, particularly having regard to his quasi-apology. He pleaded, first that he had not spoken the words complained of, secondly that if he had, the words were privileged, and last of all that the allegations made against Mr. Lambert were true.

To slander a person may or may not be a serious offence, and one for which a complete apology may be a sufficient amend, but to persist in a serious slander to the extent of maintaining that if the words were spoken they are in fact true, turns what may be a comparatively unimportant matter into one of the utmost gravity. From the very outset of the proceedings Sir Cecil had placed himself in very great difficulty; the words which he was alleged to have spoken while tapping his forehead to emphasise their significance undoubtedly meant that Mr. Lambert was, in vulgar parlance, "cracked"; that he was not honest, and was not fit to retain his position on the council. Sir Cecil had taken upon himself the burden of proving those allegations to be true. Did he himself believe them? If he did, it might be thought more likely that he had said those very words; if he did not believe them, his plea of privilege must disappear; because no one can be privileged in saying words which he knows are untrue. As an example of the somewhat rash way in which the justification had been framed, Sir Cecil had undertaken to prove that Mr. Lambert had left his house in Cobham because he believed it to be under a spell. In truth Mr. Lambert had never left a house in Cobham, for that or any other cause, for the simple reason that he had never lived there at all.

A still more surprising fact was brought to Mr. Lambert's notice during the preparation of the case which immeasurably increased his indignation. He was informed that Sir Cecil Levita had carried out his threat to communicate the slanders to Mr. Norman and Sir Stephen Tallents, two influential members of the B.B.C. Mr. Lambert was shown a memorandum which had been prepared by one of them to the effect that if Mr. Lambert persisted in his action against Levita, that course of conduct would greatly prejudice his prospects with the B.B.C. If in fact Sir Cecil had endeavoured to bring about that result the gravity of the situation could not be exaggerated; but Mr. Lambert could not prove it; the memorandum could not be used against Sir Cecil as he was not party to it, and unless he admitted the allegation in cross-examination, the matter could not be pursued. Everything must depend upon his evidence, and it is perhaps not surprising that Mr. Lambert awaited the hearing with some anxiety.

The action was tried before Mr. Justice Swift and a special jury, and it was commenced in an atmosphere very different from that into which it ultimately developed. Mr. Gladstone Murray proved the words alleged to have been spoken to him by Sir Cecil

Levita and the significant manner in which he had tapped his forehead while speaking, and he was not shaken in cross-examinations. Then Mr. Lambert himself gave evidence. He was quite definite that there was no word of truth in any of Sir Cecil's allegations against him; he did not believe in the occult, nor in the talking mongoose; he had never left any home of his in consequence of the Evil Eye, and as for the suggested house in Cobham, he had never even lived there; it was quite untrue that he had ever spent any of Price's £100 on himself.

The cross-examination of Mr. Lambert did not carry the case much further: it consisted very largely of an enquiry into the peculiarities of the talking mongoose. Counsel who appeared for Sir Cecil did not suggest that Lambert was mad, but that he was highly strung, not very well balanced and inconsistent, and based this suggestion on the allegation that Lambert believed in the mongoose and had told Sir Cecil of his belief. Any discussion upon this ridiculous animal was bound to arouse hilarity, in which the judge took part, and at this part the audience in Court enjoyed themselves enormously. Mr. Lambert left the box with his evidence unshaken, and it was quite obvious that up to this point the feeling throughout the Court was strongly in his favour.

When it became Sir Cecil Levita's turn to give evidence, the whole atmosphere changed from farce to drama. He was not a particularly impressive witness; a good deal of his evidence appeared to me irrelevant, and his account of his conversation with

Mr. Murray was somewhat diffuse. He denied that he used most of the words in the alleged slander, he said the reference to the Evil Eye was mere gossip, and while denying that he had tapped his forehead he appeared anxious to explain a possible misunderstanding by saying that he suffered from pains in the head. He particularly denied the important allegation against him that he had threatened to go to Mr. Norman. He also made the somewhat curious statement that it was Mr. Murray himself who first made the suggestion that "Lambert is a curious fellow"; a suggestion that had never been made before.

Then came Sir Cecil's turn to be cross-examined, and he did not appear to find the questions quite so easy to answer as those he had been asked by his own counsel. "If a man spoke to you about a friend and interspersed his observations by tapping his forehead and saying, 'You know,' what would you understand that to mean?"

"I saw a film a few days ago, where the tapping of the head——"

"Did you hear my question? I am not interested in your film experience. What would you understand him to mean?"

"I said that that is the conventional sign——"

"I will ask you once more. What would you understand him to mean?"

"To mean that he was lacking in intelligence."

"That he was out of his mind?"

"Not necessarily."

"You realise, do you not, that at some time your

evidence may have to be criticised before the jury? Just think once more. What would you understand him to mean?"

"That he was out of his mind."

"Supposing in addition to that he said, 'He has moved his home several times because of pursuits by the Evil Eye,' what would you understand by that?"

"I should say it was a most fantastic statement."

"I will ask you again. What would you understand by that?"

"I should not believe him."

"I will ask you a third time. What would you understand by that?"

"That he was superstitious."

"And if, while speaking, the speaker tapped his forehead significantly?"

"I have already said that according to Mr. Murray——"

"What would *you* understand him to mean? Do face it."

"That he was lacking in mental balance."

"That he was cracked?"

"Yes. But I did not do these things."

"At the date of this lunch did you honestly believe that Mr. Lambert was out of his mind?"

"No. Nor did I say it."

"Did you believe that Mr. Lambert was no longer fit to be a Governor of the Film Institute?"

"No. Nor did I say it."

"Have you ever honestly believed it?"

"No."

"So that if you did in fact say it to Mr. Murray, you were saying what you did not believe to be true."

That was an end of any defence there might be under a claim of privilege, but there remained the far more important question of the memorandum prepared by the B.B.C. Unless Sir Cecil Levita knew of its existence it could not be used in evidence, and it was to ascertain that fact we had been waiting. The next questions would decide.

"Mr. Murray has told us that you stated that if Mr. Lambert did not cease to be a Governor of the Film Institute you would go and see Mr. Norman of the B.B.C.?"

"Yes."

"Immediately on receiving Mr. Lambert's letter of complaint did you go and see Mr. Norman at his home?"

"Yes."

"About Mr. Lambert?"

"Yes."

"Did you go to Mr. Norman with a view of getting him to tell Mr. Lambert that if he brought an action against you he would be dismissed."

This question was enough to cause a rustle from the reporters' seats; notebooks were re-opened and pencils poised; everyone waited for Sir Cecil's answer. He denied the suggestion with indignation. He had never heard such a suggestion before. And his answer was final. To my intense disappointment the memorandum could not be used. And if the defence had not made what I always consider to be grave mistake, it would never have been produced in Court. They decided to call as a witness a Mr. Fuller, who was also on the Film Council and a gentleman whom I was overjoyed to see, because he had acted as an emissary between Sir Cecil Levita and the B.B.C. and I knew it. His cross-examination changed the whole course of the trial. He was taken at once to the matter I was so anxious to establish.

"Do you know the writ in this action is dated March 5th?"

"Yes."

"On March 24th did you ask Mr. Lambert to lunch?"

"Yes."

"Did Mr. Lambert appear to be quite well in health?"

"Yes."

"Between these dates had you seen Sir Stephen Tallents of the B.B.C.?"

"Yes."

"Did you go to Sir Stephen Tallents to try and effect a settlement of the action."

"Yes."

"Were you acting as an emissary from Levita?"

"Yes."

"Did anyone tell you that Lambert was suffering from a nervous breakdown?"

"I think it was Sir Stephen Tallents."

"What had that got to do with you?"

"Nothing."

"Did you tell Mr. Lambert that Sir Stephen

Tallents had said that if Mr. Lambert did not settle this action, the B.B.C. would turn him out?"

"Certainly not."

"Did you later get to know of a memorandum made by Sir Stephen Tallents about this action?"

"Yes."

And then came the vital question.

"Did you discuss that memorandum with Sir Cecil Levita?"

"Yes."

"Is this a copy of the memorandum?"

I had it in my hand. At once there came a strenuous opposition to the production of the memorandum, but it was too late; the judge allowed it to be read in Court, and its production caused even a greater sensation than had been anticipated. It was dated March 6th. Here it is.

Memorandum

"I saw Mr. Lambert at 11.10 on the morning of March 6th. I told him I was instructed:

(1) To urge him to take a week's leave, as his doctor, I understood, had advised, and to consider the matter quietly again thereafter.

(2) And to assure him:

   (*a*) That his position with the corporation was not at present in any way prejudiced or damaged:

   But to tell him

   (*b*) That if he went on with the course which he had indicated the previous morning,

there was a serious danger that he might well prejudice his position with the corporation because
(1) He could make the corporation doubt his judgment
(2) He could seem to be placing his own interest in priority to those of the corporation.
S. J. Tallents, 6–3–36.

"Do you happen to notice the date of the memorandum?"

"March 6th, 1936."

"Were you in Court when the letter was read from Sir Cecil's solicitors: letter dated March 2nd, 1936? Starting, 'We understand that the matters are being discussed by high officials of the B.B.C.'?"

"Yes."

"Do you see any similarity between the dates?"

"Now you mention it I do."

"In your opinion could that memorandum have any meaning to a fair-minded man except this: 'If you do not drop this action against Sir Cecil Levita you will get dismissed'?"

The witness would not agree to that suggestion, but from the look of utter amazement upon every face in Court there could be no doubt as to the effect which the memorandum had caused. If Sir Stephen Tallents had been called to give evidence as to what he had really meant by his memorandum, perhaps that effect might have been different; but he was not, and the evidence ended on that disquieting note.

The judge summed up impartially but gravely, and the jury answered the following questions:

"Did Levita speak the words complained of?"

"Yes."

"Are they true?"

"No."

And they awarded Mr. Lambert as damages the enormous sum of £7,500, the largest amount that I personally have ever known to be given in a slander action. The award certainly caused a sensation in Court as well as in the Temple.

But the matter did not end there. So much perturbation was aroused by the publication of the B.B.C. memorandum that the Prime Minister thought it desirable at once to appoint a special board to enquire into the whole circumstances, and within a month the report of this board was laid before Parliament. From a public point of view it was eminently satisfactory that the board completely exonerated the officials of the B.B.C. They found that they were in no way influenced by Sir Cecil Levita and were acting merely in what they considered the best interest of the B.B.C. and of Mr. Lambert himself. But the report contained this significant paragraph. "Whether the officials were wise or not is another matter. . . . the B.B.C. have only themselves to blame for the unfortunate impression caused by the singularly inapt words in the memorandum."

With that finding from a public point of view the action passed into oblivion. But for the parties themselves! A little more wisdom; a little less temper! Perhaps even one word of genuine apology and the whole trouble need never have occurred. For that reason alone, the talking mongoose might well serve as a warning to other litigants who find themselves faced with an action for slander!

THE STOCKBROKER AND THE YO-YO

Mr. Blennerhassett was a prosperous and highly respected member of the London Stock Exchange. In the course of his long experience he must, no doubt, have observed that when business in the House is slack, some of the younger and perhaps more irresponsible members are accustomed to while away the idle hours with light-hearted pleasantry bestowed upon their fellow members. Grave and elderly stockbrokers crossing the floor, deep in thought, and with a copy of the *Financial Times* tucked beneath their arm, have upon occasions discovered, to their intense indignation, that some bright spirit has applied a match to the newspaper from behind, thereby causing unbounded delight to those who observed the conflagration. If the elderly gentleman is wise, he smiles benignly; if he is unwise he loses his temper. In the year 1932, Mr. Blennerhassett was the object of hilarious attention from some of his associates upon the Stock Exchange, and he lost his temper; and the results were most unfortunate. The whole trouble arose out of a game very popular with small children, known as Yo-Yo. It was not a very remarkable or particularly skilful game, and consisted in the manipulation of a spherical object, which was allowed to unwind itself on a piece of string, and then by giving to the piece of string an appropriate jerk at the right time, caused it to wind itself up again. The owners of this somewhat elementary pastime were minded to increase its popularity by advertisement, and with that object instructed a Mr. McNulty to prepare the most humorous form of advertisement of which his ingenuity was capable. Now McNulty had a small daughter, who was accustomed to play a game of her own; this consisted in entering her father's bedroom in the morning in the capacity of a valet, bearing with her a variety of clothing. She would then ask, "Will Mr. Blennerhassett have his trousers?" If her father said, "Yes," the game proceeded, and enquiries were made as to other articles of attire; if he said, "No," the pastime came to an abrupt conclusion. The young lady had never heard of any Mr. Blennerhassett, except perhaps by a perusal of the *Bab Ballads* or some other humorous publication, in which the name appeared, but had selected it apparently at random. Mr. McNulty, being faced with the problem of inventing some individual as a suitable medium for the advertisement of Yo-Yo, had seized upon the mythical Mr. Blennerhassett for the purpose. He decided to write a poem depicting the decline and fall of a Yo-Yo devotee, illustrated with humorous drawings, and he accordingly produced an advertisement for publication in the *Evening Standard*, in which a gentleman, bearing the name of "Blennerhassett" of Throgmorton Street, was shown as a prosperous City man before being introduced to the game, and then, after a course of practice unduly prolonged, ending up with straw in his hair as the inmate of a lunatic asylum. Inasmuch as this advertisement, which appeared in the *Evening Standard* on May 26th, 1932, was the cause of all the trouble, it merits reproduction.

"Beware of Yo-Yo"

Take warning by the fate of Mr. Blennerhassett, as worthy a citizen as any that ever ate lobster at Pimm's, or holed a putt at Walton Health. "Sound man, Blennerhassett," they said in Throgmorton Street, and "Nice people, the Blennerhassetts", was the verdict over the tea-cups and in the local tennis clubs.

But Yo-Yo got him, and now . . . One day Blennerhassett brought his offspring to buy them two nice books, entertaining but instructive. Near the book department they first saw the "Yo-Yo" being played. . . .

Blennerhassett, ever responsive to the "gimme-s" of his young, bought the children one each. At home that evening, with that deprecatory condescension so familiar in parents, he offered to give them the first lesson. Strangely enough, the "Yo-Yo" was recalcitrant. It sulked. First it would and then it wouldn't. But the Blennerhassett blood was up. The dinner gong rang and cried out, but Blennerhassett kept on.

He was determined to make that little devil on the string do its stuff. The nurse took the children to bed. Mrs. B. took herself to bed. But Blennerhassett toiled on at "Yo-Yo". Came the dawn and he was still there dishevelled and wild-eyed with the "Yo-Yo" string still dangling from his trembling fingers. They tried to part him from it, but it was no use; and eventually poor Blennerhassett was taken away.

To-day, he is happy in a quiet place in the country, and under sympathetic surveillance he practises "Yo-Yo" tricks.

His old friends at Pimm's miss him at lunch, and three-

quarters of a certain foursome have had to find a stranger to make up their quorum.

So beware of "Yo-Yo" which starts as a hobby and ends as a habit.

This poetic effusion was illustrated with most unbecoming pictures of the unfortunate city magnate which left his ultimate qualification to become an inmate of a madhouse beyond question.

Most unfortunately, upon the date of publication, the Stock Exchange was passing through a period of comparative stagnation, eminently suitable, should opportunity arise, for a display of juvenile wit and hilarity, and the publication in the *Evening Standard* seemed too good a chance to miss. Upon Mr. Blennerhassett's return from lunch he was surrounded by a cheering throng who professed to see in the advertisement the unhappy life-story of their fellow member. Apart from the coincidence of the somewhat unusual name, and the fact that Mr. Blennerhassett, in company with many thousands of other City gentleman, occasionally lunched at Pimm's, there was no possible resemblance between the two individuals. The real Mr. Blennerhassett did not play Yo-Yo; he did not play golf and, therefore, had never holed a putt; and, it need hardly be said, had never been an inmate of a lunatic asylum. It may well be, and often is, a matter of annoyance to well-known men and women to see their names or portraits published under so-called humorous conditions; indeed a picture of Mr. Winston Churchill and Mr. Attlee playing spillikins until both became insane, if such a thing were possible, would no doubt depress them both, but to imagine that such a publication would be a fit matter for a slander action seems, to say the least of it, unlikely. However, that is the course upon which Mr. Blennerhassett decided. It never seemed to have occurred to him that the joke, whether good or bad, would become infinitely better or worse, as the case might be, if it was dragged into the full light of the King's Bench Division. The comparative privacy of the Stock Exchange would be exchanged for the greater publicity of the Law Courts; the hilarity which had cost him nothing would be exchanged for a trial which would cost him a great deal. But that did not matter; Mr. Blennerhassett lost his temper; so he consulted his solicitor and an action was commenced.

Thereafter the full panoply of the Law was brought into play; solicitors were employed; King's Counsel were engaged; and Mr. Justice Branson and a special jury sat in a Court in Royal Courts of Justice to enquire as to what was the proper remedy to give to Mr. Blennerhassett for the great wrong done to him.

The plaintiff's counsel must have felt it rather difficult to open his client's case with the solemnity that its importance deserved. He was able to point out that Mr. Blennerhassett was the only stockbroker of that name and that he lunched at Pimm's: there the similarity seemed to cease. In order to suggest some possibility of actual damage, he was constrained to suggest that, inasmuch as stockbrokers are not allowed to advertise, the publication complained of might have been taken to imply that his client was breaking the rules of the House by himself inserting the advertisement in the *Evening Standard*; although precisely in what way a stockbroker might be thought to be advertising himself by depicting himself in a lunatic asylum with straw in his hair was not quite clear.

Mr. Blennerhassett himself supported his counsel's opening, and the substance of his evidence was that he was laughed at so much by fellow members that he did not like to go into the House. The cross-examination consisted solely in attempting to point out the ridiculous nature of the whole action.

"Has not the name Blennerhassett been used for years by comic writers, here and in America?"

"It has been used in the *Bab Ballads* and by Mark Twain."

"Is the portrait in the advertisement in the least like you?"

Mr. Blennerhassett could not very well say, "Yes," having regard to the straw in the hair; for the purpose of the action he might not like to say "No"; so he asked if he need answer the question.

"Do you play Yo-Yo?"

"No."

"Have you ever played golf 'at Walton Heath'?"

"No."

"So you have never 'holed a putt'?"

"No."

"Have you eaten lobster salad at Pimm's?"

"Yes."

"Apart from the name, is that the only matter in which you resemble the gentleman in the advertisement?"

And the final question:

"Do you know of a living person who has thought a penny the worse of you because of the advertisement for Yo-Yo?"

Mr. McNulty gave evidence as to his daughter inventing the name of Blennerhassett, and at the conclusion of his evidence, Mr. Justice Branson stopped the case. He held that the alleged libel was merely an advertisement and not capable of a defamatory meaning. Everybody's time and money had been wasted, and for no good purpose at all.

The Law Courts are indeed the proper place in which to seek a remedy against wrong-doing and injustice, and in that capacity the Courts are open to all, but if anyone, in a sudden burst of temper, should for the moment fail to appreciate the difference between a momentary annoyance and lasting injury, it may be well that he should reflect upon the unhappy case of Mr. Blennerhassett and the Yo-Yo.

CHAPTER III

Miscellaneous

AN English jury is the foundation stone of English justice. The ordinary juryman knows nothing of Law, and is not very greatly concerned with the stricter rules of evidence, but he possesses a positive genius for arriving at the truth—possibly because no lawyer is ever required to sit upon a jury. After a not inconsiderable experience, I cannot personally remember one single instance in which a jury have been wrong; I have often been annoyed at their verdict, and may have recognised it as one which no lawyer could have given, but on thinking the matter over at a later date, I have invariably come to the conclusion that they were right. I have often thought it would be an excellent innovation if budding advocates were required to undergo a course of sitting upon juries as part of their legal education, so that they might acquire some knowledge as to the working of a juryman's mind. I have known many distinguished lawyers who claim the power of reading a jury like a book; they go further and say that they can play upon a jury as upon a musical instrument, and are always able to foretell with accuracy the verdict that will ultimately be given. These distinguished gentlemen must have been more fortunate than I was; I was never able to read anybody's mind, and as for playing upon a jury, I am afraid I must be no musician; I never had the slightest idea what they were going to decide, and was only able to form a faint idea that they were not likely to be unduly impressed by any eloquence I might bestow upon them. And yet of the many hundreds of juries I have faced there is not one that has not left behind a feeling of deep admiration; for that reason alone it would be ungrateful not to pay some slight tribute to their memory.

Perhaps the case of Gruban against Booth showed a jury's sense of justice at its highest; a German, lately freed from internment, suing an English Member of Parliament for fraud; the war at its height; hatred for all Germans inflamed by the sinking of the *Lusitania*; the word of a humble German against that of a distinguished Englishman; and yet an English jury gave a heavy verdict for Mr. Gruban. If there exist any who decry the English jury system, I could wish that they would remember the jurymen in the case of Gruban against Booth. It is for them that the record of this trial has been written.

Juries themselves form only one portion of a lawyer's memories; advocates form another—experienced advocates, less experienced advocates, and beginners. Perhaps the beginners are the most interesting of all. It has always been a matter of amazement to me that a young barrister is ever able to conduct his earlier cases with any degree of success whatever; everything is so new to him; he is quite convinced that such a case as his must be unique in the history of the Law; never have there been facts so complicated, witnesses so evasive, and a judge so irritable; he is quite unable to deal with any of them; he is travelling in a foreign country amid a hostile population, and he is lucky if he escapes unscathed. As the years go by, the atmosphere is very different. There comes a time when no case is new to him; he knows that witnesses are always evasive, and judges frequently irritable; however complicated the facts, he has known exactly similar complications a hundred times before; his task is so much simplified that it might almost seem as though experience alone is enough to develop a good advocate; but it is not. There is one essential qualification without which a long experience will be useless, and boundless industry will be cast away, and that is the ability to discover for himself the one vital point in the whole case—for there is always one and never more than one—and then, having found it, to stick to it to the exclusion of everything else. And it is not so easy as it sounds. Comparatively few people ever really see the essential point in anything. In a trial at law a client usually sees a hundred points all equally important in his eyes, but in fact of no real importance whatever; his solicitor has devoted tireless industry in the exploration of any matter in which his client is so deeply interested, with the result that his counsel is flooded with a mass of largely irrelevant material. If in his wisdom the counsel selects the one point of importance, and ruthlessly discards the remainder, he may succeed in winning the action, but he will certainly disappoint his lay client, and probably convince his solicitor that he has not read his brief. The risk may be too great for a beginner; he may be afraid to take it. But he is wrong; it pays to take risk. The case of the Diamond Syndicate is a fair example. In a trial which might well have lasted for days and weeks, and even months, when the facts were so complicated and the issues so involved that no one could understand them, Mr. Oppenheimer had made one little slip: if he could explain it the whole action might have been misconceived; if he could not the whole defence might crack and even disappear. The plaintiffs were probably appalled to find that their counsel was prepared to cast aside all their carefully selected preparations and concentrate entirely upon Mr. Oppenheimer's little slip. Perhaps a young advocate, if he cares to read, may be interested in the result.

Mere records of litigation must of necessity make dreary reading. It is only when a case conjures up a picture of human interest that it may be worth recording. When Princess Paley told her story of the Russian revolution, of her husband's murder and her own escape from St. Petersburg, those who heard it might almost have been living through her experience for themselves; when Mr. Harnett told of his years of incarceration in a lunatic asylum although a jury found that from the very beginning of his tragedy he was a sane man, his audience almost seemed to suffer with him. No one could complain that those trials displayed a lack of human interest. Why I should have chosen to record the case of Mr. Abrahams and the bookmakers, I find it hard to say; perhaps it is by reason of a sneaking regard for detective stories and the slow unravelling of secrets. Mr. Abrahams' case was a purely racing story, and anyone uninterested either in race-horses or detection may well decide to ignore it.

There is one particular form of litigation for which I have always had the greatest possible dislike and that is an action for breach of promise of marriage. It is no doubt an attempt by the law to interfere with purely domestic relationship, an attempt which usually ends in disaster, and the legal view is based upon the assumption that a promise to marry constitutes a purely legal contract, which is obviously rubbish. A promise to marry possibly is, and presumably should be, based upon a mutual desire to enjoy a happy matrimonial existence, and how in the world that desirable intention is to be achieved if one of the parties discovers that he dislikes the other intensely, utterly passes my comprehension. In a moment of joyous enthusiasm a young man invites a girl to marry him; with equal enthusiasm she accepts; the next morning he thinks better of it and suggests that they do not carry the matter any further. He is liable to an action for breach of promise of marriage, in which the damages will vary in accordance with his financial position, and a crowd of hilarious onlookers will spend a merry afternoon at the Royal Courts of Justice. Of course there may be occasions in which more serious questions arise. A young blackguard may have seduced his fiancee under a promise of marriage which he does not intend to fulfil; no one would doubt that in such circumstances some legal remedy should be available to her. But inasmuch as no woman is allowed by Law to bring an action for seduction against her seducer, she achieves the same result by bringing an action for breach of promise and introduces the unsavoury incident in order to swell the damages. In that solitary instance the present form of action may be justifiable although I gravely doubt it, and my doubts have increased with experience. My main objection to a breach of promise action lies in the fact that in no circumstances whatever can a defendant ever win. Over and over again I have felt compelled to advise men sued for breach of promise to pay money rather than to allow their case to go into Court. In almost every case the defendant has something to conceal: frequently the plaintiff has been his mistress; sometimes he himself is a married man—such cases are by no means unusual, and the full disclosure of his unfortunate indiscretions may cause his domestic ruin; even if there is nothing in his life that he desires to hide, the hilarity and ridicule which is aroused by publication in the evening Press of the many idiotic love letters and passionate endearments in which he has indulged will give him a notoriety which will take a long time to be forgotten. Whatever the result of the action, he must lose, and generally the plaintiff knows it. If anyone desires some insight into the terrors of a breach of promise action, he may be interested in the case of the three sisters.

I have chosen to record one more case, which to me was perhaps the most interesting of them all. Not because of the amount awarded to the plaintiffs, although the sum was almost astronomical, in fact by far the largest that I have known throughout my long experience, but because of the historical surroundings which lay behind the trial, and the speculations which it must necessarily arouse. If ever I attempted to recall a case in which the most important sequence of events was brought to my attention I think I should select the hearing of the arbitration between Courtaulds and the British Government.

THE CASE OF THE ENGLISH MEMBER OF PARLIAMENT

The case of Gruban against Handel Booth should always remain as a glowing example of the unswerving honesty and strict impartiality of an English jury. When it is remembered that the case was tried in 1915, at a time when the whole country was in the throes of a horrible war, and where every person possessing even a hint of a German accent was regarded as a danger or a spy, the fact that Mr. Gruban should have succeeded in convicting Mr. Handel Booth of fraud before an English Court may well be regarded as constituting a high tribute to the integrity of English justice. To my mind, it is more than doubtful whether in any other country in the world such a result could have been achieved, and for that reason alone the trial was noteworthy; to me personally it remains as an indelible memory of the first really important High Court action that I ever conducted.

Frederick Handel Booth was a sitting Member of Parliament. He was a man of unblemished character, and possessed a distinctly impressive appearance. Shortly before the outbreak of war, he had burst into prominence as a Member of a Parliamentary Commission which had been set up to enquire into the financial transactions which were popularly known as the Marconi Scandals. Certain highly placed members of the Government, including Mr. Lloyd George himself, were said to be in some way implicated, and it was their conduct in that respect which was the subject of enquiry. As a member of the Commission, Mr. Handel Booth had taken a very active part in their proceedings; he had cross-examined witnesses who had given any evidence against the Ministers concerned with considerable skill and great pertinacity, and it was no doubt due in some measure to his advocacy that the final report of the Commission was so satisfactory to all concerned. Indeed a feeling was strongly held that his part in the enquiry had been such as to arouse in Mr. Lloyd George a lasting sense of gratitude. Mr. Handel Booth was certainly a public figure of sufficient importance to be a very welcome friend to anyone in trouble or in need.

Mr. John Gruban was by birth a German. He had served in the German army, and although he had been naturalised shortly before the outbreak of war, he still possessed an unmistakably German accent. He had married a German wife, and with her came to England where he set up his home, and embarked upon a business life in England. He was a clever engineer and in time acquired his own works, which he conducted with considerable success, and there seemed no reason to doubt that his future prosperity was assured. Then came the war, and in a moment everything was changed. The possessor of a German accent became an immediate suspect; and when that suspect was engaged upon work connected with munitions, suspicion developed into fear; old ladies dreamed of mysterious lights; spinsters stayed at home as soon as it was dark in dread of German spies;

the terrors of internment began to loom on the horizon. In his anxiety and trouble Mr. Gruban looked around for some generous friend who would come to his assistance even to the extent of guaranteeing his honesty and loyalty. He was introduced to Mr. Handel Booth.

At the outset Booth was more than helpful. He visited the works and satisfied himself that they could prove not only extremely useful to the country in her need, but also extremely profitable to anyone entrusted with the management. His offer of assistance far exceeded Gruban's wildest hope. He suggested that he should join the company as a director, and by his very presence guarantee Gruban's safety. He went much further. He claimed the closest friendship with Mr. Addison, the then Minister of Munitions, and assured Gruban that with Booth as a co-director there would be no further reason for anxiety or alarm. Booth's offer of assistance came at the very moment when it was most urgently required. Mr. Addison had already appointed a government supervisor to enquire into the working of Gruban's company and it required only one word of adverse criticism to cause Gruban's instant removal from his position and possible internment as an undesirable.

Gruban was naturally overjoyed at such a generous offer, which he immediately and thankfully accepted; Booth was more than satisfied with the arrangement, which seemed to hold forth undoubted pecuniary advantage to himself. If Gruban had not been so beset with worries and anxieties, he might perhaps have been a shade suspicious of the motives which actuated the offer.

Very shortly after his appointment Handel Booth came forward with a suggestion that filled Gruban with consternation. The directors, said Booth, were not sufficiently remunerated. He claimed that they should be entitled to a commission upon all the profits, and that he, as the most valuable director, should be entitled to the largest share, which he estimated at 10 per cent. In support of this contention, he prepared a short memorandum setting out the profits of the company, to which he attached the following note: "Full 10 per cent to F.H.B." Gruban indignantly refused to be a party to any such arrangement, which he flatly characterised as dishonest, whereupon Booth in a fit of temper crumpled up the memorandum and threw it into the waste-paper basket. This was a most unfortunate act which, at a subsequent date, he must have bitterly regretted, because it was this memorandum which went a long way to throw doubts upon his honesty when it was later called in question.

From this time onward, Gruban's position progressively deteriorated; the Ministry appeared to raise a series of complaints as to the manner in which his business was conducted, and it was apparent that his German nationality became increasingly the subject of adverse comment. Outwardly Handel Booth remained his friend; perhaps because he had not yet acquired the position that he hoped ultimately to obtain. Booth's professions of loyalty became even more pronounced; he emphasised the importance of his friendship with members of the Government, particularly Mr. Addison, or, as he described him in a telegram, "the important person"; he expressed the utmost indignation at the suspicion to which Gruban was subjected, and promised his immediate and effective intervention. Yet notwithstanding all these assurances Gruban's position grew from bad to worse, and finally at a long discussion between the two of them Booth told Gruban that, in spite of all his efforts, Mr. Addison had delivered an ultimatum, namely that the only way in which Gruban's interests could be protected was for Booth to obtain a far more influential position in the business and for Gruban to sink temporarily into the apparent background. Booth was at pains to make it clear that the change would only be apparent, and made in order to please the Ministry of Munitions and to safeguard Gruban. The unfortunate Gruban, driven as he was to a pitch of desperation, had no alternative but to agree, and Booth became managing director in his stead. Even then Gruban still had confidence in the man he believed to be his friend and in the influence he was in a position to exert, and even if at any time that confidence began to wane, it could be restored by messages and telegrams from Booth, containing veiled references to the important personages whom Booth was influencing on his behalf.

Then at last the final blow was struck. Gruban received an urgent telegram from Booth arranging an immediate interview. Booth professed to be heartbroken at the news he had to bring. The Ministry was not satisfied with Gruban's large holdings in the company; that in consequence he, Gruban, was in imminent danger of internment under the Defence of the Realm Acts, and that the only possible way in which both his property and his liberty could be preserved was if Gruban would consent to transfer the whole of his shares and assets into the name of Handel Booth, and to retire completely from the company. In that event, and that event only, would the Minister guarantee Gruban's safety.

To state that Gruban was astounded is to state the position mildly. The whole disgraceful transaction was completed in the middle of the night, at a meeting at which Booth introduced a legal friend, quite erroneously stated to be a King's Counsel, who was apparently in complete agreement with the whole suggestion. Booth loudly reiterated his professions of disinterested friendship, stating that he would regard himself merely as a trustee, and that the income of the shares would constitute a trust in favour of Gruban's wife. Faced with the terrors of internment, Gruban felt he had no option except to agree to Booth's suggestion, and his future lay entirely in the hands of Handel Booth.

Within a very few days it became clearly apparent what the future was likely to be. Directly the transfer was completed Booth's demeanour changed. He treated Gruban with rudeness and contempt, and flatly refused to carry out the bargain he had made as to paying an income to Gruban's wife. Gruban was heartbroken and in despair; all he had left to him was his freedom, and even that did not last long. A few days later he was interned.

That was the story Gruban told, months later, when he stood in the witness box at the hearing of his action against Handel Booth. As he stood there, a not very impressive figure, quite alone, without a friend in the world, it was easy to understand the awful predicament into which he had been placed. He had lost everything; the business which he had built up by years of work had gone; his friend had proved false to him; the country of his adoption had disowned him; and he had been a prisoner in an internment camp. He may well have doubted the possibility of any body of Englishmen giving credence to the story which he had to tell.

But he had already received some evidence of English justice. Almost in despair he had appealed against the order for his internment to a tribunal which had been specially appointed to deal with cases such as his, and his appeal had been heard by Mr. Justice Younger and Mr. Justice Sankey, than whom no two more painstaking and considerate judges had ever sat upon the Bench. The hearing had of necessity to take place in private, and even Gruban himself was not permitted to know what had been said before them; beyond the fact that he had told his own story and that thereafter Handel Booth had been required to attend to give his version, he knew nothing. Whatever the opinion the tribunal had formed, the result had been instantaneous: an order had been made for Gruban's immediate release. The judges indeed had gone further than was usual in such cases. They recommended Gruban to seek the advice of the best solicitor he could manage to obtain with a view to seeing whether some further steps might not properly be taken to protect his interests.

Gruban was extremely fortunate in obtaining the services of Mr. Synot to represent and to advise him. Not only was Mr. Synot an extremely able solicitor, but he was a man who was prepared to expend endless time and energy in his endeavour to remedy a state of things which in his view had caused a grave injustice. Although he was not permitted to obtain a view of any evidence given before the Appeal Tribunal, I have little doubt that he found the officials of that department extremely sympathetic, and as a result of the most exhaustive enquiries Mr. Synot came to the conclusion that Handel Booth, immediately after Gruban's removal from the company, must have made some communication to the Ministry of Munitions which, so far from protecting Gruban, had encouraged, even if it did not cause, Gruban's internment. The interval between the happening of the two events had been too short for coincidence; and the merest hint given to the Minister would be sufficient to achieve the object which Booth had in view. A suggestion that Gruban was inefficient or was in some way impeding the war effort would be more than enough to dispose of Gruban, once for all. But how to obtain possession of such a document, if indeed it was ever in existence? Every effort was made to find out if such a communication had taken place. Booth flatly denied it. The Government was approached, but they refused to answer any questions or to produce any documents upon the ground of departmental privilege. It is of course permissible, and indeed desirable, that a State department should decline to afford any information which may be prejudicial to the national interest, but personally I found it very hard, in the particular circumstances of the Gruban case, to think that such a claim could be well founded. However, it had been made, and there remained only one course open to Mr. Synot. If the case should come into Court such a claim might have to be made on oath, and he decided that, if necessity arose, the head of every Government department concerned should be subpœnaed to attend the hearing to explain why such a document, if it existed, should not be produced. And there for the moment the matter had to rest.

After mature consideration Mr. Synot decided to institute proceedings against Handel Booth, and to my intense satisfaction Mr. Gruban's case was left to me. The claim, which was for damages, fell into two parts: (i) That Booth had obtained possession of Gruban's property by falsely pretending that he was acting on the advice and indeed under the instruction of Mr. Addison, the Minister of Munitions, and (ii) That Booth had maliciously procured Gruban's internment. Under the second head of claim our only hope of raising even a *prima facie* case depended on the letter which we suspected but could not produce; under the first claim, which was for simple fraud, our hopes were based upon the assumption that Booth might feel constrained to call Mr. Addison as a witness, in which case we were satisfied that, whatever story he had to tell, it would be the truth. Otherwise the case depended almost entirely upon the evidence of

Gruban himself, whose country of origin together with his German accent was unlikely to tell strongly in his favour. On the other hand his opponent was an English Member of Parliament, a man of the highest character, who would appear before the jury righteously indignant at a baseless charge of fraud. It was not surprising that poor Gruban should feel that the scales of justice were weighted heavily against him.

The first day of the trial opened at a singularly inauspicious moment. The war was at its height; our losses both on land and at sea had been enormous; the submarine menace had begun, indeed there had just occurred the awful story of the sinking of the *Lusitania* and the drowning of over a thousand of English passengers, which had stirred public indignation to fever heat; the hatred of all Germans had reached a pitch bordering on frenzy. Poor Gruban! As he took his seat in Court, I could not help wondering what would have been his chances of success if the position at that moment had been reversed, and he had been an Englishman in a German Court, suing a member of the German Reichstag before a jury who would no doubt be chanting, "Gott strafe England."

The trial took place before Lord Coleridge and a special jury, and the defence was represented by Mr. Rigby Swift, K.C., afterwards Mr. Justice Rigby Swift, and Mr. Douglas Hogg, afterwards Lord Hailsham. Both appeared extremely confident, and Handel Booth himself smiled almost contemptuously at his insignificant opponent. The Court was packed; the position enjoyed by Booth was of itself sufficient to attract a large number of curious sightseers, and as the strange story was unfolded the interest increased so largely that the Strand itself was packed with an excited crowd to such an extent that on the final day it was almost impossible to force a way into the Courts.

Gruban was the first, indeed the only, witness of importance called on his behalf. He told his story quietly and indeed with great restraint and courtesy; he faced a long and searching cross-examination without flinching. Rigby Swift was at pains to establish that from beginning to end Gruban's story was untrue; that so far from being dishonest, Booth had proved himself a loyal and generous friend; that it was Gruban who had brought the trouble on himself by the manner in which he had conducted his business and affairs, and that Gruban himself had begged Booth to come to his assistance, and to relieve him of his holding in the company which had become a danger to his safety. By the time Rigby Swift had finished it almost seemed that Gruban might easily have been a danger to his adopted country.

When it was Booth's turn to enter the witness box, he proved himself a witness of a very different calibre. Arrogant and assured, as an English Member of Parliament, he appeared only to regret so much waste of his valuable time by having to appear in Court in answer to such a ridiculous accusation, but inasmuch as he was forced into that position, he was only anxious to help the jury in any way he could. He placed himself upon a pinnacle of dignity and honesty which appeared to be impregnable.

I sometimes feel I owe to Handel Booth a great debt of gratitude. He taught me a lesson that has endured throughout my whole professional career: that with a witness standing on such a pedestal of virtue it is the first blow that counts. If within the first five minutes that pedestal can be knocked away, if the first few questions can prove him to be a liar, or what is still better can show him to be dishonest, then the great position he has sought to establish for himself will begin to crumble, and will go on crumbling until finally it disappears. That was the method I decided to employ with Handel Booth and I selected for the purpose an incident he might have forgotten, just as he might have forgotten the memorandum that he threw into the waste-paper basket not so many months before.

"Mr. Handel Booth, would it be dishonest for a director of a company to seek for himself a secret commission on his company's earnings?" Nothing could possibly exceed Mr. Booth's contempt for such a suggestion.

"If you did such a thing would you consider yourself a rogue?"

"Of course."

"Did you do that very thing when you were a director of Mr. Gruban's company?" Mr. Booth was almost speechless with indignation.

"Never—never—never."

"Then take a look at this piece of paper."

The memorandum in his own handwriting was handed to him by the usher of the Court. He took it in his hand. He turned it over. He wanted time to think. Everyone in Court was staring at him.

"Does the figure written on that memorandum correspond exactly with the amount of profit that your company had earned?"

Mr. Booth had no idea. The balance sheet of the company showing its annual profit was shown to him. The figures were the same.

"Do you know of anyone connected with the company with the initials F. H. B. except Frederick Handel Booth?"

He knew of no one.

"What is the meaning of the expression, 'Full 10 per cent to F. H. B.'?"

There could be no possible explanation. The pedestal had been knocked away. Step by step Booth was taken through the details of Gruban's accusations. He denied them all again, but his denials did not ring quite so true as formerly. He had made no representations to Mr. Addison. He could not remember what he meant by his references in his telegram to "the important person". But we were still only on the fringe of the case. What letter had been written to the Ministry of Munitions just before Gruban had been interned? He had written nothing— nothing. This might well be a vital moment in the trial. I called upon every Minister who had been subpœnaed to answer his summons. There was no reply. The Attorney-General, who was expected to deal with any question of privilege, was not in Court. The judge suggested that I should continue with the case in order to give time for their appearance. I respectfully declined. It was now or never. If there was such a letter it must be produced.

And then the defence began to creak. Rigby Swift rose in his place and said that he had a copy of a letter which might be the one I wanted, and he would hand it to me. And there it was. After all those struggles, after all this infinite delay, there was a letter. Within a few days of depriving Gruban of his position, Booth had written to the Ministry of Munitions a letter which, while not referring to internment, placed Gruban in such a light that some action against him might well have seemed inevitable. Booth had at last discovered himself in his true light, all his professions of loyalty and friendship had disappeared; his jaunty confidence had gone, and when he left the box discredited and shamed, he was a very different person from the self-satisfied individual who had first appeared.

The defence were now in a position of great difficulty. It was necessary, if possible, to rehabilitate Booth and to prove that it was not his letter which had caused Gruban's internment. They determined to call Mr. Addison into the box. That was the one thing for which I had prayed. Mr. Addison was the one person by whom I hoped to establish the charge of fraud. Mr. Addison was called. He stated that it was not Booth's letter that had caused Gruban's internment. That he, Addison, had acted upon his own initiative, aided by the assistance of his professional advisers, and that the whole responsibility was his. But that was not the issue with which I was mainly concerned. There were two questions and two only which I wanted to put to Mr. Addison.

"Had you at any time been advising Handel Booth as to what course Gruban should adopt?"

"Certainly not."

"If Booth had ever stated that you had told him that Gruban's only chance of escaping internment was that he should hand over his position and all his shares to Booth, would that statement have been a lie?"

"It would."

In the eyes of any fair-minded man, unaffected by prejudice or bias, the case was over. Unless Gruban's story was a pure invention he had been grossly defrauded by his professed friend and supporter. Who was telling the truth? Gruban or Booth? I have no doubt that the judge intended to be strictly impartial, although at the time he seemed to me to deal rather lightly in his summing up with some of Booth's more grave admissions, and I know that Gruban was cast into the depths of despair by some of the judge's remarks. But whatever doubts the judge may have felt or expressed, the jury had no doubts. All prejudice was forgotten. The jury returned to their places and gave their verdict that the little German had been defrauded, and they awarded him as damages the sum of £4,500. Mr. Booth's period of usefulness as a Member of Parliament was over.

An English jury is seldom, if ever, wrong. In my opinion twelve ordinary Englishmen and women sitting together form the best tribunal that the world has ever known. If I wished to quote one particular example of impartiality and strict fair play, I should choose the jury who tried the case of Gruban against Booth.

THE CASE OF THE DIAMOND SYNDICATE

The case of the United Diamond Fields of British Guiana against the Diamond Syndicate was one of the most difficult as well as the most interesting that I have ever known. To the general public the interest lay in the revelations as to the secret workings of the diamond industry and the effect thereby produced upon the market in precious stones. To me the difficulty lay in an endeavour to extract from a mass of irrelevant detail and a mountain of irrelevant documents some one small fact which might suffice to make intelligible that which must otherwise appear chaotic; the interest lay in the taking of a risk greater than any I had previously experienced.

The history of the Diamond Syndicate goes back to the days of Cecil Rhodes, when the great financial ingenuity of such men as the Barnatos and the Joels brought into being the industry of diamond production and made for the Diamond Syndicate a fortune almost without parallel in the world of finance. Probably they were the first people to realise the importance of the fact that a diamond is an article of little intrinsic worth and that its real value lies in its comparative scarcity; it was very shortly after the discovery of the great diamond mines in South Africa that these financiers began to appreciate that their future fortunes lay not in the unlimited production of diamonds but rather in the restriction of the quantities that were placed upon the market. If such restriction was to be effective it was absolutely essential that the syndicate should be in a position to control the output in every direction, and that could only be done if they succeeded in buying up or otherwise acquiring all the diamond production concerns throughout the world. In this task they were eminently successful; by the early part of the present century practically all the diamonds in the world were in their hands or under their control; they were able to ensure that the precise quantity of diamonds which they desired were available for sale; that the price of diamonds was maintained at a level which they were in a position to dictate; and that if too many diamonds were at any time produced, they could be kept off the market until the syndicate, and no one else, wished them to be released. The power of the syndicate was practically boundless and the wealth of its members was enormous and likely to continue; there was only one possible danger to its future prosperity and that lay in the unlikely event of a new discovery of diamonds from a hitherto unsuspected source.

In the year 1925 diamonds were beginning to appear from British Guiana in sufficient quantities to attract the attention of the Diamond Syndicate. These stones were alluvial and were obtained in a somewhat elementary manner. Two or three Creole gentlemen in British Guiana had obtained government concessions to explore for and exploit diamonds in their country. These gentlemen employed a number of natives who enjoyed the somewhat peculiar title of "Pork Knockers" and who travelled the bush throughout the concessions and obtained the diamonds by washing, and thereafter brought them back to more civilised districts and disposed of them to the concessionaires. The quantity of diamonds so obtained was growing into fairly large proportions, and probably the largest concessionaire was a man named Perez. In due course, the Diamond Syndicate got into touch with Mr. Perez and, as a result, in the month of November, 1925, a Mr. Otto Oppenheimer who was representing the syndicate entered into a contract to buy 12,000 carats from Mr. Perez over a period of twelve months. Subsequent events would appear to indicate that this contract was intended to be a preliminary step towards the possible acquisition by the Diamond Syndicate of the entire output of Mr. Perez at some later date. The price agreed to be paid by Mr. Oppenheimer for the year's purchase became of great importance inasmuch as it formed the whole basis of the arrangement subsequently made. The value of diamonds is assessed and their value is fixed by a process of assortment; frequently, this assortment is based both upon the size and the quality of the stones; sometimes, if the quality is average throughout, the assortment is based upon size alone. Generally speaking, the quality of British Guiana stones was adjudged to be very average and consequently the basis of assortment and price was fixed upon size alone; for a two-carat stone £12 2s. 6d., one-carat stone £7 12s. 6d., half-a-carat stone £4 15s. 6d., and so on in a descending scale. The price was recognised as being too low if the stones were all of best quality and too high if they were all of low quality, but on an average basis the schedule prices were agreed to be fair. Mr. Oppenheimer was a recognised expert upon all questions in the diamond industry, including the assortment and valuation of diamonds, and he was in a position to know exactly the value of the diamonds included in the original 12,000 carats. He assessed the total quantity supplied as working out at an average price of £4 10s. per carat.

The next step in the story was the formation of the United Diamond Fields of British Guiana Ltd. to take over Mr. Perez' rights in his concessions and the execution by that company of a contract between themselves and the Diamond Syndicate under which the company undertook to sell its entire production of diamonds to the syndicate at the same price paid by Mr. Oppenheimer for the 12,000 carats. Mr. Oppenheimer himself approved the prospectus of the company, in which it was stated that the average price for the diamonds to be paid by the Diamond Syndicate to the company would be £4 10s. per carat. It was well known to both sides that such a price could only be obtained provided that the assortment of the stones was made upon the same principle as had previously been adopted. It was therefore immediately apparent that the future prosperity of the company depended entirely upon the fairness with which the future assortment of diamonds should be made; and inasmuch as the syndicate insisted that the assortments should be under the complete supervision and unrestricted control of Mr. Oppenheimer, the whole future prosperity of the company lay in Mr. Oppenheimer's hands. It is only necessary to refer to two provisions of the contract then made, as these two provisions formed the corner-stone of the action subsequently brought by the company against the Diamond Syndicate. The first provision was the insistence by the syndicate that Mr. Oppenheimer, although their representative, should be appointed by the company as their technical adviser. In fact, the arrangement meant, as subsequent events showed, that Mr. Oppenheimer was the only person in a position to regulate the price to be paid by the syndicate for the stones which they acquired. The second provision, which ultimately proved the most vital of all, was a stipulation that the price payable by the syndicate under the contract for the diamonds could be reduced at the expiration of any period of six months upon an auditor's certificate being given that the value of the diamonds in stock and unsold had fallen; for the purpose of the certificate the value of unsold stock was to be arrived at by taking the price realised by the syndicate upon the sale last preceding the date of the certificate. Inasmuch as the company was never to be permitted to inspect the books of the Diamond Syndicate, it will be observed that they were to be bound completely by the certificate given to them. In substance, therefore, the company were entirely in the hands of Mr. Oppenheimer, the servant of the syndicate.

Unfortunately for the prosperity of the company, at the very moment that it commenced operations the peril which the syndicate had always visualised as a possibility became an actual fact. In the district of Lichtenberg there was discovered a totally unexpected deposit of alluvial diamonds. The quantity brought to light was so enormous that it threatened the very existence of the Diamond Syndicate. In the words of Mr. Solly Joel, a leading member of the syndicate, spoken in December, 1926, "the Lichtenberg discovery was a find which might conceivably undermine the corner-stone of the diamond industry." In the words of Mr. Oppenheimer himself, "the syndicate are off their heads with worry about the find". It was quite obvious that unless the syndicate could do something to restrict the output of diamonds from Lichtenberg and elsewhere, the world market in diamonds might be flooded, with the result that the price of diamonds would crash and the syndicate as it then existed might be ruined. It was at this very moment that the company was starting business and more diamonds were to be expected from British Guiana.

It was therefore very fortunate for the syndicate that Mr. Oppenheimer was in control of the company operations. It was fairly obvious that if the price paid by the syndicate was substantially reduced the company would not be able to trade at a profit and the flow of diamonds from British Guiana would cease, and the price depended upon the assortment; the method of assortment was decided solely by Mr. Oppenheimer. From the commencement of business Mr. Oppenheimer made up his own mind that the assortment should no longer be made by size alone but also by quality and that the assignments should be made "finer", that is to say that the contract prices should only be paid in respect of best-quality stones. If that course were adopted, it became immediately obvious that the anticipated average price of £4 10s. per carat could not be obtained. Under the contract between the parties no one except Mr. Oppenheimer could ever know the basis upon which he was instructing his servants to make the assortments. It was not until many months later that the company discovered that Mr. Oppenheimer was writing regularly to those servants in British Guiana to make the assortment of diamonds "finer and finer".

The result of Mr. Oppenheimer's changed method of assortment was obviously disastrous to the company. The average price per carat dropped from £4 10s. to £3 and less per carat; the prices were so low that the suppliers in British Guiana would not produce diamonds at that price and the company's output dropped from 2,000 to less than 300 carats per month. Truly, the syndicate was being well served by Mr. Oppenheimer. Not unnaturally the company in London protested vigorously against the disaster which appeared to be threatening them, but they could do no more than protest. Mr. Oppenheimer was their technical adviser and they were compelled to rely upon him.

But there was worse to come. In May of 1927, almost exactly eighteen months after the company had commenced business, Mr. Oppenheimer told them that he would be compelled to reduce the price of diamonds paid by the syndicate still further;

he reminded them that the reduced prices must depend upon the value of the company's then unsold stock and that value would depend upon the price obtained "upon the last preceding sale". He stated that the profit of the last preceding sale was only 5 per cent above cost and that price justified a further reduction in the price to be paid by the syndicate of 10 per cent. The company had no means of checking these figures or calculations; they were not allowed to see the syndicate's books; they were bound by a certificate, if they desired one, and Mr. Oppenheimer in fact gave them a certificate establishing that the last preceding sale had realised no more than a profit of 5 per cent. The company made almost pathetic appeals to Mr. Oppenheimer, pointing out that if he insisted upon this 10 per cent reduction the company was ruined, but Mr. Oppenheimer was adamant. The result of Mr. Oppenheimer's action was immediate. By September, 1927, deliveries of diamonds from British Guiana had been reduced by 75 per cent and the average price had dropped to £2 15s. and the company was ruined.

Fortunately for the company there was upon its board a gentleman of great ability, by name Victor Coen. Mr. Coen was a tobacco merchant and knew nothing about diamonds, but he became quite satisfied in his own mind that his company had been unfairly treated and he determined to bring the matter before the Courts. Mr. Oppenheimer struggled hard to persuade Mr. Coen to consent to some form of arbitration but Mr. Coen refused. He obtained a considerable amount of support from shareholders in the company and ultimately in May, 1929, two actions were started: one for conspiracy and fraud against the syndicate and Mr. Oppenheimer, and the other for an account against the syndicate. The damages claimed must of necessity be very large and Mr. Coen took the view that they should be in no case less than £300,000.

From the moment that the action started, the syndicate appeared determined to render its ultimate trial, if not impossible, at least extremely difficult. From the date of the issue of the writ it was quite obvious that the proceedings were going to develop into quite unmanageable proportions. The syndicate insisted upon producing more than 4,000 letters; bundles of documents increased to an incredible size and one incident alone was sufficient to establish in my mind that if we were not very careful the action would grow entirely out of hand. It was necessary to take Mr. Perez' evidence on commission, and although the evidence he could give was very slight, he was cross-examined for days and was questioned about matters which to my mind had nothing whatever to do with the real issues involved. It began to look as though, unless we were very careful, the intricacies of the case would render it practically impossible for any jury ever to appreciate what they would have to try. I had known such a state of circumstances to have arisen before in other cases, but never to such an exaggerated extent. Unless we could discover some one incident, however small, upon which to concentrate our attention, the merits of our case would be swamped in the mass of detail and our prospects of success would be practically non-existent. And then came a stroke of luck. During the preparation for the trial it became necessary for the syndicate to show us some entries in their books, and amongst these entries we saw the "last sale" upon which Mr. Oppenheimer had certified that the profit was 5 per cent and that the cut of 10 per cent in price was justified. It was a sale to a Mr. van Antwerpen. It was unfortunate for the syndicate that they had been obliged to show us that entry. It was apparent that the profit upon that sale was not 5 per cent, as Mr. Oppenheimer had certified, but was in fact 16 per cent or 17 per cent. There was no explanation of this discrepancy and no explanation by Mr. Oppenheimer. Immediately I was informed of this discovery, I thought I had found a way of cutting through the immense intricacies of the action. Either there was a proper explanation of this incident and of Mr. Oppenheimer's certificate or there was not. If there was, it would probably completely exonerate Mr. Oppenheimer in the eyes of the jury; if no explanation was forthcoming, the certificate was a fraud, and if such a fraud had been perpetrated, all our suspicions would seem to fall into line. I determined to throw over all the 4,000 letters and the bundle of documents and tell the jury from the outset that we were prepared to stand or fall upon one issue in the case. If Mr. Oppenheimer had given us a false certificate, we had been robbed and nothing else mattered. If his certificate was honest and he was an honest man, our case must fail. Basing our entire hopes of success upon this one small point was a terrible risk to take, but I determined to take it. In that way and that way alone I saw a possibility of rendering the case coherent and making it intelligible to a Court.

The action came on for trial on the 17th March, 1930, before Mr. Justice McCardie and a special jury. It is seldom that a special jury Court can have been littered with so many documents and papers. Mr. Stuart Bevan, K.C., who appeared for the syndicate, was provided with his 4,000 letters and his bundles of documents, which increased day by day as the case proceeded; and Mr. Norman Birkett, K.C., who appeared for Mr. Oppenheimer, also had his 4,000 letters and even more documents than Mr. Bevan. There seemed to be no end to the books and papers with which he was necessarily provided as the case dragged on. I, of course, had to be armed with all the letters and documents that any of them might want. There were some other defendants in the case, but there turned out to be no evidence against them and they were dismissed from the action.

The case was not an easy one to explain to a jury. The course which I decided to adopt necessarily incurred the risk that the Court might suspect the reasons for which I had decided to eliminate practically all the voluminous documents, and might come to the conclusion that there was something contained in these documents which I was anxious to conceal. But the risk had to be taken. I explained the story in a few words concentrating entirely upon Mr. Oppenheimer's method of assortment, and then told the jury that in the view I had put before them there was only one short point in the case which it would not take them more than a few minutes to understand and decide. Mr. Oppenheimer's certificate was either honest or not. If it was not, they would have no difficulty in coming to the conclusion that the whole course of conduct had been to prevent the production of diamonds and thereby ruin the company. I told the jury that they would have to listen to hours and possibly days of cross-examination upon matters which in my view would be absolutely irrelevant. At some time or another the defendants would have to explain Mr. Oppenheimer's certificate. If they succeeded, they would win; if they failed, they would lose. When the syndicate's advisers heard this short epitome of the case, they gave some signs of being overjoyed at the test put to the jury. I was not so sure that their joy was well-founded.

Substantially, the only evidence which I had in support of my case was that of Mr. Victor Coen, and he proved to be without exception the best witness that I have ever seen in a witness box. As I had anticipated, he was cross-examined for days on end, taken through piles of documents and letters, and never once was he at a loss for a date or a fact or an answer. He was courteous and restrained, although obviously suffering from a sense of grave injustice, and never once showed the slightest sign of exasperation at the questions which he must have felt to be irrelevant. Mr. Stewart Bevan cross-examined him for four days and during every moment of the time

I waited for the point when he would explain Mr. Oppenheimer's certificate, but that point never came. At repeated intervals I ventured a suggestion that we were waiting for that explanation, but my suggestions remained unanswered. At the end of four days Mr. Bevan sat down, and we were not one iota nearer to the explanation for which by this time the jury were impatiently waiting.

Then it was Mr. Norman Birkett's turn and, as he was representing Mr. Oppenheimer, no doubt the explanation would be left to him. He also cross-examined Mr. Victor Coen for days. Hour after hour I listened to questions which again seemed to be quite irrelevant, until it was quite obvious that I had been right. The explanation was delayed because they were afraid of it. At last, after many hours, it came, and I think everyone in Court must have heaved a sigh of relief. "Now," said Mr. Birkett, "I want to ask you about Mr. Oppenheimer's certificate." At last, after ten days, the moment had come for which we had all been waiting. Poor Mr. Birkett! He must have found the explanation as difficult to give as we found it difficult to understand. Apparently, the explanation that Mr. Oppenheimer was going to give was something like this: After the vital sale of diamonds to Mr. Antwerpen, Mr. Antwerpen had been dissatisfied with his bargain and, as the syndicate would not relieve him, Mr. Oppenheimer had come to his rescue and bought the diamonds back himself. What bearing this was supposed to have upon the truth or falsity of the certificate I was quite unable to understand. At any rate, it was the first moment that we had ever heard of a suggestion that Mr. Oppenheimer had bought the diamonds for himself. Mr. Justice McCardie, whose mind had obviously been centred on this point for days, was apparently as much puzzled by this explanation as we were. The learned judge thought it necessary to interpose. He asked: "Do you mean that Mr. Oppenheimer bought them back for himself, or for the syndicate, or what?"

Mr. Birkett: "He bought them back for himself. Even if it was done wrongfully (that is to say, if his action cannot really be justified) and mistakenly, it really cannot be a fraud."

Mr. Justice McCardie: "If it was secret, of course, I say no more than that it might well be the grossest fraud. Where are the accounts by which he adjusted this transaction?"

Mr. Birkett: "With all due deference, no such accounting would be necessary."

Mr. Justice McCardie: "Mr. Birkett, are you going to suggest that the books showing a sale to Mr. van Antwerpen do not represent the truth of the matter, mark this, at the moment when the certificate was given?"

Mr. Birkett: "Yes, my Lord."

Mr. Justice McCardie: "Is the truth contained in any other documents or document whatsoever?"

Mr. Birkett: "It is, my Lord."

Mr. Justice McCardie: "But not entered in your books. Just reflect on what you are saying, Mr. Birkett, not entered in your books! Is that what you mean? If you say that, it means that these accounts which you are now putting before me as the accounts of the defendant syndicate are not worth the paper they are written on. Reflect, Mr. Norman Birkett. At this stage the action may assume a grave aspect.

Mr. Birkett: "All these matters have been the subject of most anxious consideration by the adviser of Mr. Oppenheimer, my Lord."

Mr. Justice McCardie: "Let me tell you at once, Mr. Norman Birkett, that curtains of ingenious suggestions or veils of ingenious suggestion will be no good in the end as far as I am concerned. I shall put them aside and get at the truth and I am sure the jury will assist me in that."

I had been right. There was no explanation forthcoming. Not one of the thousands of documents could afford any explanation at all of what had been done. It is true that the case dragged on, more irrelevant questions were asked and more voluminous documents were read, but from the first moment of the attempted explanation it was quite obvious that only one question was present to the minds of the jury: "When are we going to hear from Mr. Oppenheimer's own lips his own explanation of the certificate he gave?" The jury never heard. Instead, there were conversations behind the scene. The defendants said that Mr. Oppenheimer had become unwell. The syndicate were anxious to make good any loss the company had suffered, but they could only consent to pay in the action for an account, and not in an action charging them with fraud; Mr. Victor Coen did not mind in which action they paid as long as the claim was paid; they asked him how much he wanted; he replied, exactly the same sum as he had always claimed; they offered him a much smaller sum; Mr. Coen refused. I am afraid the syndicate found Mr. Coen quite as skilful as a bargainer as he had been as a witness; he obtained the precise sum he required.

When the Court reassembled, the judge was told that the parties had come to terms. The action for fraud would be withdrawn and under the action for account the syndicate would pay a sum sufficient to satisfy the company's claim. The charges of fraud against the syndicate were withdrawn and the company accepted the statement of Mr. Oppenheimer's counsel that he was justified in the course he took and that his conduct, although unjustified, was not dishonest. Mr. Coen's triumph was complete.

The action had already lasted for ten days, and we were only at the beginning; the enquiry into Mr. Oppenheimer's certificate had only lasted for five minutes, but it had been enough. When I had first announced to my own clients that I was going to risk everything upon that one small point, they were much perturbed and gravely anxious. I often wonder what would have happened to this action if I had not decided to run the risk.

THE PRINCESS FROM ST. PETERSBURG

By the year 1928 we had all heard the story of the Russian Revolution; we had been told of the Royal family done to death in a cellar; we had heard of robbery, rape and murder, and, memory being so short, we had almost forgotten this terrible story; it seemed too horrible to be true, and, after all, Russia was far away. When the Princess Olga Paley went into the witness box in one of the Royal Courts of Justice and told her own story of what she had suffered in St. Petersburg, the Revolution ceased to be a figment of the imagination; it became a living thing. Her home had been torn from her, her husband had been murdered, and she herself had barely escaped from Russia with her life. As we listened, we seemed to see the whole story re-enacted before our eyes. I have heard many tragedies in my life, but the story, as told by Princess Paley, I shall never forget.

The Princess was the widow of the Grand Duke Paul of Russia, a Royal Prince of the Imperial House. She had married without the consent of the Czar, and in consequence her marriage was morganatic; it is perhaps by the irony of fate that she may well have owed her life to the fact that she never became legally a member of the Romanoff family. She lived with her husband in the Paley Palace at Tsarskoe Seloe, a district just outside St. Petersburg, where she maintained a household of dignity and affluence; the palace was furnished with articles of great beauty and immense value and was undoubtedly one of the great homes of Russia.

When the Revolution broke out in St. Petersburg there was a short period during which the palace appears to have been left unmolested by the mob; it was not until a month or two later that the Revolutionaries appeared upon the scene; from that moment the Grand Duke and the Princess were never allowed to live in their home again. Thereafter their story was one which has become only too familiar. For a time the Princess was allowed to perform the menial task of escorting round the palace such comrades of the revolution as desired to inspect her treasures, but that respite did not last for long; within a few months the Grand Duke was arrested and thrown into prison in St. Petersburg. The Princess herself was not arrested, but she voluntarily followed her husband into the city in order to visit him on such rare occasions as were permitted; that also did not last for long. Within a short period her husband was murdered in prison. Thereafter all that was left for the Princess was to escape with her life; she fled from Russia without a passport, and finally arrived in England, where she lived like so many of her compatriots without a country or a home.

Ten years later the then Russian Government were anxious to obtain foreign currency from abroad and, amongst other means which they adopted, they decided to sell the palace treasures. With that object in view they entered into negotiations with an English business man named Weisz, and finally sold to him the effects from the Paley Palace for the sum of £48,000. It is only fair to Mr. Weisz to say that he bought the property in absolute good faith for the purpose of resale in England or elsewhere, being firmly under the impression that the Russian Government were the legal owners of that which they were selling. In due course, Mr. Weisz shipped the goods to London, and news of their arrival reached the Princess. She made enquiries and was afforded an opportunity of inspecting the consignment, when she immediately recognised it as coming from the Paley Palace. She thereupon consulted lawyers and was advised to institute proceedings in the English Courts, claiming that the original seizure by the Bolsheviks was illegal and that in consequence all the effects remained her property.

Mr. Weisz was in an extremely difficult position. There was no doubt that the property originally belonged to the Princess; there was equally no doubt that it had been taken from her in circumstances which in any civilised view would have amounted to theft; the only possible way in which he could defeat her claim to its recovery was if, and only if, he could establish that everything which had happened was legal according to Russian Law.

At this time any investigation into the system of Law as practised in Russia was extremely difficult, indeed it was almost impossible to understand the conditions which existed in that country. It was known that people had been murdered indiscriminately and that property had been seized wholesale in the name of the Soviet Republic, and further that some sort of laws or decrees had been passed from time to time in order to afford a justification for such acts, but as to who passed them, and with what authority legislation was enacted, very little definite information could be obtained. There were in London one or two Russian lawyers who had practised in the Czarist Courts before the Revolution, and they had endeavoured to translate and indeed to understand the various documents and publications which emerged from Soviet Russia, but the results of their investigations were very inconclusive. One thing, however, was abundantly clear whatever form of jurisprudence existed in Russia, it was a system quite unknown to any other community in the civilised world, and it must be that system upon which Mr. Weisz must rely if he were to defeat Princess Paley's claim. It was in those circumstances that the action came before the Courts in the year 1929. It was tried before Mr. Justice MacKinnon, a judge of great learning, eminently qualified to adjudicate upon a difficult point of Law, with a mind divorced from any feelings of sentiment however natural that sentiment might be. The Court was crowded; it had become public knowledge that the Princess was going to tell a story of more than ordinary human interest, and many people were anxious to get a glimpse into a page of history of the truth of which they had only a dim idea. When she entered the witness box, the Princess appeared to be the most unmoved person in the Court. I have often noticed that when a witness has a particularly tragic or unhappy story to tell, the witness gives the evidence in a manner singularly devoid of all feeling or emotion; perhaps because of the subdued atmosphere of the Court itself, or perhaps because of the self-imposed restraint of the witness. It was so in this case. Never throughout her story did the Princess show the slightest sign of the strain from which she must have been suffering. She was calm and dignified and seemed totally unaware of the intense interest she was creating amongst the onlookers. Even her own counsel seemed to be at pains to make her story as undramatic as was possible. Her evidence was very short, as there could be no dispute as to the facts, but the vital elements in her case had to be proved.

"In January, 1918, did some people come to your home?"

"Yes."

"What happened?"

"I had to show them through the house. They said, "Yes, certainly, this house is worth taking."

"At that time had you any servants in the palace?"

"Only an old Sweitzer—a door-keeper."

"After these people came, were you ever allowed to live in your own home again?"

"Never."

"Then were the public allowed in your house?"

"Yes. I had to show them round."

"A few months later, was your husband taken away, to prison?"

"Yes."

"What did you do?"

"I followed him to St. Petersburg, to be near him."

"Were you ever allowed to see him?"

"Sometimes."

"While you were in St. Petersburg, did you hear that the palace had been confiscated?"

"Yes. I went to Tsarskoe Seloe. I was not allowed into my home. I was allowed to take an ikon and say farewell."

"When was the last time you heard anything from your husband?"

"January 25th, 1919."

"What happened to your husband?"

"Five days later he was murdered in prison."

"And what happened to you?"

"The next month I escaped from Russia, without a passport."

"And is all the property we are discussing in this case your property, taken from your home, the Paley Palace?"

"Yes."

That was all. When the Princess left the box, it was quite clearly apparent from the faces of the onlookers in Court that there would not be any doubt as to the result, if the decision were left to them. It was in that somewhat depressing atmosphere that I was constrained to argue that everything had been perfectly legal according to the Law of Russia. There were two documents upon which we sought to rely. One was a decree passed by a body known as the Council of Peoples' Commissaries published on March 6th, 1921, No. III, in which it was stated, "all moveable property of citizens fled outside the confines of the Republic is declared to be the property of The Russian Soviet Federal Socialist Republic"; and secondly, a decree of the All-Russian Central Executive Committee and of the Council of Peoples' Commissaries, dated March 18th, 1923, which provided that "Works of art and antiques—being in museums—are recognised to be State property". We maintained that the Princess was a person who had fled outside the confines of the Republic within the meaning of the first decree, and that after the seizure by the Revolutionaries the Paley Palace was a "Museum" within the second, and that inasmuch as the British Government had diplomatically recognised the existing Russian Government since the year 1924, an English Court was bound to give effect to the Russian Law.

The extreme difficulty in arriving at an interpretation of that Law, or indeed of obtaining a correct translation of the language employed, could not be better expressed than in the words of one of the judges of the Court of Appeal who subsequently considered the case, and who dealt exhaustively with the political situation in Russia at the time. He said, "Great difficulties have arisen in this case in ascertaining the exact effect of the Soviet Law. The parties cannot agree on a proper translation; their experts differ as to the Russian meaning of the legislation, while the English translation is obviously susceptible of various meanings; over and above that, the legal principles involved are so different from our own that it is difficult to appreciate and apply them. In the early days of the Revolution, the position, as was natural, was vague and uncertain. The local Soviets seem to have been endowed with, or assumed, power. A formal constitution was promulgated on July 10th, 1918, under which three bodies were created: (1) the All-Russian Congress; (2) the Executive Committee; and (3) the Council of Peoples' Commissaries. The first two had legislative powers, the third mainly administrative, although their decrees were from time to time accepted as legislation.

"At first an attempt was made to nationalise almost everything, but there were express enactments in favour of 'toilers', which provided that in cases where they were concerned the Law might be administered to some extent in their favour. After a time it was found that the policy of complete nationalisation could not be maintained, and the beginning of a new economic policy occurred in 1922, ending with a Civil Code in January, 1923, which to some extent recognised private property, subject to certain exceptions in the case of property already transferred to the State."

That was the whole crux of the case. The Court held that the Princess was in Russian Law "a person who had fled outside the confines of the Republic" within the meaning of the decree, and that the consequent confiscation of her property had been confirmed by the Civil Code, and further inasmuch as the British Government had recognised the Russian Republic as a sovereign State, the English Courts were bound to give effect to Russian Law.

For similar reasons the Court decided that as the Russian Government had confiscated the Paley Palace as a museum, its whole contents became the property of the Republic.

I have no doubt that the Court was right. The Law of England is inflexible, and it is not to be influenced by considerations of mere sympathy, however justifiable. Only in one sentence of his judgment did Mr. Justice MacKinnon allow a glimpse to appear of what may have been his private feelings. "I am constrained to come to the conclusion," he said, "that this was an effect in Law, and that this property has become the property of the Soviet Republic."

Poor Princess Paley: her last hope was gone. Her home had been taken from her, and an English Court had pronounced that to have been legal. Well may she have said to herself, "My husband has been murdered. Would an English Court tell me that was legal too?"

THE TRAGEDY OF THE KENTISH FARMER

No sight can be more painful than to see a man being cross-examined as to his own sanity. The issues are so vital and the consequences may be so terrible that no jury should be called upon to enter into such enquiry; indeed it is more than doubtful if any jury can be competent to do so. The state of a man's mind, the degree of his mental stability, depends so much upon so many factors that it can only be decided, if at all, by persons who have had years of experience and training in such matters.

There is on record in the Assize Courts of a county town the case of a man who was being tried for a brutal assault upon the warder of a lunatic asylum. The man himself had been an inmate and according to his own story he had committed the assault with the sole and definite purpose of being brought before a jury, so that at last he might have an opportunity of establishing beyond any doubt that he was completely sane and that he should never have been incarcerated. He conducted his own defence. For hours he had cross-examined witnesses for the prosecution and had conducted legal arguments in a manner so reasoned and restrained that he had satisfied every person in the Court that he was as sane as they were; and then quite suddenly a point arose, of no materiality, which seemed to incense him without reason. He burst into a tirade of abuse, particularly directed against the Royal Family, so violent and absurd that within two minutes the same people were satisfied beyond all question, not only that he was mad, but probably a homicidal maniac. Without that outburst the jury could quite possibly have been induced to make a grave mistake. If no jury should properly be called upon to enter into such enquiry, no advocate should be required to cross-examine a person for the same purpose. I can remember few more unhappy experiences than the day when I had to cross-examine Mr. Harnett.

Mr. Harnett was a well-to-do Kentish farmer. He was married and in the year 1912 he was fifty-one years of age. From a medical point of view his family history was unsatisfactory. His father and mother were second cousins and his mother had died in an asylum, although the actual cause of her insanity was never explained in Court. His elder brother was there described as "eccentric, bordering on insanity for years". Of Mr. Harnett himself the main characteristic described to us was that he possessed views upon religious matters that were perhaps eccentric and certainly beyond those more usually held. In October, 1912, he became seriously unwell, and was so unwise as to consult a person whom he described as a quack doctor, with the result that he received a treatment which proved far from beneficial. He was injected with some substance, the nature of which he did not know, but which caused him to become seriously ill, to such an extent that he became delirious, and remained in that condition for about a month. Very shortly afterwards, and as he thought in consequence of this treatment, he engaged upon certain activities which were no doubt very largely responsible for his subsequent misfortunes. One of the most peculiar was a visit that he paid to Borstal prison. He hired a motor-car for the purpose, in which he was accompanied by a solicitor and a land agent whom he desired to be present as guarantors of his position and reputation, as he wished to ask the Governor's permission for him to preach to those prisoners who were under sentence of death. As there were of course no prisoners at Borstal under such sentence the visit may well have seemed peculiar.

On November 12th, 1912, he summoned to his house the reporter of a local newspaper, to whom he imparted a remarkable account of certain visions, of which he gave detailed particulars.

On the same day he wrote a letter to the local post office which may well have caused amazement to its recipient, and which subsequently remained annexed to his medical records.

"Dear Postal Official (or Officials),

"Jesus has touched my eyes. If I have done wrong I am willing to make things right. I love you. If you love Jesus and love me, you will come and see me and make me happy.

"Yours sincerely,
"W. S. HARNETT (a sinful man)."

Mr. Harnett's medical advisers took a very serious view of this document, which they attached to the report which they made upon his mental condition.

In addition the report stated that Mr. Harnett was suffering from delusions, one of which was that his wife had been unfaithful to him. It is right to state that no evidence whatever was given in any way supporting the truth of this suggestion, but at the same time it might well have been argued on Mr. Harnett's behalf that many a married man might possibly be under a similar misapprehension in regard to his own wife without necessarily being regarded as a fit subject for detention in an asylum.

However, this combination of circumstances satisfied Mr. Harnett's family that his mental condition had become affected, and they accordingly consulted two medical men, who certified him as insane, and he was on November 12th, 1912, accordingly removed to a private asylum presided over by a medical superintendent named Doctor X.

Mr. Harnett only remained at this asylum for about a month. At the end of this period the medical superintendent formed the opinion that Mr. Harnett was sufficiently recovered to be able to return home to his family. Mr. Harnett was thereupon seen by two visiting justices, who upon December 12th issued an order that he should be released on leave for twenty-eight days. The order was made under the Lunacy Acts and the effect of it was that if Mr. Harnett showed signs of a recurrence of his malady within that period he could be returned to the asylum; otherwise he would be a free man. Mr. Harnett's brother was requested to attend at the asylum for the purpose of escorting the patient to his house.

Mr. Harnett evinced great displeasure at being accompanied by his brother, whom he considered was the cause of his original certification, and indeed stated that he would prefer to be escorted by the police, but this was thought to be unreasonable, and on December 12th Mr. Harnett left the asylum in his brother's company and in high dudgeon. He refused to occupy the same railway carriage with his brother, and succeeded in leaving the train undiscovered, finally arriving that night at his own home alone.

On the next day he saw many different people. Two of them, both doctors, thought that he was not in his right mind. Many others, some of them business men, took a directly contrary view and considered that he was perfectly normal.

On December 14th, the second day of his freedom, Mr. Harnett came to London. After paying certain business calls, one of which was on his bank, during which he appeared to be quite normal, he called at the office of a Commissioner of Lunacy at the Board of Control Offices in Victoria Street. There was some dispute as to what actually occurred on this occasion, upon which Mr. Harnett presumably desired to raise questions as to the propriety of much that had happened to him, but it was clear that on his first arrival the commissioner himself was not present in the office. Mr. Harnett was seen by an assistant, who stated that he could not make head nor tail of what he wanted, although Mr. Harnett talked incessantly. When the commissioner appeared upon the scene he interviewed Mr. Harnett personally and came to the conclusion that he was not in a fit condition to remain at large. Accordingly a telephone message was sent to Doctor X, requesting that a car be sent to convey the patient to the asylum, and Mr. Harnett was detained in the commissioner's office until the car with two male attendants arrived. This actual detention during that very short period was the only possible act the responsibility for which could be held to rest upon the commissioner personally.

From that day, December 14th, 1912, Mr. Harnett remained as a mental patient in various asylums until October, 1921, a period of almost exactly nine years. During that time he was detained at Croydon Public Asylum; then at the Holloway Sanatorium at Virginia Water; and finally he was removed to a home in Aylsham. He was periodically visited by visitors in lunacy and examined by many doctors, all of whom were of the opinion that his delusions were still continuing and that his mental condition was such that his further detention was justified. During the latter part of his stay at Aylsham his condition was improved to an extent that permitted permission being given to him to call upon persons who lived in the neighbourhood, all of whom formed the opinion that his mental state was normal. In October, 1921, Mr. Harnett escaped from Aylsham, and remained at liberty for fourteen days, after which interval of time he could not, according to the Lunacy Laws, be retaken under the original reception order, but if it was desired further to detain him as a lunatic it would be necessary to have him recertified. This was never done; indeed Mr. Harnett voluntarily submitted himself to further medical examination, at which he was pronounced to be sane and consequently no longer liable to restraint.

Thereupon Mr. Harnett determined to institute proceedings in the Law Courts and to claim damages for the wrongful detention he had suffered and also for the many years of mental anguish which he must have undergone. He did not bring his action against the doctors who originally certified him, as they would be protected by the Lunacy Laws, but he named as defendants (i) the commissioner who detained him in his office in Victoria Street, and (ii) Doctor X who took him back to his mental home. Mr. Harnett contended that all his subsequent incarceration was the direct result of these two acts.

The action was tried before Mr. Justice Lush and a special jury and from the outset attracted an enormous amount of public interest. Mr. J. B. Matthews, K.C., who conducted the plaintiff's case with the greatest care and skill, alleged that from the very outset his client had been completely sane, and that any actions upon his part which might have seemed peculiar were entirely due to the improper treatment and injections he had received from the quack doctor. In particular he complained that the Commissioner in Lunacy in December, 1912, had made a tragic mistake in detaining Mr. Harnett at his office in Victoria Street and causing him to be sent back to the care of Doctor X, and the whole of the subsequent detention was directly attributable to that initial mistake; he categorised all the subsequent examination by visitors in lunacy and medical experts as being incompetent and careless and drew

SIR PATRICK HASTINGS WALKS TO THE LAW COURTS
(Photo: Keystone)

a picture of his client as being a man in full possession of his faculties who had struggled vainly for nine years to free himself from detention in a lunatic asylum to which he should never have been sent. He challenged the Crown, who were representing the Commissioner in Lunacy, to call as witness any one of the experts who had visited and examined Mr. Harnett during all those years to produce the slightest evidence that he was otherwise than completely normal. It is not surprising that such a story aroused a great deal of public anxiety and indeed indignation.

It was in that atmosphere that Mr. Harnett was called into the witness box. His demeanour was beyond reproach. He told his dreadful story calmly and with extreme moderation, without the slightest appearance of rancour or indignation, and no one who had not heard that story could ever have imagined that his sanity had once been in question. He offered himself unhesitatingly for cross-examination.

How could anyone possibly cross-examine such a man? By this time he had been pronounced by experts to be completely sane. To such curious incidents as had occurred nine years before there was the clearest answer. To a man who has suffered from the treatment of a quack doctor anything may have happened. Even the curious letter to the postal officials could be explained as the case of a man with extreme religious views who had suffered from temporary delusions. Upon one incident he was unshaken. On the day he visited the office in Victoria Street he was completely normal; he was able to call witnesses to prove it; and anyone who alleged the contrary was wrong.

In accordance with the wish of Mr. Harnett himself, and indeed in fairness to both sides, many witnesses were called by the defence, doctors and mental experts who had visited the asylums at which at different times Mr. Harnett had been confined; all of them expressed the opinion that the detention had been justified, but their position in the witness box was very difficult. It was admitted that Mr. Harnett had never been violent or in the least degree dangerous either to himself or anyone else, and their evidence as to his mental condition was of necessity composed of generalities. The one definite point of apparent substance lay in the alleged delusions, which had from time to time been certified as continuing, but that point so far from assisting the defence was turned to ridicule by the briefest cross-examination.

"One of the delusions from which Mr. Harnett was stated to be suffering was that his wife had been unfaithful to him?"

"Yes."

"And you stated in your report that the delusion was still continuing?"

"Yes."

"And continued during all these years?"

"Yes."

"Did you happen to find out whether or not his wife had in fact been unfaithful to him?"

The witness had no idea.

How could a man properly be found to be suffering

from delusions upon evidence such as that? The responsibility for releasing the inmate of an asylum is very great, and the difficulty in forming a definite opinion upon his condition may be still greater, but I confess that I was much disturbed by some points of the evidence given as to the different examinations made of Mr. Harnett during his detention.

Unfortunately the sympathetic considerations which arose in the case of Mr. Harnett tended to swamp the legal issues which were really fundamental to his claim for damages. With regard to Doctor X, that gentleman had been appointed under the Lunacy Acts which defined his duties and responsibilities. Provided that he acted in good faith and honestly believed that Mr. Harnett was a fit person to be detained under his care and further took reasonable precautions in his investigations, then he personally could be under no liability for that detention, and Doctor X contended that there was not and could not be the slightest evidence that he acted otherwise than in the honest belief that Mr. Harnett's mind was deranged and that he took all reasonable precautions in his investigations. With regard to the Commissioner in Lunacy, he contended that even if he was wrong in his belief that Mr. Harnett was insane on December 14th, 1912, the only injury that he had caused to Mr. Harnett was to detain him in the office at Victoria Street for two hours until the car from the asylum arrived, and that any damages which the jury awarded should be limited to that short period of time.

By the time the case drew to its conclusion popular

feeling was running so strongly in Mr. Harnett's favour that even the learned judge was temporarily deflected from a true interpretation of the necessary legal implications. He ruled that the jury were entitled, if they thought fit, to regard all the many years' incarceration as being the direct result of the original detention and that they might award damages upon that basis. He also held that there was evidence upon which the jury might find that Doctor X did not in fact take reasonable precautions to satisfy himself that Mr. Harnett was insane.

With that interpretation of the Law before them the jury had no hesitation as to the verdict they should return. They found against both defendants and awarded to Mr. Harnett by way of damages the sum of £24,000.

It was a most unfortunate result. There was an immediate appeal to the Court of Appeal, who took a different view of the Law from that expressed by Mr. Justice Lush. They held that there was no evidence of lack of reasonable care having been taken, and further that any damages which would be properly payable by the commissioner must be limited to such amount as would be attributable solely to the short detention in the Victoria Street offices. Accordingly the action against Doctor X was dismissed entirely, and a new trial was directed as against the Lunacy Commissioner.

Poor Mr. Harnett! That was not the end of his misfortunes. The next I saw of him was when he was sitting, a lone figure, outside the room I occupied, as Attorney-General, in the House of Commons.

Night after night, he sat there alone, and I was compelled to pass him as I went to and fro from my room. What he was doing there I never knew. He never moved and never spoke, but his continued presence became more than I could endure. I sent my policeman to tell him that I found his presence to be embarrassing and to ask him not to sit there any more. He received my message very apologetically and courteously; I never saw him again.

Within a comparatively short time he was dead. His body was recovered from the Thames. He was drowned.

THE CASE OF THE ILLUMINATING DOT

It is no part of the duties of an advocate to investigate the evidence that is to be brought before the Court. The facts are placed before him by a solicitor who himself questions the proposed witnesses and satisfies himself both as to their ability and reliability. If necessary, enquiry agents may be employed to probe still further into suspected sources of information. An advocate is not a detective, although in the case brought by the bookmakers against Mr. Abrahams I felt very like one.

Mr. Abrahams, under the soubriquet of "Beaufort", was the racing correspondent of a well-known London newspaper. Inasmuch as his principal employment was to foretell winning horses for those who pored daily over his prophecies, it is perhaps not surprising that his own ventures with the bookmakers were not very successful. In fact he had a consistently bad time. However, there came a period when his fortunes changed and from being a very regular loser he changed into a winner successful beyond the dreams of tipsters, so much so that the bookmakers with whom he dealt, and there were many of them, came to the conclusion that his luck was too good to be true. They decided that the time had arrived when they might well make some enquiries as to the methods by which he had achieved such a remarkable success

Bookmakers are not wholly unaccustomed to being swindled; indeed there are quite a considerable number of sportsmen whose main object in life appears to consist in an endeavour to discover new methods by means of which that desirable object can be best obtained. The more usual system is based upon the use of the telegraph, and it takes many forms. It is practically the universal custom of bookmakers to accept bets by telegram, provided that the telegram is despatched prior to the "off" of the race in respect of which the bet is made. In consequence much dishonest ingenuity has been expended in endeavouring to discover new methods by which a backer could despatch a telegram before the race had started containing the name of the winner, while at the same time being in possession of certain knowledge that the selected horse had in fact already won. Success in this form of swindle requires at least two confederates. One watches the race upon the course itself, while the other, at some distant village post office where one telegram is an event and a large bundle quite unknown, floods the unhappy post-mistress with a batch of wholly irrelevant telegrams, in the midst of which there is one making a bet upon a race with the horse's name blank. All these telegrams are duly stamped as having been dispatched before the race has started. Meanwhile the gentleman upon the course, having watched the winner pass the post, is able to telephone the result to his friend waiting at the post office, who thereupon dashes to the post mistress explaining distractedly that he has wrongly addressed one of the telegrams. The unsuspecting post mistress hands him back the batch of forms, which by then are duly stamped with the time of despatch, in order that the error may be corrected, and thereby affords him the required opportunity of filling in the winner's name. Everything appears to be in order and the defrauded bookmaker has no course open to him except to pay.

In the case of Mr. Abrahams, however, no suspicion that this course had been adopted could possibly attach, by reason of the fact that all telegrams sent by him or on his behalf came from the race-course post office, where only skilled and experienced officials were employed, far too astute to be taken in by such a well-known ruse. It therefore became apparent that if there was a trick it could only have been perpetrated in collusion with some member of the post office staff. Mr. Abrahams himself, although the racing correspondent of a highly respected daily newspaper, was held in no very high esteem by members of the ring by reason of his marked reluctance to pay upon his wagers when he lost. In consequence of which unhappy fact they refused to bet with him except in comparatively small amounts. Also, the information which they acquired, that he was using the name of more respected clients in which to make his bets, was one of the first reasons which induced them to make some more intimate enquiries. They decided to investigate the activities and personality of every telegraphist who was on duty at a race-course at which Mr. Abrahams had been operating, with particular attention to those occasions on which Mr. Abrahams had been exceptionally successful.

They discovered that among these, there was one telegraphist who was invariably present when Mr. Abrahams enjoyed a particularly good day. He was a man named Harvey. Harvey had been employed in the post office for many years and he bore the highest character, indeed not the faintest breath of suspicion had ever attached to him; but a very close, indeed minute, examination of his attendances revealed a state of circumstances which was, to say the least, suspicious. When Harvey was in the post office at the same time as Abrahams was betting on the course, Abrahams almost invariably won; when Harvey was absent Abrahams almost invariably lost. Among the firms with whom Abrahams dealt were the Pari-Mutuel Ltd., and his accounts with them over some months were closely scrutinised by chartered accountants, when some rather remarkable coincidences appeared. Between the months of December, 1933, and June, 1934, there had been fifty-seven racing days. Of these Harvey had not been on duty for forty-six days, during which Mr. Abrahams, betting account showed a loss by him of £264. Upon eleven days Harvey had been on duty, and on those occasions Abrahams had won thirty-three bets out of thirty-seven made, ending up with a profit of £719.

Abrahams also betted with a bookmaker named Day. The case of Mr. Day was equally peculiar. Between June, 1934, and February, 1936, there had been 134 racing days during which Abrahams had made bets with Mr. Day, and out of 134 days Harvey had been on duty upon fourteen occasions. During his absence Abrahams' account showed a loss to him of £137, but during the fourteen days upon which Harvey had been present Abrahams made thirty-one bets, of which he won twenty-nine, and his account showed a profit of £394.

Abrahams' account with Messrs. Ladbroke only differed in that the amounts were larger. Between June, 1935, and June, 1936, a summary of Mr. Abrahams' dealings upon occasions when Mr. Harvey was absent showed but a trifling profit of £78, but when Mr. Harvey was present in the post office, Abrahams, betting in the name of Smith, succeeded in winning £1,812.

The result of these enquiries decided the bookmakers to probe more deeply into the whole circumstances and in consequence they communicated their suspicions to the postal authorities. They in turn, being jealous of the reputation of their employees, sent an inspector accompanied by a police officer to take statements not only from Harvey but also from every one of the postal clerks who had attended the race meetings at the relevant times. From the point of view of the bookmakers the results obtained were not very encouraging. Not only was Harvey's character and reputation of the highest, but he indignantly repudiated any possible association with Mr. Abrahams. Indeed he went much further; he said he did not know Abrahams and had never even seen him, and there was not the faintest evidence that his statement was untrue. And more was to follow. It was discovered that Harvey was never alone in the telegraph office; there were at all times several other clerks working with him, each one of whom was equally beyond suspicion. Each one was interrogated. They were all unanimous that it was absolutely impossible for Harvey or anyone else to tamper with a telegram after it was handed in, or in any way whatever to alter or manipulate the record of the exact moment at which it was so handed in. There was only one discovery that might seem in the smallest degree important. The actual telegrams themselves were unearthed and it was discovered that in every case the name of the horse, unlike the body of the telegram, had been written in printed characters and therefore might conceivably have been inserted at a time later than the other portions of the telegram. But even this would be by no means uncommon in racing telegrams despatched by a perfectly honest backer, as it is quite usual for punters to leave the name of the horse selected to the very last moment before the actual despatch.

But the bookmakers were still far from satisfied; the coincidence of Harvey's presence on the occasions upon which Abrahams had been so uniformly successful was too remarkable to be lightly swept aside. The idea which they had formed as to the possible working of the swindle was something to this effect: That Abrahams had handed in a telegram with the horse's name blank, and that telegram would be duly stamped with the precise moment of acceptance; that Harvey would then take up a position at the window of his office from which he could keep his eye upon a confederate, who would, in his turn see the winning-post; that the confederate would signal the winning horse to Harvey, who thereupon could insert the name in the blank space left in the telegram, using for the purpose printed characters in order to avoid leaving any record of his handwriting, and the completed telegram would appear to be complete and regular. The theory was of course easy to formulate but much more difficult to prove; very direct evidence indeed would be required to establish such an ingenious fraud. There was, however, one small incident discovered that might turn out to be important. Abrahams had made a substantial bet through Harvey and had lost, but subsequent enquiries established the fact that the loss had been a little out of the usual course of events. The horse specified in the telegram had in fact been the first to pass the winning-post but unfortunately had subsequently been disqualified upon an objection. A confederate watching the race would of course have been unaware of such objection and would merely have signalled to Harvey the name of what he fondly imagined to be the winning horse. It was at least a possibility and possibly one more coincidence.

All sources of enquiry upon the race-course had been exhausted, and the results had fallen far short of producing the evidence which would be required before Abrahams and Harvey could be charged with any form of conspiracy. As a rule people do not enter into a conspiracy except with the fixed determination to make money and there was not the slightest indication that Harvey ever received a penny piece of Abrahams' winnings. Consequently it was necessary to make some effort to discover what

Abrahams had done with the money he had received as the result of his successful speculations. Enquiries to that end were set on foot and they proved to be both delicate and difficult, particularly as the bets were usually made in some name other than that of Abrahams himself; but as a result the following facts emerged. Upon every occasion upon which the bookmakers had sent a cheque in respect of winnings either to Abrahams or his nominees, the whole or a substantial amount had found its way into Abrahams' banking account. Abrahams thereupon drew a bearer cheque in his own favour, receiving in exchange either one-pound or five-pound notes. All the five-pound notes were traced, and there could be found not the slightest indication that any of the money found its way into Harvey's pocket—until at the very end of the enquiries one note turned up that was suspicious. It was a five-pound note and bore upon its back the initials "W. H." Those were the initials of Harvey himself. Immediately the inquiries were intensified. The note had been passed into the hands of a tobacconist, part of whose business it was to supply tobacco to different branches of the post office; at one of the branches he supplied Mr. Harvey was employed. The tobacconist himself was closely questioned; he was quite unable to connect the note with any payment made by Harvey, all that he could say was that it was his usual practice to require any person handing him a five-pound note either to sign or initial it upon the back. He did not know Mr. Harvey or his handwriting, and he had no recollection as to the person who had given him the note. The only possible course then open was to submit the note to an examination by handwriting experts. And juries do not much like experts. Moreover all that could be shown to them were the initials W. H., and the examination of initials could at the best be a very slender foundation upon which to found a very definite opinion. It was not surprising, therefore, that the best report which could be obtained was to the effect that while undoubtedly there were elements of suspicious similarity, it was impossible to consider them conclusive. At the conclusion of the enquiries the evidence taken as a whole appeared to be very slight upon which to launch a charge which must be in the nature of a criminal offence. However, the bookmakers were satisfied that they had been defrauded, and considered themselves amply justified in placing the whole facts before a jury; accordingly an action was commenced against Harvey and Abrahams claiming damages for conspiracy to defraud. Other defendants were mentioned, but as they were completely exonerated it is unnecessary further to refer to them.

The action was tried before Mr. Justice Lawrence and a special jury. From the very outset it had been apparent to me that the bookmakers required the assistance of a detective rather than an advocate. An advocate cannot make bricks without straw, and the facts put before me amounted to very little more than grave suspicion. Suspicion is not enough to support so serious a charge, and unless some new factor could be discovered, I was more than doubtful as to the result.

An action about theatrical or racing matters is always popular, and it was a motley crowd that thronged the Court at the commencement of the hearing. In addition to many bookmakers there were large numbers of unsuccessful plungers, some of them hoping to view another form of sport, and many more no doubt anxious to learn a trick or two which might possibly avail them in their future speculations. All the defendants were adequately represented and consequently the number of counsel engaged was very large. Both Abrahams and Harvey of course were present and I observed them both with interest. Abrahams was a shrewd-looking person, with a somewhat self-satisfied manner and an ingratiating smile; Harvey was a nondescript individual in whose appearance there seemed nothing of sufficient importance to attract attention. Both appeared supremely confident and wore an air of conscious innocence which must have appealed to all beholders.

I presented the facts of the case to the jury very much as they have been given here; there was the strange sequence of Abrahams' winning bets and the theory of a conspiracy by which such successes could have been obtained; there was the fact that the names of the horses had been printed and not written; there was the grave suspicion of the initials upon the five-pound note. We had very little additional direct evidence to offer. At the conclusion of the plaintiffs' case there was suspicion, but very little more.

But it was enough to require that an answer should be made and Mr. Abrahams himself went into the witness box to repudiate with the utmost indignation any suggestion that he had been guilty of a fraud. And here Mr. Abrahams allowed himself to make a very sad mistake. So anxious was he to prove his honesty and his great position on the turf that he went too far. "Why," he said, "these bets were nothing but a bagatelle to me. In the past I have won as much as £1,500 upon a single bet." The complacent arrogance of Mr. Abrahams was to me a gift from the gods. I knew all about that bet for £1,500, and as he himself had introduced it I was enabled, not only to cross-examine him about it, but also if necessary to give direct evidence as to the true facts.

It was the first matter I dealt with in cross-examining Mr. Abrahams.

"Did you at one time carry on a business as a bookmaker with a man named X?"

" I did."

"Was Mr. X generally employed as a bar-tender?"

That appeared to be the case.

"Did X obtain the money to finance the business from a rich gentleman whom we will call Y?"

That also appeared to be an accurate suggestion.

"Did the business purport to make an unsuccessful bet with a man named Abrahams, and as a result owe Mr. Abrahams the sum of £1,500?"

"That is so."

"And were you yourself the Mr. Abrahams concerned?"

This question appeared to cause Mr. Abrahams grave unhappiness. But there was more to follow.

"When Mr. Y innocently discharged the debt to

Abrahams, did you and X cut up the £1,500 between you?"

At this point Mr. Abrahams became involved in some most confusing explanations. If only, he said, he could discover the whereabouts of X, so as to be able to call him as a witness, everything could be satisfactorily explained. Even then I was able to assist him. X had resumed his occupation as bartender, and I was even able to offer to Mr. Abrahams the actual address of his employment, but however grateful Mr. Abrahams must have been at the information, his friend X never appeared in the witness box and no further information was forthcoming. Mr. Abrahams must have regretted very deeply that the bet of £1,500 had ever been introduced.

Although gravely discredited, Abrahams still adhered to his protestations of innocence on the issue then before the Court. He still maintained that he had not known Harvey; that he had never paid him a penny in his life; and that there was no ground whatever for suggesting a conspiracy between them.

When Abrahams left the box the case was not much more advanced than when we started. Truly it was most unlikely that Abrahams would be regarded as a truthful or indeed an honest person, but we had set out to prove that he and Harvey were joint conspirators, and that we had failed to do. Unless some admission could be obtained from Harvey our prospects of success were far from rosy.

Harvey himself was a witness of a very different

G

calibre. His character was irreproachable. Witness after witness was called from the post office on his behalf, to prove, not only that fact, but also that it was physically impossible for him to have manipulated the telegrams as we alleged. In a voice that appeared to carry complete conviction he swore that he did not know Abrahams, and had never received a penny of his money; if there was any fraud, he said, he at least was completely innocent. He was asked to take a pen and print the names of the winning horses so that his printings could be compared with the printed names appearing on the telegrams. But there is all the difference in the world between words written in printed characters and in ordinary handwriting. We could get but very little further. He was shown the initials on the five-pound note, and swore without the slightest hesitation that they were not written by him and that as far as he knew he had never seen the note before.

And then like a bolt from the blue came a discovery that altered the whole case. It was not advocacy that turned the scale. It was detection. When Harvey had first been examined by the police, in the early stages of the enquiries, a long and detailed statement had been taken from him. In accordance with the usual practice in similar cases, he had affixed his signature at the end, while every one of the preceding pages bore his initials for the purpose of verification of the accuracy of the record. That statement was produced in Court and the initials were examined. It was observed that the initials bore a somewhat unusual appearance. While it is not uncommon for a person to place a full stop after his initials, Harvey had an invariable habit of placing a dot immediately after writing W. H. and the dot was not in the place usually occupied by a full stop, but was placed halfway up the letters. Every page was examined and upon every page the dot was found to have been placed precisely in the same place, and at the same angle. The importance of this discovery was immediately apparent. Harvey was said to have initialled the five-pound note. If the same dot, placed in precisely the same distinctive position was found after the initials upon that note the conclusion would appear to be irresistable. The note was sent for; the initials were examined; and there, precisely in its proper place, was found the distinctive dot.

The case was over. Where the experts had been in doubt before, now they were convinced beyond all question. The initials had been signed by Harvey upon a note paid to him by Abrahams. They both shared in the proceeds of the fraud.

From that moment the ultimate conclusion was beyond doubt. What before had been a coincidence now had become an obvious sequence of events; what had been a suspicion now became a certainty. The jury returned a verdict convicting both Abrahams and Harvey of a conspiracy to defraud, adding a rider to the effect that the main responsibility lay with Abrahams.

That the final result was correct I was quite satisfied; that it was brought about by the sudden and unexpected discovery of Harvey's method of signing his initials I am convinced. What would have been the result if that discovery had not been made, I do not know. But of this I am quite certain: the bookmakers owed a debt of gratitude to Harvey's illuminating dot!

THE CASE OF THE THREE SISTERS

Kathleen, Susan, and little Deirdre were three very remarkable sisters. They lived together upon terms of mutual affection and regard and their respective outlooks upon life were curiously similar. Kathleen, who was the eldest, had enjoyed some experience of life, having been married twice; Susan, the second sister, had only been married once; while little Deirdre, who was the youngest of the three, was recognised as the baby of the family. The only business occupation upon which the sisters had ever been engaged was in the management of a tea shop, which they conducted together, but they were obviously a broad-minded family, indeed so broad-minded was Kathleen that she had for some years been living as the mistress of a wealthy manufacturer whom we will call Mr. Robinson. Throughout this period Mr. Robinson was residing with his unsuspecting wife, and as he was a man long past middle age, he was quite old enough to have known better. As was only to be expected, the association was a somewhat expensive matter, and during its continuance Mr. Robinson had regularly become aware of the existence of little Deirdre, although he had seldom, if ever, spoken to her. When the liaison drew towards its close, the acquaintance with the baby of the family suddenly developed into a very intimate relationship and this was brought about in a remarkable manner; there were two very different accounts of that development. According to the version told by little Miss Deirdre, Mr. Robinson appeared one afternoon at the family flat attired in garments of the deepest mourning. In heartbroken tones he told of the sudden death of his dear wife, and his grief was so intense that Deirdre's heart was touched and after a short interval she consented to marry him herself. The fact that Mrs. Robinson was happily alive at the moment was presumably unknown to her.

Mr. Robinson's account was very different. According to him, he had met Miss Deirdre one day quite unexpectedly in Oxford Street. She had pressed him to return with her to the family flat, which he did, and there intercourse had immediately taken place between them on the drawing-room sofa. Support for this latter view is perhaps to be derived from the fact that Deirdre had to admit that there were some peculiar features about her suggested engagement. In the first place she received no ring; indeed the whole affair was so completely wrapped in secrecy that it was never known to anyone except her sisters and herself; but what was more surprising still, the marriage was to be postponed for eighteen months, and inasmuch as Mr. Robinson would soon be seventy years of age, a prolonged delay might seem to be a trifle hazardous. It was no doubt in order to get over the disappointment caused by this delay that Mr. Robinson installed Deirdre in a small flat in Mayfair Court where he could visit her at his pleasure. Susan, who of course was well aware of the prior liaison with Kathleen, told us that she strongly objected to this arrangement, but was overpersuaded by Mr. Robinson, who told her she must be broad-minded. As broad-mindedness in such matters was an obvious attribute of all three sisters, it is perhaps not surprising that her scruples were overcome. Undoubtedly Mr. Robinson paid handsomely for such privileges as he enjoyed; considerable sums of money found their way into the hands of one or other of the sisters; in particular there was a sum of £300 which Mr. Robinson understood that he was paying in order to relieve Susan from some pressing need, but which Deirdre thought was a present to herself. Whatever the reason for the payment, the money was undoubtedly shared by all three sisters, who expended it upon a holiday in Germany.

During the next few months Mr. Robinson was occasionally abroad on business, and upon his various returns he continued to pay his periodical visits to the flat at Mayfair Court until one day his association with Deirdre was suddenly brought to conclusion in a most unpleasant manner. The final visit took place on the 16th of September, a date which later became of considerable importance. Upon that day there unexpectedly appeared upon the scene a gentleman who was introduced as an ex-detective inspector from Scotland Yard. Being not unnaturally surprised at his appearance, Mr. Robinson demanded to know his business, when the visitor replied that he was making enquiries as to whether Mr. Robinson was keeping the flat as a place of assignation for himself and sister Kathleen. Mr. Robinson was furious at the suggestion and indeed suspicious of his visitor, and his indignation was not lessened when Deirdre interposed with the information that she was going to have a baby. To this Mr. Robinson made the not unnatural reply, "For God's sake let us deal with one thing at a time." He left the flat and from that moment never saw Deirdre again. She wrote to him. He received one letter in particular dated September 17th, the day after he left the flat so hurriedly. It was in these terms:

"My darling Bobbie,
"I have always trusted you, and I am sure it is not misplaced. Try and have a nice quiet week-end Darling and do not worry. I am sure everything must come right in the end. With all my love and faith in you, because Bobbie there are so few people in the world one can trust. I do hope you believe in me.
"Your Deirdre."

He made no answer and the next thing he received was a writ for breach of promise of marriage.

I suppose that circumstances may exist in which an action for breach of promise is justifiable, although personally I have never met them, but in a case in which a proposed defendant is faced with disclosures of a very unpleasant nature and in particular has a perfectly good wife of his own living at the time, the motives for bringing such an action may well have been suspect. It was so in the case of Mr. Robinson. He was faced with two alternatives. Either he could hush the whole matter up, and pay; or else he could confess the whole story to his wife, and obtain her consent to fight the action and repudiate the whole claim, which he knew to be dishonest. He chose the braver course. He made full confession to his wife, and with her approval decided to contest the action.

There were already two suspicious circumstances about the claim, and not the least remarkable was the fact that no living person had heard a word as to the suggested engagement except the two sisters Kathleen and Susan. The other was the date of the suggested breach. It was said to be September 16th, the day when Mr. Robinson left the flat, and when, it was said, he definitely refused to carry out his promise to marry. If that suggestion were true and Mr. Robinson had behaved in such a blackguardly manner, it was certainly odd that Deirdre should have written her affectionate letter of next day hoping that he would have "a nice quiet week-end". Moreover there would be time to make some more detailed enquiries about the life and habits of the plaintiff and her sisters.

Meanwhile they upon their part were far from idle. No doubt they were fully of opinion that the last thing Mr. Robinson would want would be publicity, and they decided to give him as much of it as possible. They started upon a regular campaign for that purpose. The first method selected was to make a public application in Court to fix a date for the hearing of the trial; upon that application all three sisters appeared solemnly, but quite unnecessarily, in Court. A few days later some remarkable forecasts of the hearing appeared in the public Press, accompanied by photographs of little Deirdre, beautifully dressed and described in the following manner:

"Beautiful, twenty-year-old photographer's model, who is bringing an action for alleged breach of promise of marriage against Mr. Robinson, a wealthy industrialist."

Of course if Deirdre was really only twenty, at the time when she first met Mr. Robinson she would have been about fourteen, with her hair hanging down her back, and it was difficult to see where the Press could have obtained this information except from the plaintiff herself.

It may have been a disappointment to the sisters that this preliminary announcement did not produce some offer from Mr. Robinson to settle the proceedings satisfactorily and it may have been as a direct consequence that they decided upon stronger measures. Unknown to them their movements were being strictly watched and it was discovered they were staying together at an hotel in Ireland, where they were no doubt resting in anticipation of their forthcoming struggle in the Courts. While staying at the hotel Kathleen, the eldest sister, hit upon the expedient of herself communicating with Mr. Robinson, in order to warn him of the ordeal he must expect. No doubt she was the wisest choice as a letter writer as her previous intimacy with Mr. Robinson made it extremely unlikely that she would herself be put into the witness box; moreover she had already had some experience of a breach of promise action of her own, in which curiously enough she had employed the same solicitor as Deirdre. It seemed therefore that she could write in safety without fear of any subsequent risk of cross-examination.

Her first communications were apparently directed to explaining the enormous benefits which would accrue to Deirdre if she was compelled to pursue her action. One letter in particular contained the following optimistic passage:

> "Her publicity agent will state in Court the exact amount of financial injury to her health and future life, but Deirdre will make thousands of pounds and dollars in film contracts, etc., which will compensate her in one way for the irreparable harm you have done her."

This moving passage proved quite insufficient to bring Mr. Robinson to the desired state of mind, and therefore Kathleen was forced to have recourse to threats. By this time apparently Susan had been selected as the one witness who should be called to corroborate the promise of marriage, and accordingly she had supplied the solicitor with a proof of the evidence she would be prepared to give. And a terrifying document it was. No doubt, thought Kathleen, if Robinson once sees this he will collapse, and to ensure that he should see it, she posted him a copy. In it Susan had been at great pains to emphasise her baby sister's age; she described her at the time when she first met Mr. Robinson as "a child with her hair hanging down her back." But the real sting of her evidence came at the end. She stated that when Deirdre knew she was going to have a child, Mr. Robinson wanted her to undergo an illegal operation. Mr. Robinson was therefore a criminal and as such should be regarded. As these documents were dispatched from the hotel in Ireland where all three sisters were staying together, the whole action began to assume rather a sinister aspect, and so far from having the desired effect, they only tended to strengthen Mr. Robinson's determination to contest the claim; and accordingly the parties duly appeared at the Royal Courts of Justice.

The action was tried by Mr. Justice Charles and a special jury. Mr. Hemmerde, K.C., appeared for the plaintiff and must indeed have been impressed by the justice of his claim. He was almost poetic in his opening address, and expressed the view that there was practically no limit to the amount of damages which the jury might properly award little Deirdre. At the same time he must have seen some elements of danger in Kathleen's correspondence because he castigated her unmercifully for disclosing Susan's proof of evidence, which he suggested she must have stolen, and even suggested that it should have been the duty of Mr. Robinson's solicitor to have returned that proof unread. From this denunciation it seemed extremely unlikely that Kathleen would be called before us, and as I was particularly anxious to know which of the loving sisters we should be allowed to see, I made some enquiries. Where was Susan? Susan was standing beside the plaintiff in the witness box. Susan was asked to remove herself to another more remote position which she reluctantly proceeded to do. Where was Kathleen? Nobody knew. Was she in the building? Deirdre didn't know. 'And then a loving voice was heard from the body of the Court, "Here I am, Darling," and up popped Kathleen. This unexpected appearance, although gratifying as evidence of a deep affection, was apparently somewhat embarrassing to her sisters, particularly having regard to what Mr. Hemmerde had said about her, and Kathleen departed, to be seen no more. However, it was discovered that she had only gone as far as the Waldorf Hotel two hundred yards away, where she remained throughout the trial, so she could easily have returned if she so desired, but in spite of my repeated suggestions, she did not do so.

When Deirdre entered the witness box, she ably supported the speech of her own counsel, and appeared a gentle timid creature entitled to expect and to receive the chivalrous treatment due to one of her tender years, and it was only upon the first question put to her in cross-examination that a small difficulty arose. She was asked when she became twenty years of age, and as she appeared to have some slight difficulty in remembering, she was shown her birth certificate, which had been discovered with some difficulty and which showed that in truth she was not twenty but was really thirty-five. This discovery seemed to upset her greatly, and she was even more distressed to be asked if she had a publicity agent. At first she said she had not, but then in broken accents she confessed that she had although she did not know him by sight, and indeed this question of publicity was so abhorrent to her that she burst into tears, and begged me to desist from asking her such unkind questions. From this point she sobbed without ceasing, so much so that I was constrained to request her to restrain her tears as much as possible at this early stage, as there were so many more unpleasant things to ask her and it would be a mistake to exhaust herself so soon. Not unnaturally this observation resulted in an increased degree of weeping until the judge interrupted by remarking that she was not really crying at all, as he had watched her carefully and there had not appeared one single genuine tear. This unsympathetic observation may have had some effect, because then Deirdre somewhat pulled herself together and announced that she had never had a publicity agent after all, and deeply resented any suggestion that this action had been brought to get money out of Mr. Robinson. Upon which the judge politely enquired, "Then why are we all wasting our time here in Court?" To which in turn Deirdre asserted that all she wanted was that honour should be returned to her. Upon hearing this remarkable statement, I felt bound to point out that if she insisted upon having intercourse with old gentlemen upon the drawing-room sofa, it would be impossible to comply with her request.

In spite of her timid simplicity Deirdre was a very astute witness. Any questions which might possibly cause embarrassment were met by floods of apparently synthetic tears, or else by a total absence of recollection which she excused by explaining that she had been compelled to take a sleeping draught the night before. The visit to Germany was one of those occasions. She indignantly denied that the £300 had been obtained by Kathleen upon the ground that

Susan was in some urgent trouble; that money, she said, had been a present to her, although it was admittedly expended on a pleasant holiday enjoyed by all three.

The visit of the mysterious ex-chief inspector was another matter upon which she displayed extreme innocence. She knew nothing about it and any enquiries must be made of whichever of her sisters elected to give evidence. She did not know which one that was likely to be; she did not know why Kathleen had so suddenly left the Court nor if she was at the Waldorf Hotel, nor whether she was likely to come back; she knew nothing about her sister Susan's proof. She had heard that her sister Kathleen had herself brought an action for breach of promise and that she had been represented by the same solicitor as Deirdre herself. But she indignantly denied that the defendant in her sister's case was a man of colour; he was merely dark-complexioned. She agreed that she had never had an engagement ring, and that no one in the world, except her sisters, had ever heard of her prospective marriage, and finally she left the witness box in floods of tears with her innocence a trifle tarnished, and the unpleasant suggestion ringing in her ears that the whole case was nothing but a conspiracy by three extremely dangerous sisters.

The next morning it was apparent that it was Susan who had been chosen as the corroborating witness, and she loyally confirmed her sister's evidence in every respect. As she had the night to think things over and as the Waldorf was only two hundred yards away it is perhaps not surprising that her cross-examination was punctuated by continual requests to know if Kathleen was still sitting in the hotel; whether her health was good enough to enable her to attend the Court if she so desired, and whether we might expect to see her. However, Kathleen never did appear and we had to do the best we could without her. Susan was far from tearful and indeed extremely cross, and her temper was in no degree improved when it was bluntly suggested to her that she was a senior partner in the conspiracy. She knew of the long intrigue with her sister Kathleen, and it was a little difficult to explain her acceptance of Mr. Robinson's rapid change of affection to little Deirdre. It was still more difficult to explain her broad-mindedness in approving of the installation of Deirdre in the flat at Mayfair Court. She quite recognised that Deirdre was in fact a little older than had previously been represented, but she explained that slight inaccuracy by stating that Deirdre had always been particularly sensitive on the question of her age. The advance proof of her evidence that had been purloined by Kathleen was a document she must have found extremely annoying. In it she had stated that she was a "femme sole"; that when she first met Mr. Robinson she was a widow; that she had divorced one husband and that she had then married again, all of which romantic episodes were pure invention. With regard to Deirdre her proof stated that when Mr. Robinson had first become acquainted with her she was a little girl "with her hair hanging down her back", a somewhat picturesque description which, if true, might tend to show that little Deirdre had preserved her childish ringlets a little longer than was customary. The statement in her proof that Mr. Robinson had suggested the desirability of procuring an illegal operation upon Deirdre was far too serious to be explained by the possibility of mistake, so she gallantly averred that it was true, although by this time it must have been apparent, even to her, that the possibility of anything she said being believed was most unlikely.

It was, however, with regard to the visit of the mysterious ex-chief inspector that she finally came to grief. Her explanation of this visit was indeed remarkable. On being closely questioned she was driven to confess that it was she herself who had arranged this interview. According to her, she was at that time under the impression that Mr. Robinson was in the habit of personally conducting her sister Kathleen to a brothel, a practice of which she strongly disapproved. In her natural distress she had appealed for assistance to a gentleman who, by a curious coincidence, happened to be the same solicitor who was now conducting Deirdre's breach of promise action, and she had instructed him to dispatch the so-called policeman to Deirdre's flat in order, if possible to frighten Mr. Robinson into a state of mind in which he could be induced to desist from taking Kathleen to such undesirable resorts.

This truly amazing explanation was too much for any of us. With a last request for information as to the whereabouts of Kathleen, which remained unanswered, sister Susan left the witness box, feeling,

I am afraid, that any chance of obtaining money from Mr. Robinson had receded into the very distant background.

Kathleen never appeared. That fact caused me very considerable disappointment, as I had been greatly looking forward to asking her some questions as to previous experience in the matter of a breach of promise action enjoyed by this broad-minded family of sisters. But the jury had already heard enough. Without desiring even to hear the evidence of Mr. Robinson they returned a verdict in his favour and the action was dismissed.

Mr. Justice Charles himself must have formed a very strong opinion on the whole case. These were his final words:

"I shall consider whether it is not my duty to report this matter to the Director of Public Prosecutions. This case was no more than a conspiracy to extort money from the defendant. I will consider what steps I shall take in the matter in order to put a period to the activities of these three dangerous women."

THE COURTAULD ARBITRATION

The arbitration which took place between Courtaulds and the British Government in the year 1942 told a story of the development into enormous prosperity of a great business enterprise which was probably unique in commercial life; the record, which lay behind the arbitration, of the great international difficulties and dangers which had beset England in the previous year, and of the assistance given to the government by Mr. Samuel Courtauld and his co-directors in order to overcome those difficulties, may well have written a page in English history. What would have been the political result, if on the 14th of March, 1941, Mr. Courtauld had refused the request of the Chancellor of the Exchequer that Courtaulds should on that very day sell to the government the whole of their immense American resources, must be a matter of pure speculation. Would it have delayed the giving by the United States of that financial aid of which England was so urgently in need? No one will ever know; everyone must be free to form his own opinion; after all, the arbitration was not concerned with speculation, it was merely required to assess compensation. For that purpose it was necessary to know something of the Courtauld history.

The founder of the English family of Courtauld was one Augustine Courtauld who came from France in the seventeenth century as a Huguenot refugee, and his descendant George Courtauld set up the first of the Courtauld silk mills at Braintree in Essex in the eighteenth century. His son Samuel set up a similar factory at Bocking in the same county in 1816. From these comparatively small beginnings sprung the enormous enterprise now conducted by a limited company, Courtaulds Limited, possessing a nominal capital of £32,000,000.

At first the Courtauld business consisted mainly, if not wholly, in the manufacture of natural silk, but as the years passed by, chemical research discovered the possibility of manufacturing an artificial substitute by treating vegetable cellulose with caustic soda, and as a result of that discovery artificial silk, or rayon as it is now called, was born. Courtaulds were quickly to realise the importance of this discovery and they devoted a great deal of time and money to its development. At the beginning of the present century they commenced to manufacture artificial silk, and from that date it may well be said that they were pioneers in the rayon industry.

The arbitration was not concerned with the company's English business, but only with such part of their undertaking as existed in America. In 1910 Courtaulds had decided that a useful and profitable extension of their business could be developed in America, where, at that time, the rayon industry was scarcely in existence. Accordingly in that year they formed a company in Pennsylvania under the name of "American Viscose Company", to develop a business on precisely the same lines as that carried on in England. The development of the American company and the immense success which it achieved is almost as remarkable as that of Courtaulds themselves. It erected many mills in Virginia and Pennsylvania and in its early years the business increased with immense rapidity. Not unnaturally this great enterprise soon began to attract American competitors. Large American companies sprang into existence, all of which started with manifest advantages in that they were in a position to benefit from much of the early experience of their English rival, and in addition they were in a position to instal the newest and most up-to-date machinery, while that of the Viscose Company had been in existence for a considerable time. By the year 1937 the Viscose Company was seriously affected by this competition. The manner in which the danger was overcome is by no means the least of the company's achievements. Immediate and stringent re-organisation was essential and was at once adopted. Enormous sums of money were devoted to that re-organisation, new mills were erected on the most modern lines, old machinery was scrapped and new plant on the latest lines was installed, with the result that by the year 1941 the competition had been overcome to such an extent that the company was able to show for the year 1941 the enormous trading profit of approximately fourteen million dollars, with an estimated increase for the next year to a sum of no less than twenty million dollars. Inasmuch as Courtaulds owned practically the whole share capital in the American Viscose Company, it cannot be a matter for surprise that they regarded the Viscose Company as one of their most valuable assets.

The cruel misfortune which resulted in the arbitration with the British Government fell upon Courtaulds in the year 1941. At that time England's fortunes were at their lowest ebb. She was fighting the World War practically alone; all her financial resources were exhausted; her only hope of obtaining the munitions and supplies which she needed lay in such help as she could obtain from America, and that help was almost at an end. In order to provide the dollars with which to pay for their requirements in the United States, the Government had compulsorily acquired all the marketable American securities in private hands, and there were no more left. England was practically penniless.

It was in those desperate circumstances that Mr. Roosevelt, perhaps England's greatest friend, decided upon the introduction of the American Lend-Lease Bill. If that Bill, together with its necessary adjunct, the Seven Billion Dollar Appropriation Bill, became law, American aid to a practically unlimited extent would be available to the United Kingdom; if those Bills failed to obtain the approval of the American legislature, disaster would seem to be inevitable.

Unfortunately the passing of those two Bills was by no means a foregone conclusion. America at that time had not entered the war and there existed in that country a large body of political opinion, particularly the Isolationists, who were against any form of American participation in the European struggle, and consequently were bitterly opposed to the projected legislation. They put forward many contentions in support of their views, of which perhaps the financial arguments were thought to carry most weight. While fully aware that England had disposed of all her marketable securities, they contended that inasmuch as there still existed large business concerns in America owned entirely by English shareholders, those concerns at least should be sold to Americans before the United States should be asked to supply further aid to Britain; in the forefront of their argument they placed the case of the American Viscose Company. As the date for the passing of the Bills approached, the opposition of the Isolationists appeared to harden, until at last a moment arose when it seemed possible that the two Bills might never become law unless the British Government first agreed to acquire these businesses and then to resell them to America.

This fact placed the British Government in a position of considerable difficulty. On the one hand it was quite impossible to place upon any of their business concerns a value which could be assessed with any degree of accuracy, and it seemed an extreme hardship to acquire by compulsion property the true value of which it might be impossible to ascertain. Upon the other hand the danger to the country was imminent. There was no possible alternative to acceptance of American wishes, and accordingly the British Government announced their willingness to acquire the businesses in question and in due course to resell them to America. For the moment this announcement acquired the desired result.

The Lend-Lease Bill passed through the Senate

upon March 8th, 1941, and received the signature of the President of the United States upon March 11th.

Within a few hours a further grave issue arose. The Seven Billion Dollar Appropriation Bill would come before the Appropriation Committee almost at once, and unless that too were passed the Lend-Lease Bill would be comparatively useless. The Isolation opposition were not satisfied by the announcement already made; to them it appeared as nothing more than a pious hope. They insisted that some tangible proof should be given of English good faith; they insisted that at least one of these businesses should actually be sold to America by the British Government before the Seven Billion Dollar Appropriation Bill should become Law, and for the purpose they selected the American Viscose Company. The British Government were officially informed that it was absolutely essential that actual sale of the Viscose Company to America should be completed immediately, and indeed before March 15th.

Accordingly on March 14th, the Chancellor of the Exchequer asked Mr. Samuel Courtauld to call upon him at the Treasury. The Chancellor received Mr. Courtauld with the utmost sympathy; he explained that the reasons necessitating the acquisition by the Government of the shares in the American Viscose Company were not only imperative but of the utmost urgency; he expressed the wish that Courtaulds should assist the Government by voluntarily consenting to the transfer of those shares, but at the same time he made it clear that if the transfer was not voluntary the Government would have no option except to acquire the property compulsorily. The Government themselves were in a great difficulty. While they already possessed power under the Emergency Powers Act to acquire by compulsion all marketable securities, they possessed no powers sufficiently wide to enable them to acquire the American Viscose Company's shares, and although they would undoubtedly be able to obtain sufficient power by passing a new regulation, that would take some little time and could not be done before March 15th, the last date by which the whole transaction had to be completed. It was in those circumstances that Mr. Courtauld was virtually asked for his assistance.

This request placed Mr. Courtauld and his co-directors in a position of the greatest difficulty. If they had been free agents practically no sum of money would have been large enough to induce them to part with their American holding, but they were bound to appreciate the grave and indeed dangerous situation with which His Majesty's Government were faced. At all costs the American legislation must be passed. It would have been impossible for them to refuse such help as lay within their power. With the utmost reluctance Mr. Courtauld informed the Chancellor that Courtaulds were prepared to part with their American holding that day. The whole transaction was completed within a matter of hours. By the morning of Monday, March 17th, the New York Press was able to state that England had sold the Viscose Company to America.

All opposition to the proposed legislature disappeared and the Seven Billion Dollar Appropriation Bill was unanimously approved by the Appropriation Committee upon the next day. The danger was over.

The amount of money to be paid by the British Government to Courtaulds for their property was impossible to assess at that time, and accordingly it was left for future agreement, or subsequent arbitration; the price to be paid by America to the English Government was defined in a somewhat complicated agreement but can be expressed in simple language: American bankers who appeared as the purchasers were to make a preliminary payment to the British Treasury and thereafter the shares in the Viscose Company were to be issued to the American public; the amount of money realised upon such issues, if greater than the preliminary payment, was to be handed over to the British Treasury. The preliminary payment was agreed at the sum of 36,456,000 dollars (roughly nine million pounds). Although this preliminary payment amounted to an enormous sum of money, Courtaulds were horrified at the smallness of the amount when compared with their estimate of the value of their asset, and they expressed their disapproval in no unmeasured terms, but they had no option except to wait the pending issue, and then if still unsatisfied to resort to arbitration. The disposal of the shares in America took a good many months to complete, and the final realisation was found to amount to some 62,000,000 dollars, which amount, when adjusted in a manner considered by the

Treasury to be reasonable, resulted in a sum payable to Courtaulds of £16,700,000.

Even this sum, large as it was, was considered by Courtaulds to be insufficient, and they informed the Treasury that they were not prepared to accept that figure as representing the true value of what they had lost, and that they would require the proper amount to be assessed by an arbitrator; and accordingly the arbitration was commenced.

The only question to be decided by the arbitrator was the real value of the American Viscose Company, and the ascertainment of that value gave rise to the greatest difficulties. Both sides agreed that the sale had been forced upon Courtaulds and consequently the value to be ascertained must be based upon a hypothetical assumption, namely that of an assumed purchase by a willing buyer from a willing seller, in other words a sale at a fair price. What was a fair price? And upon what basis was it to be ascertained? Upon the one hand the Treasury contended that in a matter of such magnitude the only possible way of arriving at the proper figure was to take the actual sum in fact realised by the American issue, namely £16,700,000. On the other hand Courtaulds maintained that the actual sum realised would be no criterion whatever by reason of the fact that the sale had not only been forced upon them, but had been a rushed sale taking place at a most inauspicious moment. If the Treasury were right in their view, the arbitration would be a very simple matter, as there was no possible dispute as to the amount paid by the investing public; if the Treasury were wrong, there would of necessity be a very intricate inquiry into the amount of the enormous assets of the Viscose Company and the realisable value of those assets.

The arbitration took place in July, 1942, before Mr. Justice Simonds, assisted by two eminent chartered accountants, and lasted for many days. The Attorney-General appeared for the Treasury and stoutly supported the Crown's main contention. Inasmuch as the learned arbitrator gave no reasons for the award at which he finally arrived, it is of course impossible to know upon what actual grounds he arrived at his decision, but from the award itself it was apparent that he did not regard the final result of the American issue as by any means conclusive. The greater part of the time occupied during the arbitration was taken up in an attempt by both sides to establish the true value of the American Viscose Company, and the evidence given was certainly remarkable if only by reason of the extraordinary differences between the views of great financial experts. As far as I am aware there never had been a prior occasion when the value of a business of such magnitude had been the subject of judicial enquiry, and the difficulties in the way of arriving at a true result were obviously present to the minds of everyone concerned. Having regard to the important position of many of the witnesses called to give evidence, it was impossible to imagine that they were not endeavouring to assist the arbitrator to the best of their ability, but their opinions were, to say the least of it, irreconcilable; the variations ran into millions of pounds.

The view which Courtaulds sought to maintain was in its essence extremely simple. They suggested that the only fair way in which to assess the true value of a business was to ascertain the real value of its assets, and the amount when ascertained, subject to any possible difficulty in realisation, formed the basis upon which the true value could be fixed. If those assets earned a reasonable amount of interest, all that remained was a matter of almost mathematical calculation. In support of this contention I was supplied with figures which certainly showed that the success of the American Viscose Company had been remarkable, and that its financial position was extremely good. The realisable assets had been carefully valued and showed the following results: the net current assets, such as marketable securities, cash and stock were valued at £11,727,267; capital assets, such as buildings, etc., at cost less depreciation, were valued at £19,995,820, making a total for assets alone of over £30,000,000; and these figures allowed nothing for the value of goodwill. In addition the figures showed that the company earned an extremely good commercial profit. Eminent financial witnesses were called on behalf of Courtaulds to give evidence that upon those figures they would expect, under normal conditions, to realise upon a sale of the Viscose Company a sum in the neighbourhood of £30,000,000.

The expert witnesses called on behalf of the Crown took a very different view, and it was upon their cross-examination that the remarkable difference of opinion between almost all of them became apparent. Detailed examination of financial evidence is of necessity wearisome, and it may be sufficient to say that in the main they supported the Government's contention.

Those were the kind of differences with which the learned judge was confronted. How in the world was it possible for him to arrive at any possible conclusion! So far from his being assisted by the evidence, it seemed to me that all the witnesses, although no doubt with the best intentions, had combined together to make his task more difficult. During the time which elapsed between the conclusion of the hearing and the announcement of the award I amused myself by trying to imagine upon what basis I should have acted if I myself had been the arbitrator. Upon the whole I think I should have started with the fact that the business realised £16,000,000 under a forced sale taking place in abnormal conditions, and to that amount I should have added such further sum as in my opinion would have been realised if the sale had been entirely free and the conditions were entirely normal. Whether or not that would have been the proper method, or indeed have any relation whatever to the principles upon which the learned judge acted, we shall never know. All that remains certain is that when the award came to be made it was for a sum of £27,125,000.

The arbitration had been a most interesting experience, and it left with me a reflection that was even more absorbing. If, on that day in March, 1941, Mr. Courtauld had refused the Chancellor's request, would the Lend-Lease legislation have passed through the American Senate, and if not, what would have been the result upon subsequent history? If the risk of failure was at that time a very real one, what sum of money would the British Government have been prepared to pay to obviate the risk?

CHAPTER IV

The Central Criminal Court

CRIMINAL COURTS are no doubt a necessary evil in a civilised community. If society is to be preserved and law and order maintained, presumably crime must be punished, and nowhere in the world is that punishment administered more fairly and impartially than in the Central Criminal Court. But crime is a sordid business, and to anyone who has practised in that Court the recollection of his experiences will bring him little that he could possibly wish to record. I have no memories of the Central Criminal Court beyond a sense of undiluted melancholy; the whole atmosphere reeks of misery and squalor; it almost seems as though no human feeling could possibly exist within its walls, no hope, no sympathy, nothing but indifference and, above all, monotony. The same cases tried one after another, each one apparently a replica of its predecessor; the wretched procession of criminals who pass from the cells into the dock, and then back from the dock into the cells, appear to share the general lethargy, almost as though they had done it all so frequently that they were used to it. Except in the comparatively rare case of a trial for murder, when a few sadistic onlookers eagerly await the possibility of witnessing the death sentence, even the verdict of the jury appears to awake but little interest.

That atmosphere is apparent from the moment of entering the main hall from which all the many Courts extend. There are a few unemotional policemen, a few peripatetic lawyers, a few poorly dressed women, waiting in melancholy silence to learn the fate that is shortly to descend upon their unhappy menfolk. If they exhibit any feeling whatever, it almost seems as though they recognise that they are passing through a not uncommon experience, in fact one to which they are well accustomed.

Within the walls of the Courts themselves the atmosphere does not seem very different. With the exception of the dignified figure of the judge whose duty it is to control the progress of the trial, and who, in consequence, is keenly aware of every incident which takes place before him, there is little to indicate that a human tragedy is to be unfolded. It all seems so much a matter of routine. It has all happened so many times before. Nobody cares.

The Court is peopled with persons all of whom appear to share the general indifference. There is an associate who has a seat below the judge's bench, a jury in the jury box, a few apparently uninterested onlookers and of course still more policemen. To anyone visiting the Court for the first time it might almost seem as though he was looking at a stage before the rising of the curtain. Suddenly there comes a knock on the floor. It announces the entry of the judge. Everybody rises. When he sits, everybody sinks back into their seats. The performance is about to begin. It is the associate who rings up the curtain. He rises to his feet. "Put up John Smith." The name is taken up by innumerable warders, and their voices rumble down into the cells below, apparently in the bowels of the earth, and then a melancholy individual is pushed up the stairs into the dock. The warder standing beside him introduces him to the Court. "Number 148, John Smith." Sometimes John Smith merely looks unhappy; sometimes he assumes the indignation that one associates with a bull upon his first appearance in the arena. The associate intervenes again: "John Smith, you are charged that you" on some date or other, did something or other, probably burglary, robbery, forgery, indecency, or any other of the innumerable offences usually before the Court. "How say you, John Smith, are you guilty or not guilty?" Occasionally John Smith says he is guilty. Everyone is quite indifferent, except perhaps the officials, who are slightly relieved that the case will not take long. A policeman mentions that John Smith has done precisely the same thing on many previous occasions, so he once more returns to prison.

Sometimes John Smith is more hopeful, and states in tones of synthetic indignation that he is not guilty, and he may even call upon the Almighty to witness the truth of his assertion. Everyone in Court is equally indifferent. The jury is sworn and the sordid case proceeds upon its dreary course. Whether or not John Smith is convicted seems to remain a matter of complete indifference to everyone. If he receives a sentence of imprisonment, John Smith himself appears unmoved, although occasionally he announces that upon his release from prison he proposes to deal violently with the policeman who has given evidence against him, which savage threat appears to affect no one. England has been a civilised country for many centuries; to anyone who spends a day in the Central Criminal Courts, a reflection must arise as to whether civilisation has very much advanced.

There is, however, another side to the picture, when the dreary procession of habitual criminals is interrupted and a name is called by the warder of a man perhaps known to almost everyone inside and outside the Court, a name hitherto honoured and respected and now included in the calendar of prisoners to be tried. What can a trial mean to such a man! To the burglar and the pick-pocket, a sentence of imprisonment is the worst that can befall, perhaps soon to be forgotten, but to a man who has enjoyed a high position and the esteem of all who knew him, imprisonment is the least of all his punishments. His name will be remembered as long as he may live as a symbol of the ruin of a most distinguished life. I have known such a case myself. When Lord Kylsant and Mr. Harold Moreland stood in the dock everyone in Court knew that they were in the presence of a living tragedy. I am glad to remember that Mr. Moreland left the Court with his name untarnished, but that is my only happy memory of a long and painful case.

I have recorded only one other instance of the Criminal Courts, and in that case the trial was of little interest. It was the man himself who left behind a memory that has remained. I could not understand him then, and I am not sure that I can understand him now. Perhaps a student of pyschology could be more successful. I have called him a gambler, and that name must suffice. Strictly speaking, the case of the Lost Pearls should find no place in these recollections, as it never actually came into Court. It is a detective story. But it interested me very greatly, and perhaps it may interest anyone who cares to read it. I have no other memories of the Central Criminal Court that I care to record.

THE CASE OF THE ROYAL MAIL

Lord Kylsant was the chairman of the Royal Mail Steamship Line, and Mr. Moreland was a partner in one of the largest and most respected firms of accountants in the world. Lord Kylsant was a man who, until the moment of his trial, was universally acclaimed, not only as a great shipping magnate, but as one of the most respected figures in the country. He had been made a peer in 1923. He was a Grand Cross of the Order of St. Michael and St. George. He was the Lord Lieutenant of the County of Hereford West. He had been president of the Chamber of Shipping of the United Kingdom and of the London Chamber of Commerce. In fact, his whole career had been one of personal triumph and achievement.

Mr. Moreland stood equally high in the opinion of all who knew him. Not only was he one of the heads of a great profession, but he was a gentleman whose private and public life had earned the respect of everyone who knew him.

On the 20th July, 1931, these two gentlemen stood side by side in the dock at the Central Criminal Court, charged with publishing balance sheets of the Royal Mail Steamship Company which were false and fraudulent. It was alleged against them that they had wilfully deceived the shareholders by representing that the company was in a very prosperous condition when they knew that it was on the verge of ruin.

The Royal Mail Company owned one of the largest shipping lines in England and, like many other similar concerns, had undergone periods of violent fluctuation in its financial condition. During the period of the First World War, it had made extremely large profits, and with commendable foresight the board of directors had placed a large portion of those profits to reserve, with the object of being in a position to meet any possible liability to income tax and excess profits tax. At one time, these reserves had accumulated to an amount exceeding two million pounds, and after all the requirements of the Revenue had ultimately been settled there remained in their hands over a million pounds, which could be used as the directors thought proper. During the years 1921–1925, the profits of the company had largely decreased, and the directors had decided to use some portion of their accumulated reserves for the purpose of increasing their annual profits, and no complaint was made at the trial of the method by which a portion of those reserves had been so utilised.

It was in respect of the years 1926 and 1927 that the trouble arose. In 1926 the company applied to the Treasury to extend the period during which certain repayments were due from the company to the Treasury, in respect of loans which had been made. The Treasury thereupon desired an enquiry to be made into the financial affairs of the company, and for that purpose appointed an accountant to look into their books. It was as a result of that enquiry that the prosecution was commenced. It is, therefore, necessary to see exactly what was the position of the company in the years 1926 and 1927. An intricate examination of financial detail is always tiresome, and therefore, it will be sufficient to state broadly what the balance sheet purported to show, and what were the true facts.

The balance sheet showed that in the year 1926 there was a trading profit earned by the company of £439,000. The Government enquiry discovered that, so far from there being any trading profit for the year 1926, the company had in fact been running at a loss, and the way in which the alleged profit was arrived at was by crediting the accounts with the sum of £750,000 drawn out of the tax reserve, and that in fact instead of a trading profit of £439,000, the company had really incurred a loss of about £300,000. In consequence of this discovery, the Treasury maintained that the balance sheet was fraudulent, and decided to institute criminal proceedings against Lord Kylsant, as chairman, and Mr. Moreland, as auditor. Sir John Simon, K.C., and Mr. Singleton, K.C., were instructed to represent Lord Kylsant, and I and Mr. Stuart Bevan, K.C., represented Mr. Moreland.

At the outset, the case appeared to be a very difficult one, and it was necessary to make some very careful enquiries, not only as to the practice of preparing balance sheets generally, but also as to the precise figures in this particular case.

Of Lord Kylsant I saw but little, but I was supplied with information as to his views on the matter. According to his understanding of shipping business, he took the view that great fluctuations in the earnings of shipping companies were only to be expected, and gave no indication of the true financial position of the company. His experience had taught him that periods of prosperity occurred in regular cycles, and it was necessary, from a business point of view, to accumulate large reserves in prosperous years, in order that in leaner periods the company should be able to draw upon them to make up the losses which might well have been anticipated. He pointed out with considerable force that, unless this course was adopted, an untutored body of shareholders, being faced with a sudden drop in their annual profits, might well fall into a panic, which would be unfair alike to them and the investing public, and, generally speaking, he justified everything that appeared in the balance sheet upon that basis. He moreover maintained that his company had employed the best possible firm of accountants as auditors, and that he relied upon them to see that the company's balance sheets were properly prepared. There was a further point upon which Lord Kylsant very naturally relied, although I personally never thought quite enough weight was attached to it at the trial, that he was supported by a board of directors of the highest position, some of them very eminent lawyers, and no one of them had ever queried the propriety of what was being done.

From the outset, it was apparent that the main burden of this part of the trial would fall upon those representing Mr. Moreland, and it was to him that we looked for a more thorough elucidation of the facts. Although Mr. Moreland was no doubt an admirable accountant, as a client he was a little trying. Being completely conscious of his own integrity, he treated all the allegations made against him with supreme contempt, and absolutely declined to recognise the very grave position with which he was faced and the danger in which he stood. Moreover, being a devoutly religious man, he was convinced that a divine interference would necessarily decide the issue, a view which, although no doubt satisfactory to him, was a little trying to his harassed and even exasperated legal advisors.

However, in the end, we were able to get a clear view of the facts, particularly as to the manner in which the 1926 balance sheet had been prepared. Apparently the accounts were prepared in the office of the Royal Mail, and the balance sheet in its proposed final form was then submitted to Mr. Moreland for his certificate and final approval. Mr. Moreland was, of course, aware that the revenue reserves had, to some extent, been utilised to increase the profits for some years prior to 1926, and said that such utilisation was quite usual and proper. In the year 1926, inasmuch as it was proposed to utilise so large a sum as £750,000 to change an admitted trading loss for the year of £300,000 into a declared profit of £400,000, Mr. Moreland considered that the time had arrived when some indication of that fact should be given to the shareholders.

When the draft balance sheet was submitted to him in the year 1926, Mr. Moreland, when dealing with the amount of profit, himself wrote into the draft balance sheet the words "including adjustment of taxation reserves". He did this entirely of his own initiative, and he stated that those words were the ones usually employed by accountants, to give notice to shareholders and anyone who might be concerned with the declared profit that such profit had only been arrived at by a utilisation of reserves. Lord Kylsant had nothing whatever to do with the words which Mr. Moreland inserted in the balance sheet, but he made no comment upon them, and the final balance sheet, as published, contained Mr. Moreland's addition.

On receipt of this information, it immediately became apparent that the whole defence must necessarily turn upon the one question, as to whether or not the words used by Mr. Moreland were well recognised in accountancy circles, and were sufficient to give notice of the manner in which the trading loss had been turned into an apparent profit. From that moment, every effort was made to obtain balance sheets in other companies, certified by accountants of the highest position, in which a similar phrase had been used in similar circumstances. Whether or not this accountancy practice was to be commended was, in our view, wholly immaterial. The charge we had to meet was a charge of dishonesty, and if it could be shown that Mr. Moreland had merely adopted the customary practice, it would be very difficult for anyone to accuse him of dishonesty. Infinite labour had been expended by the solicitors instructing me in obtaining instances of such practice, and before the preliminary hearing in the Police Court, I had been provided with a pile of balance sheets, all more or less to the same effect, with which to cross-examine the distinguished accountants who were to be witnesses for the prosecution.

The great difficulty with which we were then faced was whether or not to disclose our main defence at the preliminary hearing. If we cross-examined the accountants at such an early stage, no doubt each witness cross-examined would endeavour to draw great distinction between the cases in which he had used such a phrase and the case of the Royal Mail. Thus we had to decide whether or not it would be wise to let them know in advance what our line of defence would be, while at the same time gaining an opportunity of finding out what distinctions could be raised against us. Conversely, should we leave the point entirely until the hearing at the Central Criminal Court? As subsequent events proved, we were well advised in adopting the former course.

The preliminary hearing took place at the Guildhall before the Lord Mayor, when the first important witness was Sir William McClintock, the head of the well-known firm of accountants bearing his name. In front of me were piles of balance sheets, some of them having been audited by Sir William himself, and it was fairly obvious that the cross-examination was likely to be prolonged. Upon my first question directed to the main point of the defence, namely that the actual words "including adjustment of taxation reserves" were precisely the words customarily used by wise accountants in similar circumstances, the magistrate adopted what was to my mind a most extraordinary and unprecedented course. He refused to allow any of the questions, as being irrelevant. Sir Phené Neale was then Lord Mayor and the senior magistrate in the City of London. He was also a solicitor, and perhaps a little over-conscious of his own importance, but how in the world he took upon himself to reject, at a preliminary enquiry, a cross-examination which was obviously based upon the considered opinion of a large number of somewhat eminent counsel has always passed my comprehension. His ruling necessitated an immediate decision. I saw at once that the defence might in the end benefit extraordinarily by reason of the course he had adopted. I rose in my place and stated that having regard to his ruling no one of the counsel present could possibly take any further part in the hearing before him, and in a procession we all left the Court. I should imagine that such an event has never previously occurred in the Guildhall, and Sir Phené may well have regretted his ill-advised and perhaps hasty decision.

I immediately communicated with the Attorney-General, and obtained from him permission for my solicitors to interview the prosecution's witnesses, in order to obtain from them a statement of their views, which we had been prevented from obtaining in the Police Court by the action of the Lord Mayor. There was only one witness whom we really desired to see, and that was Lord Plender, perhaps the doyen of accountants. He also in the past had verified balance sheets containing words substantially similar to those complained of in the present case. Accordingly a very carefully prepared questionnaire was submitted to him, with a view to obtaining his agreement with the principles upon which we so strongly relied. As was only to be expected in the case of a man such as Lord Plender, the replies were absolutely frank and, in our opinion, entirely satisfactory. It was upon the material supplied by Lord Plender that our defence was mainly based.

The trial took place on the 20th July, 1931, at the Central Criminal Court before Mr. Justice Wright and a jury. No doubt the atmosphere which prevailed at the time was none too friendly towards the defendants, and the Court was packed with onlookers, most of whom had suffered severely.

From the exposure which had, of course, taken place in consequence of the preliminary proceedings, I could not help wondering whether the distinguished accountants who were to be called by the prosecution were a little unhappy that they had not been already asked to give a little more explanation of the prevailing practice as to certifying balance sheets, as by this time they were of course aware of the information in our possession. They must also have known that we ourselves were in a position, in case of necessity, to call into the witness box the heads of their own profession to give evidence in support of the suggestions which we had already made to Lord Plender. We, upon our part, were gravely anxious in case Lord Plender himself should in any way qualify the answers which he had already given to us; accordingly our pile of balance sheets was given a prominent place upon the desk before us.

The case was opened by the Attorney-General, who appeared for the prosecution, and as I listened to his speech, I could not help wondering if he too would not have been better served if the defendants had been allowed to outline their defence before the Lord Mayor; once or twice it seemed to me that he had been completely misinformed as to what the defence was going to be. There were two charges against the defendants: the first was based upon the alleged fraudulent balance sheets, and in that both Lord Kylsant and Mr. Moreland were implicated; the second was against Lord Kylsant alone, and in that I took no part. It was upon the first charge that I felt that the Attorney had been somewhat led astray. After outlining the facts and figures, he made this specific allegation against Mr. Moreland: "the phrase 'adjustment of taxation reserves' was a phrase quite deliberately prepared and selected and chosen as a phrase which would convey nothing whatever to the mind of the ordinary person, but at the same time would enable anyone to say in case the need thereafter arose, 'Oh! but all this is covered by the phrase "adjustment of taxation reserves."' It betrays, members of the jury, on my submission to you, an uneasy conscience about what was being done."

It was upon that very point that Lord Plender had been questioned, and it was upon Lord Plender's answers to those questions that the defence relied. The Attorney-General was right in thinking that to be the whole basis of the prosecution; if Lord Plender's evidence turned out to be that which we anticipated, could that prosecution be maintained?

Lord Plender himself was the first witness called before the jury, and his evidence for the prosecution was merely formal. It was upon his cross-examination that everything depended. I never remember to have approached a cross-examination with more anxiety, and inasmuch as the questions and answers formed the basis of the whole defence I have recorded them in full.

"Lord Plender, is it quite a usual and a proper thing for companies to set aside large sums against their liability for excess profits duty and income tax?"

"Yes."

"If they were not required for the next year, could they properly be brought back into profits for subsequent years?"

"That would be quite a regular credit."

"In many cases, would they not be disclosed in a profit and loss account as having been brought into credit?"

"Sometimes no reference is made, but, generally speaking, it will be found that an indication is made that some transfer has been made."

"Do I understand you to mean by that that if the secret or inner reserves are used for that purpose, there might properly come a time when an auditor would say that some indication should be given to the shareholders that those transfers are being made?"

"Yes."

"Are there not many cases in which a reserve of

this kind is made into the credit of the year's profit and loss, and no mention is made that reserves have been called upon?"

"There are such cases."

"Is it done by firms of the very highest repute?"

"Yes."

"Is it your view that no exception could be taken to that practice?"

"As a principle, no exception could be taken."

"Might there come a time when the auditor would say: 'Now if these reserves are to be used again, some indication must be given to the shareholders that the profit and loss account is augmented by transfers from the excess profits duty reserve'?"

"Yes."

"Are there common phrases used by auditors to indicate such augmentations in one or other of these forms: 'Excess profits duty adjustment,' or 'after adjustment of reserves for excess profits duty,' or 'taxation adjustment,' or 'adjustment of taxation reserve?'"

"Yes."

"Are all these phrases commonly used by auditors to indicate transfers to the profit account from taxation reserve?"

"That is so."

"And those transfers, according to the facts of any particular case, might be either small or large?"

"Yes."

"That being so, if you saw such words as those which I have described in a profit and loss account, would you understand from them that there had

LORD KYLSANT, WITH HIS SON-IN-LAW, THE EARL OF COVENTRY, LEAVES FOR MR. JUSTICE WRIGHT'S SUMMING UP IN THE ROYAL MAIL STEAMSHIP CASE

(Photo: New York Times)

been a transfer from an excess profits duty or other reserves, which might be small or large?"

"Certainly."

That was all we could have hoped. Mr. Bevan's relief was quite as great as mine. When I sat down he whispered, "That has done them!"

Whether or not anyone in Court immediately realised the importance of those answers, I never knew. Certainly the action of Sir Phené Neale had prevented the prosecution from learning what was our real defence, and it may be that the answers of Lord Plender took them by surprise; the judge at any rate seemed to take comparatively little interest in them at that stage of the proceedings. But those answers were vital, and what was of equal importance to us was that the Attorney-General asked no questions in re-examination of Lord Plender to minimise the effect of the evidence he had given. But what was still more remarkable was that none of the subsequent witnesses for the prosecution were ever invited to express a view in contradiction of Lord Plender's, and, in our view, the propriety of Mr. Moreland's conduct was completely established by the accountancy evidence given by the Crown.

After that evidence how was it possible to contend that Mr. Moreland had deliberately prepared that phrase in order to hide an uneasy conscience?

As Lord Kylsant justly contended that he had nothing whatever to do with the wording of this suspicious phrase, and that he relied in that respect entirely upon his accountants, the main burden of the defence fell upon Mr. Moreland, and whatever else he might succeed in doing, I did not envy the Attorney-General his task of trying to establish criminal dishonesty against Mr. Moreland. As I called Mr. Moreland into the witness box, anything less fraudulent in appearance it would be impossible to imagine. His demeanour was precisely as it had been upon the first occasion when I had seen him. He treated any allegation made against him with supreme indifference, and regarded his accusers almost with good-natured contempt. He accepted full responsibility for the wording of the phrase "adjustment of taxation reserves", which he said was perfectly well-recognised throughout the entire profession of accountancy to indicate exactly what had been done. He stated that those words gave the fullest notice of the inclusion of monies previously reserved for taxation, and it was perfectly open to anyone interested in the accounts to ask a question as to the extent to which they had been so utilised.

Although he was cross-examined at some length, he declined to budge one inch from his original statement. When asked about his interest in the company, he said that he had no interest financially or otherwise, except to the extent of his auditor's fee, which was, of course, shared with all the many partners in his firm, and which, after payment of tax, resulted to him in a benefit of only £20.

If any jury could have convicted kind old Mr. Moreland of fraud, my faith in juries would have been gravely shaken. Many of the heads of his profession followed him into the witness box to give evidence on his behalf, all of them stating that, if called upon to do so, they would have signed the balance sheet exactly as Mr. Moreland had done, and upon that note the evidence closed. The judge summed up at very considerable length, no doubt by reason of the importance of the case and the many complexities in which we had been involved. As I listened to him I began to feel that he had been, at the end, very deeply impressed by the defence we had put forward, but he must have recognised, as we all did, the tremendous amount of public prejudice which existed at that time against anyone connected with the Royal Mail Company. The jury retired and were absent for some hours. The period of waiting while a jury is considering its verdict is one I have always hated. In this case I hated it more than ever; I was so determined that my clients should be acquitted, and the jury were out so long. All the devoted band of most skilful lawyers who had worked so hard, and had helped me so much, shared my anxiety. Nerves began to fray and tempers became short; Mr. Moreland alone maintained his attitude of confidence almost amounting to indifference. That same attitude which had exasperated us so much during the preparation for the trial now became intolerable, and when it was found to have extended to Mr. Moreland's own domestic hearth it became more than those instructing me could bear. While the jury was still out of Court the telephone rang up from Mr. Moreland's home; somebody wanted to speak to my solicitor. He hurried to the telephone, deeply distressed that there was still no news. A sweet and gentle voice addressed him: "Could you kindly tell me if Mr. Moreland is likely to be late for dinner?" That was the last straw. "Yes, Madam," he replied, "I should think about twelve months late." But he was wrong. When the jury came back into Court, they returned a verdict of Not Guilty, and both Mr. Moreland and Lord Kylsant were acquitted.

Unhappily for Lord Kylsant, that was not the end. Against him alone there was a further charge based upon the issue of debentures in the same company, and in that charge I was merely an onlooker. My client Mr. Moreland was no party to that indictment, but Lord Kylsant was convicted and sentenced to a term of imprisonment. As a mere observer my opinion is completely valueless, but I was never completely satisfied of the justice of that conviction. I was very sorry for Lord Kylsant.

THE GAMBLER'S STORY

He was a gambler. I will not mention his name because although it is a long time ago there may still be someone who might possibly be distressed to be reminded of the whole story. It will be enough to call him the Gambler. By profession he was a bookmaker, although anything less like the popular idea of a bookmaker it would be difficult to imagine. His appearance was remarkably distinguished; he was tall, good-looking and extremely well dressed, but his most outstanding characteristic was an absolutely unwavering imperturbability. I do not think I have ever seen a man with such a sphynx-like countenance. He must have been a perfect gambler.

The other person concerned in the subsequent trial was a young American named Doyle who had come to England and had soon become a well-known member of the sporting fraternity. He was a good-looking young man with a pleasant manner and a quick wit and he rapidly acquired popularity among a large circle of friends. He lived extravagantly although the source of his income was never clearly defined beyond the fact that it was probably derived from the race-course. Doyle had been a friend of Danny Maher, the American jockey who had lately come to England, where he had achieved immediate and outstanding success, and for some time Doyle had undoubtedly profited by backing Maher's mounts. It was through his racing activities that he had become acquainted with Solly Joel, the millionaire race-horse owner. By reason of the fact that Maher was accustomed to ride many of Joel's horses, Doyle was soon included among Joel's racing friends. He was a constant visitor at Joel's home as well as being a guest upon his yacht, and in consequence was well known to the whole Joel family, including Woolf Joel, a son. For some time Solly Joel was a good and generous friend to Doyle; it was a few years later that he became a vindictive enemy.

During the First World War, Woolf Joel became old enough to join the Flying Corps and he was seriously injured in an aeroplane crash, which kept him in hospital for some time. When sufficiently recovered he came to London for a short period of leave. It was during that leave that he again met Doyle. He was dining one night at a restaurant when Doyle came up and spoke to him as an old friend of his father. Young Joel was not aware that Doyle was at that time in a very precarious financial position. Doyle was very sympathetic about the flying accident and offered his services, as an older man, to help young Joel to spend a pleasant leave. An appointment was made to dine together a few nights later, and the dinner duly took place.

Thereafter events followed an almost stereotyped course. Doyle pointed out various well-known personalities in the room and finally called attention to a solitary figure dining in the corner. It was the Gambler. Doyle described him as a well known bookmaker and a particularly interesting companion. An introduction was soon effected. The Gambler was invited to join them at dinner and in due course he suggested that both Doyle and young Joel should go round to his flat for a drink. Then came the suggestion of a friendly game of chemin de fer. As was to be expected, when the stakes were low young Joel won. Doyle suggested that they should be increased, and then the luck changed! By midnight Woolf Joel had lost between three and four thousand pounds. Doyle himself complained loudly that he too had been a loser to the extent of a couple of thousand pounds. To what, if any, extent the game had been dishonest, it is impossible to say. In all probability young Joel had about as much chance of winning, even in a straight game, from two such experienced gamblers as he had of reaching the moon. But whatever the nature of the game, it was disastrous for Woolf Joel. Naturally enough he had not the money to pay, so he gave a cheque. The cheque was promptly discounted with a money-lender and in due course the matter came to the ears of Solly Joel.

As was to be expected, the father was furious. That his son should have been inveigled into the hands of two gamblers was bad enough, but that one of them should be the man he had befriended was more than he could overlook. He decided to prosecute them both for a conspiracy to cheat at cards.

The case for the defence was brought to me and it did not seem to possess any particular interest or unusual feature; just an ordinary case of card-sharping. The trial took place at the Central Criminal Court and I came into Court just as the prisoners were placed in the dock. Everybody seemed to be staring at the Gambler. He certainly was the most remarkable figure I have ever seen in any dock. He seemed to be devoid of any human sentiment whatever. From first to last he never showed the slightest feeling or emotion. His face was the colour of ivory. He might almost have been taken for a statue of some well-known actor or other distinguished person. He reminded me instinctively of the hero of Bret Harte's famous gambling stories. He was certainly not a man whom a father would select as a gaming companion for his son.

C. F. Gill, K.C., conducted the prosecution and he gave full dramatic force to the somewhat sordid story. He painted a picture of the young flying officer, badly injured in the war, and coming home to find himself the victim of two heartless gamblers. From the very outset it was fairly obvious that the result was almost a foregone conclusion. The only possible interest in the case would lie in the cross-examination of the Gambler himself.

Gill was a prosecutor of the old school. The moderation and restraint which marks the prosecuting counsel of to-day was unknown to him. An extremely able cross-examiner, he was accustomed to use every artifice of the skilful advocate to obtain a conviction in any trial in which he prosecuted and this was essentially a case in which he would undoubtedly employ them all. I was more than curious to see if he would be able to goad my client into some display of feeling, possibly of anger or possibly of fear; but

Gill was quite unsuccessful in any such attempt. When the Gambler went into the box, his demeanour remained precisely the same as it had been when standing in the dock. He was perfectly calm and perfectly courteous; if he gave any indication of being affected in the slightest degree by Gill's taunts, it was merely perhaps that some of his answers indicated a slightly amused contempt. His demeanour was irreproachable and he was quite frank in all his answers. Certainly he had invited young Joel to his flat; certainly he had suggested a game of cards; that was how he lived. But to suggest that there was anything dishonest in the play was utterly ridiculous. There was no possible need for it. Anyone who played cards with him did so at his own risk; he was a very good card player. The cross-examination was long and skilful, well calculated to provoke an outburst from the prisoner. But it never came. If anyone was roused to anger, it was Gill himself. When the Gambler went back into the dock, he was quite as unemotional and unperturbed as when he left it.

But the facts were too strong for him. The judge summed up severely. The young officer on leave; the spider's web; it was all too clear for words. The jury were of the same opinion; they convicted both prisoners and they were sentenced to long terms of imprisonment.

As I was leaving the Court, I received a message that my client was anxious to see me before he was taken away. I hate those interviews, but it is always impossible to refuse, so I saw him. He looked precisely as he had done before the verdict; equally unmoved and apparently quite unaffected by what had happened. To my intense surprise he said he was going to appeal and the appeal must be brought on at once. I told him that in my opinion any appeal would be utterly hopeless and was at some pains to point out my reasons for that view. He listened politely until I had finished. "Perhaps," he said, "you would be interested in knowing why I am appealing. I have a son of my own, who is now fighting the Turks in Palestine. He has no idea that I am in this trouble. If he got to hear of it, it might be very awkward for him with his brother officers. That is why I am appealing and the appeal has got to succeed." If, even then, he had displayed the slightest feeling, I could have understood him, but he did not. He merely stated a fact; then the warders took him away.

Why had he told me that story? I could not understand it, it was so unlike him. Had he thought it would be a good move to try and arouse my sympathy, or was the whole thing pure invention? I made some enquiries the next few days and found that it was quite true that he had got a son who was fighting in Palestine at the time. I was younger in those days and perhaps a trifle sentimental, but whatever the reason, the whole case began to worry me. He had appeared so confident that his appeal was going to succeed. It might be that I had missed some point which ought to turn the scale; but I could not find one. However much I worried, I felt that the case was hopeless, and I knew that I should be glad when it was over. In the end I came to the conclusion that his interest in his son was some sort of pretence.

As I went into the Appeal Court some weeks later, an usher gave me a message; once more the prisoner asked me to see him. This time I almost refused. I did not want to be burdened with any more sentimental stories, but in the end I consented and saw him in a room beneath the Court.

He was exactly the same; no sign of anxiety or emotion of any kind; he was utterly unmoved. He thanked me for coming to see him. "I am afraid this case has worried you," he said, "I beg you will not worry any more. This morning the governor of the prison told me that my son has just been shot down in Palestine and killed. It is quite immaterial now what happens in my appeal." His interest in his son had been quite true.

The appeal failed completely as I knew it would and once more the Gambler showed no sign either of disappointment or distress. I never saw him again, but I have often wondered whether his face remained equally imperturbable at the moment when the prison governor told him that his son was dead.

THE LOST PEARLS

I first heard of the lost pearls from Mr. Price, senior partner in the firm of Price & Gibbs, the well known assessors to Lloyds Underwriters, who had received notice of a claim from Mr. Max Meyer of Hatton Garden. Max Meyer was probably the largest wholesale dealer in pearls in England and was a man of unimpeachable integrity. His stock of pearls was enormous; in the safe of his small office in Hatton Garden were to be found pearls absolutely beyond price. He once showed me a bunch of pearls, strung together rather like a bunch of bananas, and told me their value. It seemed incredible that so much money could be tied up on little bits of string.

Mr. Meyer, it appeared, had recently made a large and important purchase from a firm of pearl merchants in Paris and the pearls had been sent to him by post. They had been packed in a small parcel, little bigger than a matchbox, and of course registered as well as being heavily insured. In due course the parcel was delivered at Mr. Meyer's office and when opened it was found to contain nothing but pieces of sugar; the pearls had been stolen. Mr. Meyer at once communicated with the underwriters, who in turn handed the matter over to Mr. Price for investigation.

The case presented many unusual features. The French firm, equally with Mr. Meyer, were beyond suspicion, and enquiries from them carried the matter very little further. The pearls had been safely packed, the parcel had been sealed and registered and duly despatched. The conveyance of precious stones by registered post, although it might be thought a somewhat risky operation, was by no means unusual and a loss in those circumstances was extremely rare. Investigations in Paris satisfied Mr. Price that the pearls were perfectly safe when they were handed over to the French post office. The parcel was examined with meticulous care; the seals were found to have been intact on arrival; there was not the slightest evidence of any tampering with the package and yet the pearls had disappeared. How and when the theft had taken place remained a complete mystery.

Mr. Price had a great deal of experience in the investigation of mysterious losses. By a process of elimination he came to the conclusion that the pearls must have been stolen in transit, and that the theft could not possibly have been the work of one man; there must have been a gang of skilful thieves working in collaboration. The careful organisation showed clearly that the thieves were not only extremely clever in arranging the actual theft, but in all probability were equally astute in their plans for the ultimate disposal of the pearls themselves, for which they would no doubt expect to receive a very large sum. No clue was discovered sufficient to afford the slightest hope of tracing the perpetrators of the robbery and the underwriters were thrown back upon the expedient of offering a reward to any person who was willing to give any evidence leading to the recovery of the lost jewels.

The problem of the amount of reward to be offered

was extremely difficult. If Mr. Price was right in his surmise, the secret of the theft would be very carefully guarded and probably known only to the actual perpetrators, who would expect their share of the proceeds to be very large; consequently the offer of a small reward would be useless. Moreover, any member of the gang of thieves who might be persuaded to betray his confederates would in all probability be running a grave risk of personal danger, and that fact had to be taken into consideration. Mr. Price took a large view; he advised the underwriters that any offer less than £10,000 or thereabouts would be of no avail and moreover the reward must be advertised at once as it was practically certain that the pearls would be sent abroad within a matter of days or even hours. The underwriters took his advice and the next day the advertisement appeared.

Thereafter there was nothing to do but wait, but the period of waiting was very short. Almost immediately Mr. Price received information that some person had appeared upon the scene who claimed to be in a position to effect the return of the stolen property, provided that he was satisfied that he would receive the reward and further that he would run no possible risk on his own account, either from the police or, what was still more important, from his quondam friends. From such enquiries as he was able to make Mr. Price was satisfied that his informant was genuine in his offer and that he was, if not one of the thieves himself, at least wholly in their confidence. Thereupon Mr.

Price devised a plan which would ensure the recovery of the jewels and at the same time remove the not unnatural fears of the informer. How the plan was devised and what were the means of communication employed I was never told, and I thought it wiser not to ask. But undoubtedly the informer was satisfied with the promises made to him for he proceeded to tell his story with a remarkable degree of frankness. The pearls had been stolen in transit and there were several persons involved. They were to be taken abroad for disposal, and the informer himself was the person who was to be entrusted with the task of conveying them out of the country. The final arrangements for his journey were to be made that day at a meeting in a hotel in Holborn, where the pearls would be handed over to him with complete and detailed instructions as to how and where he was to travel. The informer would give no further information beyond stating that he was quite unable to hand the pearls over to Mr. Price as he was certain that his every movement would be watched, and this statement was confirmed by the fact that it was quite obvious that he was in a state of terror lest he should be suspected of betrayal by his associates.

Mr. Price's plan to meet these difficulties was delightfully simple. The informer himself was to be robbed of the pearls as he carried them away from the meeting at the hotel. The arrangements were quite simple; it was decided that he should carry the pearls in the right-hand pocket of his overcoat and that for the purpose of identification he should display a handkerchief in his breast pocket. He was to walk down Holborn and then to turn into Hatton Garden at precisely five minutes to 3 o'clock, walking on the left-hand pavement. At the same moment, another man, this time wearing a carnation in his button-hole, would enter Hatton Garden from the other end; this second man was an emissary from Mr. Price. The two men, walking at a normal pace, would pass each other about halfway down the street, and at the moment of passing the man with the carnation would slip his hand into the informer's pocket, abstract the pearls, and continue his walk as though nothing had happened. Thereafter arrangements would be made for the protection of the informer if protection became necessary.

This was the best plan that could be devised in the shortness of the time at Mr. Price's disposal and it was duly carried out. The meeting took place at the hotel and the pearls, together with his instructions, were duly handed to the informer. He in his turn proceeded slowly down Holborn, no doubt with his eyes on the clock, and precisely at five minutes to three o'clock he entered Hatton Garden. The pearls were then in a loose parcel in the right-hand pocket of his greatcoat.

At the same moment, the gentleman with the carnation in his button-hole entered Hatton Garden from the opposite end. Inasmuch as each party to the plan was eagerly awaiting the appearance of the other, no doubt both of them were immediately aware of each other's presence. The informer moved slightly to the left to ensure that his right-hand pocket was in the most easily available position; no doubt the prospective pick-pocket stretched his fingers to ensure their flexibility; the walk of each grew more and more nonchalant as the distance between them decreased. And then, all of a sudden, a policeman in uniform stepped out of a side turning and crossed into Hatton Garden between them.

Immediately the informer jumped to the conclusion that he had been betrayed. The whole plot was plain before him. He was to be arrested with the missing jewels upon him; there could be no defence; he would be sent to prison as the thief and the underwriters would get their pearls without the necessity for payment of the reward. At any rate that should not happen! In a flash the pearls were in his hand, the parcel was burst open and every pearl was thrown into the gutter behind his back; he crossed the road, passing the carnation bearer at a safe distance, and disappeared. The uniformed policeman, who was merely an ordinary officer on his usual patrol duty, passed on, totally unaware that anything untoward had occurred.

Within a few minutes Mr. Price was informed that the plan had failed. His emissary could give him no explanation beyond the fact that the man with the handkerchief had crossed the road, obviously in order to avoid a meeting. No one had observed the action of the informer when he threw the pearls into the gutter and the emissary was quite unaware of any reason for the change of plan. Mr. Price in his turn thought he had been tricked. Immediately a net was spread for the informer and with some difficulty he was found. At first he was both furious and frightened and it was with some difficulty that he could be persuaded to tell his tale. All he would say was the pearls had been thrown away. Naturally no one could believe such a story. A search party was sent to Hatton Garden, and the gutter was raked from end to end. At first nothing could be found, but at last, on the very edge of a drain running down into the sewer, was found one solitary pearl. What had happened became only too clear; the remainder must have fallen down the drain and been swept away in the sewer itself.

All Mr. Price's work had been useless; his ingenious plan had failed. A large fortune had been lost, merely because an ordinary patrolling police officer had happened to step into Hatton Garden at five minutes to three on that very afternoon.

But fortune intervened once more, only this time fortune was more favourable. Within a very few hours Mr. Price received a suggestion from an unexpected source that it might be a good thing if he were to pay a visit to a certain public house in the vicinity of Hatton Garden and take a look at a bead necklace which was adorning the neck of the barmaid in the public bar. Not very hopefully Mr. Price drove to the public house and saw the barmaid. Round her neck were the missing pearls.

The story was quite simple. A roadman who was a usual customer of the house had been sweeping the gutter in Hatton Garden when he came across a parcel of beads. They were no use to him and apparently of no value, but he had put them into his pocket and when he came into the public house for his evening refreshment he had given them casually to the barmaid as a present. She thought they looked rather pretty and she had strung them on a piece of cotton and had hung them round her neck thinking the whole affair to be a joke. But in truth the joke had been worth the best part of £100,000 and for a short time the barmaid had worn a king's ransom round her neck.

CHAPTER V

Murder

THERE is no doubt whatever that to a sensation-loving public a trial for murder is the most enthralling of all trials that come before the Courts; there is equally no doubt that such trials are usually the most sordid and frequently the most tedious; they are tedious because of the enormous amount of detail which requires the most minute and exact proof; they are sordid, either because of the revolting nature of the crime itself or of the parties immediately concerned. A murder case of any real human interest is extremely rare; murders of a policeman by an escaping criminal, of a night watchman by a burglar, of a prostitute by a drunken sailor, they are all equally absorbing to the crowd of sightseers in Court whose presence would seem to be explicable only upon the assumption that they are moved by the sporting spirit of enquiry as to the prisoner's chances of acquittal, or else by a sadistic desire to see a man sentenced to death. If the execution were permitted to take place in public, the same crowd would not, no doubt, be in their places to see the sentence carried out.

To a lawyer, a trial for murder must stand in a class by itself; to defend a man for his life, knowing full well that one indiscreet question, one momentary lack of concentration, may perhaps cause his death, places upon any counsel a responsibility which he must undertake with dread; to prosecute a murderer and to be compelled to ask him questions from which there is no possible escape is an experience which no one who has ever known it would desire to repeat. I have done both and my dislike for the duty placed upon me has never lessened; consequently, my appearance at murder trials has been rare, although the memory that each case has left behind is very vivid. In theory, the social position of a person charged with murder should make no difference to the feelings with which an advocate approaches a defence; in practice it is very different. The memory of Mrs. Barney standing alone in the Central Criminal Court, in the dock so lately occupied by pick-pockets and burglars, facing a crowd of well-dressed men and women, many of them her friends and relations, is a most unhappy one. The mere evidence of luxury and perhaps refinement which permeated the atmosphere of the Court appeared to accentuate a hundredfold the horror of her position. The memory of the distinguished Polish officer who stood in the same place is perhaps even more vivid. He was alone, in a foreign country, facing a trial under a legal system of which he was necessarily ignorant, with the tragedy of his life behind him, and without a friend to offer him either sympathy or support. I never saw him before that day or since; I only remember him as a very gallant gentleman.

The case of Jean Pierre Vaquier was very different; by virtue of the office which I then held it was my duty to cross-examine him to his death. Although it is no part of the duty of an advocate to form any opinion of his own as to the innocence or guilt of the prisoner in the dock, it was an immeasurable relief to me to feel, as I did, that there was only one verdict possible in his case although no one ever knew the reason which prompted him to commit the crime of which he was convicted.

Perhaps the trial of the Hooded Man, containing as it did a revolting story of betrayals, has left behind the most vivid memory of all. I was very young, and it is the only occasion upon which I have defended a murderer who was found guilty. Moreover, to this day I am satisfied that he should never have been hanged. It was many years ago, yet the anxiety which haunted me throughout that sordid trial remains with me to-day. Each of these trials had peculiarities of their own, sufficient to make them memorable. Taking murder as a whole, there is one remarkable feature common to nearly all cases in which a murderer is found guilty and that is the apparent desire of the accused man to talk to a policeman and thereby hang himself. When he appears in a Court ready to support a most excellent defence carefully prepared by his legal advisers, it is practically certain that, sooner or later, there will step into the witness box a police officer who will produce a "voluntary statement" signed by the prisoner which is completely different in most essential particulars from the story which the accused desires to tell. Faced with this statement, or even statements, for there are often several of them, the prisoner flounders about in an effort to reconcile the statement with his present evidence, with a result that almost invariably ends in disaster. How come these "voluntary statements" to be so universal? It is a rule of legal procedure that no prisoner may be questioned by the police unless he is cautioned against the risk of so doing and no statement may be used in evidence against him unless it is made voluntarily; in consequence, every such statement begins with a caption to the effect that the prisoner has been warned that he is not obliged to say anything, but that if he does, his statement may be used against him at his trial. In spite of this warning the prisoner proceeds to pour out a long rigmarole, in the optimistic belief that it is going to be of some use to him, which is later the despair of his legal advisers upon his subsequent trial. I have seen dozens of these statements and the effect of them on my mind is always the same: how in the world was the prisoner so foolish as to talk! It is quite easy to picture the scene: the prisoner is probably seated in a police station, surrounded by policemen, one of whom is taking shorthand notes; he is perhaps being comforted by a cup of tea and a cigarette, notwithstanding which he is certainly terrified out of his life and ready to clutch at any straw; he may even hope that if he talks to the kind policemen they may let him go; instead of which desirable result, immediately he has affixed his signature to the statement he has made, he is clapped into a cell where he remains until his ultimate appearance in the Central

Criminal Court. Sometimes the interrogation takes place in the middle of the night and lasts for hours; and yet, it is purely voluntary.

Of course, there are two possible views upon these statements. On the one hand, it is no doubt eminently desirable that a murderer should be convicted of his crime and the police are only doing their duty in bringing about that result; on the other hand, the one thing abhorrent to our sense of justice is any form of third degree; when it is remembered that any person in possession of his normal faculties must realise that to say nothing is in all probability his only hope of safety, these "voluntary statements" by a man in state of terror which may well render him incapable of exercising any reasoned judgment on his own course of conduct are, to say the least of it, disquieting. There are some thoughtful persons who allege that our natural characteristic is that of compromise, others consider that we are a nation of hypocrites, but whoever is right, neither compromise nor hypocrisy should find a place in a trial for murder. I have never liked these "voluntary statements", and I never shall. The trial of Rouse for the murder in the blazing car may well afford food for thought, and for that reason alone has been included.

THE CASE OF THE BLAZING CAR

If Alfred Arthur Rouse had only kept his mouth shut, he would never have been hanged. His loquacity was too much for him. His purely lying conversations with friends and strangers alike immediately after the murder were sufficiently damaging to make his position perilous, but his "voluntary statements" to the police rendered his ultimate fate inevitable. I took no part in the trial, which came to be known as "The Case of the Blazing Car", but was only brought in for the purpose of the Court of Criminal Appeal, by which time the evidence had all been given and I was therefore in a position to assess exactly all the evidence of which the police were in possession apart from any facts supplied by Rouse himself in his "voluntary statements"; and those statements supplemented and indeed supplied all the missing links which the police required to establish the identity of the murderer. To anyone interested in the so-called "psychology of murderers" an examination of those facts may be of interest.

The case itself was certainly remarkable and probably unique.

Rouse was a commercial traveller of moderate means who lived with his wife in London, and if his appearance in the witness box afforded any true guide to his character, he must have been a most unattractive person. Unfortunately, his unattractiveness was not apparent to women and he had a large number of illicit attachments, the details of which are unimportant beyond the fact that one of them was a young woman who lived in Gellygaer in Wales, whose father had been told that Rouse was in fact her husband. The only thing known about Rouse of any importance was that he had received a severe wound in the head in the First World War the nature of which was never investigated in Court but which, as I always thought, may have had something to do with the subsequent tragedy. For the purpose of his business Rouse used a car, a "Morris Minor", which was registered in his name, and he was a sufficiently experienced driver to have made himself thoroughly familiar with the mechanism of motor vehicles.

At about two a.m. in the morning of the 6th November, 1930, a motor-car burst into flames some 200 yards from the village of Hardingstone, near Northampton. It was first noticed by two young men returning home from a dance, who saw a bright light farther down the road. At the same time a man came out of a ditch by the side of the road and walked past them without speaking. Just after he had passed them, he looked back and said: "It looks as if somebody has had a bonfire." He then walked on down the road, seemed to hesitate as to which way to go, then turned towards London and disappeared. That man was Rouse. He was subsequently identified by the two young men and his identity must be taken as sufficiently established without the necessity for any admission of his own. The two men ran towards the flame and then saw that it was a motor-car blazing furiously by the side of the road. They ran on to the village and came back with the village constable.

They were unable to approach the blazing car until the flames died down. They then discovered something inside which turned out to be the body of a dead man. They could make no further investigation until the fire was extinguished, by which time the car was completely demolished. It is not perhaps surprising that the trial of Rouse for the murder of the man found inside the car was described as a mystery, because from that day to this no one has ever known who the dead man was, or how or for what purpose he was killed.

The action of the police on discovering the body was not particularly helpful to themselves. No photographs were taken of the body or the car before it was moved, and the car itself was left unwatched by the police for a considerable period. It was therefore impossible to say conclusively what portions of the car, if any, or its contents might not have been moved from their original position by some curious onlooker. The actual position of the body, which subsequently became of great importance, had to be proved by verbal evidence of the police from their recollection of what they saw without the assistance of any photographic record. The body seemed to be lying across the near side seat and extending on to the driver's seat. One leg was drawn up under the body and the other was projecting through the space normally occupied by the near-side door. The projecting leg had been burnt off somewhere between the ankle and the knee, other portions of the body had been destroyed by fire and the face was quite unrecognisable. The car itself was subsequently examined by experts and their examination established to their satisfaction certain facts. According to their evidence, the violence of the fire was caused by a joint having been loosened between the petrol tank and the carburettor which would allow petrol to escape and fall underneath the car. The experts took the view that that joint had been loosened before the fire and, as they thought, deliberately. It is right at this point to state that experts for the defence gave a considerable amount of evidence that excessive heat in a burning car invariably results in the loosening of that joint and they took the view both that there was no evidence of the fact of the joint being loosened, or that the loosening had been done before the fire, or that it was deliberate. Further, the top of the carburettor was found to be off, and although at first the Crown witness thought that it had fallen off through the melting of the body of the carburettor, he seemed to be a little doubtful of that fact as the case proceeded. Upon the whole, I think, it would be a fair summary of the experts' evidence as to the origin of the fire to say that while there was undoubtedly evidence for the Crown that the origin of the fire was probably deliberate, it was by no means conclusive. There was also evidence that some portion of the deceased's clothing smelled of petrol and from that fact the Crown thought to draw the inference that the deceased had been soaked with petrol before the fire. There again, I think it would be a fair comment to observe that when a car bursts into flames, there is at least a possibility that small portions of petrol may fly anywhere. There was one further piece of evidence available to the police: a wooden mallet was found some yards in front of the car to the head of which three hairs were found to be attached. There was no blood upon the mallet nor indeed any other factor to show that it had been used as a weapon. Upon microscopic examination one of the hairs, which was broken off, was found to be human. The other two hairs probably were not. Upon the whole the evidence derived from the mallet was so inconclusive that the judge advised the jury to disregard it. The number plate on the car was intact and that showed it to be registered in the name of Alfred Arthur Rouse.

From their own investigation the police were able to trace the movements of Rouse after he left the scene of the fire with some exactitude. Almost immediately he stopped a lorry that was travelling to London and asked for a lift. He told the driver he was waiting for a friend with a Bentley car and he had missed him. The driver took him to Tally Ho Corner on the Barnet Road, which he reached about six o'clock. There Rouse left the lorry. At 8.30 that morning Rouse spoke to a man employed by the Transport Company and asked if he could get to Newport in Wales. He then quite gratuitously said: "I am in a bit of a mess. I lost my car or had it pinched." At about the same time he spoke to the manager of the Transport Company and said he wanted to go to Wales. He said that he had a car of his own and that he had had it stolen during the night somewhere on the Great North Road, outside a coffee stall. All these remarks appear to have been quite gratuitous. He then got on to a coach for Wales about 9.15 in the morning and made a precisely similar statement to the driver. At about eight o'clock in the evening of the same day he arrived at the house of his young lady at the village of Gellygaer, where he told her father that he had had his car stolen in Northampton. He stayed the night at her father's house and in the morning he was shown a copy of the *Daily Sketch*, dated 7th November, which contained a photograph of a burnt car with a headline: "Body found in a blazing car"—"The car is registered as belonging to Mr. A. A. Rouse." By this time there can be no doubt Rouse was thoroughly frightened.

At ten o'clock on the morning of the 7th November Rouse begged a lift to Cardiff, which he got. By this time people were asking him about his burnt car and he adhered to his statement that it had been stolen. Later in the morning he took a motor coach and arrived at the Hammersmith Bridge Road in London at about 9.20, and on descending he was approached by the police.

Substantially speaking, that is the whole of the evidence that the police had against Rouse. It is true that a police constable at a later stage gave evidence that he had seen a man, whom he identified as Rouse, driving with a passenger a few hours before the murder, but inasmuch as Rouse had himself informed the police of that fact, it is very doubtful whether the evidence of the police constable would have been of much value or, indeed, possibly available if it had not been for Rouse's own statement. At any rate, the officer did not take the number of the car, and as the night was pitch dark it must have made any identification extremely unreliable. To any fair-minded person it might well seem that there was considerable suspicion against Rouse, but very little more. There was no apparent motive for the crime, if crime it was. It did not seem as though Rouse had wished to disappear, because within a few hours he had turned up in Wales among people who knew him well. It is true that Rouse had an insurance policy of £1,000 which would be payable in respect of the death of a passenger in the car or of the owner if driving at the time, but it could hardly be imagined Rouse could make such a claim; there was also a sum of £150 payable in respect of the car itself if destroyed, but nobody could reasonably suggest that such insurance could afford a motive for murder upon the evidence available.

The police had practically no evidence at all against Rouse. They could prove that he owned the car and that it had been burnt; they had some expert evidence that the fire had probably been started by human agency, although that evidence could be formally disputed; they could not identify the dead man, nor could they establish that Rouse ever knew him; they could not even prove that Rouse had been the driver of the car except for the statement of the solitary police constable, if it could have been available to them; they knew that Rouse had been seen near the burning car and they could trace his movements afterwards, but the only statements by Rouse of which they had any knowledge were to the effect that his car had been stolen. Suspicion there may have been, perhaps even grave suspicion, but that was all. A conviction for murder upon that evidence would have been impossible. That was the position when Rouse stepped down from the motor coach on the Hammersmith Bridge Road on the night of the 7th November.

From now on, the evidence depended upon a series of statements made by Rouse himself to the police. About these statements it may be enough to say that if Rouse's only object in making them was to hang himself, he could not possibly have said anything more likely to achieve his object. In the first place, he told the police everything which they wanted to know and which they had not yet been able to establish; in the second place, he gave himself a character which would necessarily cause abhorrence to everyone who read it; and thirdly, it proved conclusively that every statement he had made to people he had seen within the previous two days had been a complete and deliberate lie.

When the police first spoke to him in the Hammersmith Bridge Road, they told him they wanted him to accompany them to the police station. This was his reply: "Very well, I'm glad it's over." "I was going to Scotland Yard about it." "I'm responsible." "I'm very glad it's over." "I've had no sleep." He was taken to the police station, when he made the following "voluntary statement": "I suppose they wish to see me about it. I do not know what happened exactly. I picked the man up at Great North Road; he asked me for a lift. He seemed a respectable man and said he was going to the Midlands.

ALFRED ROUSE

(Photo: *Topical Press*)

I gave him a lift; it was just this side of St. Albans. He got in and I drove off, and after going some distance I lost my way. A policeman spoke to me about my lights. I did not know anything about the man, and I thought I saw his hand on my case which was in the back of the car. I later became sleepy and could hardly keep awake. The engine started to spit and I thought I was running out of petrol. I wanted to relieve myself and I said to the man: 'There is some petrol in the can; you can empty it into the tank while I'm gone,' and lifted up the bonnet and showed him where to put it in. He said: 'What about a smoke?' I said: 'I've given you all my cigarettes as it is.' I then went some distance along the road and had just got my trousers down when I noticed a big flame from behind. I pulled my trousers up quickly and ran towards the car, which was in flames. I saw the man was inside and I tried to open the door, but I could not as the car was then a mass of flames. I then began to tremble violently. I was all of a shake. I did not know what to do and I ran as hard as I could along the road where I saw the two men. I felt I was responsible for what had happened. I lost my head and I did not know what to do and really don't know what I have done since." The narrative of the police officer who took the statement added: "I noticed he had his case and I said: 'I see you have your case now. Did you rescue it from the car?' and he said: 'No. Owing to the fact that I had seen the man's hand on my case when it was in the back of the car, I took it with me when I got out of the car and went along the road. I did not want him to take it.' "

At one o'clock in the morning on the 8th November the Northampton police arrived and interviewed Rouse again. He made another "voluntary statement", which it took some four hours to complete. It is not necessary to set out this statement again as it was really a very amplified form of the one he had previously given to the police. During the course of it he was obviously asked a very large number of questions, as for instance about the mallet and the presence of human hair upon it. He amplified his account of how the fire may have started by saying that he had given to the unknown man a cigar just before he left the car. In fact, if the police had been anxious to provide material to enable a prosecuting counsel at a subsequent date to cross-examine Rouse, they could scarcely have afforded to him better material. After the completion of this "voluntary statement" Rouse was taken to the police station at Northampton, where he arrived at 9.30 a.m. on the 8th November. A little later Rouse asked if he could see his wife and on being told that he could do so a little later, he made the following truly astounding statement; when it is remembered that Rouse was a man in imminent danger of standing his trial for murder, it seems almost unconceivable that a man with anything approaching normality could have said what he did:

"She is really too good for me. I like a woman who will make a fuss of me. I don't ever remember my wife sitting on my knees, but otherwise she is a good wife. I am very friendly with several women, but it is a very expensive game. I was on my way to

Leicester on Wednesday when this happened, to hand in my slip on Thursday morning to draw some money from my firm. I was then going to Wales for the week-end. My harem takes me to several places and I am not at home a great deal. But my wife does not ask questions now. I was arranging to sell my house and furniture. I was then going to make an allowance to the wife. I think I should clear between £100 and £150 from the sale."

If ever Rouse had hoped to arouse sympathy on his behalf in anyone, his final statement must inevitably have put an end to his hopes, and the result in my view was appalling. It was given full publicity in the Police Court at the preliminary hearing and was blazoned abroad to such an extent that Rouse's disgusting mode of life became known to everyone throughout the country. At the trial at the Assizes it was not given in evidence but all the harm that could possibly be done had been effected. Not one of the jury could have been unaware that Rouse was an utter blackguard and the one thing against which English justice so rightly sets its face, namely evidence of a prisoner's bad character, had been brought to light. However much the jury may have struggled, which I had no doubt they did, to be impartial, it must have been impossible for any one of them not to have regarded Rouse in the witness box as a man beneath contempt. The proceedings before the magistrate ended on the 16th December. On the 26th January Rouse was tried at the Assizes before Mr. Justice Talbot and the jury. He was defended by Mr. Douglas Finnemore with great skill and pertinacity. But what could he do?

The evidence for the prosecution, at one time so inconclusive, had been strengthened a hundredfold by Rouse's statements to the police. Rouse was practically compelled to go into the witness box to tell his own story and ask the jury to believe him, knowing full well that he must stand before them as a self-confessed liar, everyone in Court knowing that his character was beneath contempt. He was bound to support, if he could, his detailed statements to the police and to confess that all his previous stories had been lies; the merest glance at the quite obvious cross-examination with which he was inevitably faced is enough to show what a hopeless task lay before him. How could he explain his lies? He couldn't.

"Did you drive in a lorry from the scene of the fire to Tally Ho Corner?"

"Yes."

"Did you tell the driver that you had lost your car or had it pinched?"

"Yes."

"Was it a lie?"

"Yes."

"When you wanted to drive to Wales, did you tell the manager of the Transport Company that your car had been stolen from a coffee stall on the Great North Road?"

"Yes."

"Was it a lie?"

"Yes."

"Did you tell your friends in Wales that your car was stolen in Northampton?"

"Yes."

"Another lie?"

"Yes, it was unfortunate."

"What do you mean when you say that the lies you told were unfortunate?"

"I have always been noted for telling the truth. At the time I thought it was the best thing to do."

"Why was telling lies better than telling the truth?"

No answer was possible. And then, to sum it up:

"Do you think an innocent man might have told the truth?"

"Yes, no doubt, to your way of thinking."

He had never told the truth. Why should he be telling it in the witness box? Inevitably the jury must have had in the back of their minds the story of the women and the harem although it had not been proved before them. Equally the jury must have asked themselves why he had told all those lies if he were innocent. Rouse had admitted to the police that he had driven the dead man in the car. The jury knew that the car was burned and the man was dead. And now all these lies. Why?

Even with all the admissions the case was none too strong. Mr. Justice Talbot made that clear to the jury in a summing up which was beyond criticism or reproach. After recapitulating the evidence he said, "Of course, there can be no doubt about it that these facts create grave suspicion against this man who was the owner of the car and who had driven it to that place and was within 600 yards of it when it was in full blaze. There is no doubt of that at all. If he is an innocent man, he has created suspicion, or a great deal of it, by his own folly. He no doubt realised that himself, because you recollect what he said to the policeman when he first asked him to go to the police station:

"'Very well, I am glad it is all over. I was going to Scotland Yard about it. I am responsible.' Of course, that does not mean 'I committed the murder', that would be unfair.

"'I am very glad it is over. I have had no sleep.' No, the question is, is it more than suspicion?" What was the position after all the 'voluntary statements' had been given? What would have been the position without them?

At the conclusion of the summing up the jury returned a verdict of GUILTY and Rouse was sentenced to death. In due course he appealed to the Court of Criminal Appeal against his conviction, mainly upon the ground that there was no evidence which the jury could have found against him. But it was too late. All his "voluntary statements" had combined to hang him. A strenuous argument was raised in the Appeal Court, based upon the introduction at the Police Court hearing of the statement about his "harem", upon the ground that the prejudice against him thereby publicly aroused had made an impartial trial impossible, but the Court rejected the argument although the Lord Chief Justice characterised the introduction as unfortunate.

After Rouse's execution there was published in the Press yet another statement which appeared to be a confession of his guilt. Apparently he talked to the end.

THE TRIAL OF MRS. BARNEY

At midnight on a night in 1932 a well-known London physician was called from his bed by the telephone. A woman's voice was crying hysterically: "It is Mrs. Barney. Oh, doctor, come at once. There has been a terrible accident. For God's sake, come at once." This was the first warning of a tragedy which was to result in an unusually sensational trial.

Mrs. Elvira Dolores Barney was a spoilt child of fortune. The daughter of wealthy and titled parents, in early youth she had drifted into an atmosphere of idle luxury. She married young, but the marriage was not a success, and the husband and wife soon separated; although there was no divorce, the separation was obviously final and complete. Thereafter her life and habits rapidly deteriorated; she had no interests except those to be found in night clubs and similar haunts; she drank a great deal too much, and soon drifted into flagrant immorality. At the time when her existence became the subject of public notoriety she was occupying a maisonette converted from a garage in the Knightsbridge district where she lived with a young man named Stephens. He was as worthless as she herself had become; he had no money and no occupation although it was said that he had at one time been engaged as a dress designer, and he was apparently quite content to exist upon such funds as Mrs. Barney was prepared to provide for him. He was a good-looking young man and she was said to be very fond of him although the menage was punctuated by repeated altercations, and the noise caused by their domestic discord together with that of the hilarious parties in which they were accustomed to indulge was a constant source of annoyance to the respectable inhabitants of the mews in which they lived.

It was to this establishment that the doctor was summoned on the telephone. Upon his arrival he found an appalling sight. Stephens was lying upon the stairs and he was dead; Mrs. Barney was in a condition of extreme hysteria alternately trying to revive the dead man and crying that it was an accident; by their side was a revolver which had been recently fired. In spite of her frenzied protests, the doctor rightly insisted upon sending for the police and they arrived soon afterwards. No doubt Mrs. Barney was scarcely in a condition of mind to give a very coherent account of what had happened, indeed it was stated by the police that in a hysterical outburst she struck a police officer who was endeavouring to question her, although she immediately apologised for so doing, but fortunately for her the story which she then told was one to which she adhered from beginning to end throughout her subsequent ordeal. She said that there had been a quarrel, and that the young man was proposing to leave her, that she had threatened to commit suicide by shooting herself with a revolver that she kept by the side of the bed; that she had taken the revolver from the drawer and that he had struggled to prevent her carrying out her threat, and that in the struggle the revolver had gone off, accidentally shooting him through the body. She was taken immediately to the police station for further questioning, but there she adhered to her previous story, and as no further information was available, she was released and allowed to go home under the care of her mother.

At that moment Mrs. Barney may perhaps have thought that her troubles were over, but unfortunately for her the investigations by the police brought to light some new and startling facts. People in the adjacent flat had heard the noise of the quarrel, and it was said that more than one shot was fired; moreover, one witness stated that she had heard Mrs. Barney shrieking, "I will shoot you." And there was worse to follow. Inhabitants of a flat somewhat farther down the mews had been the witnesses of an earlier quarrel and their evidence was distinctly ominous. It was alleged that after a violent altercation Stephens was seen to leave the building and walk away; as he did so, the upper window was opened by Mrs. Barney, who was heard to scream, "Laugh, baby. Laugh for the last time." She then produced a revolver and fired at him from the window. If both or indeed either of these facts were established, the theory of suicide and accident became somewhat difficult, and thus it was not surprising that Mrs. Barney was arrested and charged with murder. Immediately the affair developed into a society scandal of the first magnitude; Mrs. Barney's family were well-known in Mayfair and both Mrs. Barney and the dead man were notorious members of the so-called young "smart set". A murder in high life had not been before the Courts for years.

She was brought before the magistrate and I was instructed to defend her; my junior being Mr. Walter Frampton, who was without doubt one of the most able criminal lawyers of his day. His assistance to me throughout the case, and indeed throughout every one of the many cases in which we have been associated, is one of my happiest recollections at the Bar. It is a very salutory rule of criminal practice that in a capital charge the less that counsel for the defence have to say in the Police Court the better it is for their client. It is a very dangerous thing to ask questions until you know all the facts that are going to be brought out against you, and silence, except in rare cases, is not likely to do much harm. The only incident of any interest to me in the early proceedings of Mrs. Barney's case was the difficulty I experienced in getting into Court. The crowd round the building was something I have never experienced before or since and a cordon of mounted and unmounted police was required to keep unauthorised people from approaching. I had the greatest difficulty in forcing my way through the various cordons, and finally endeavoured to obtain admission to the Court by giving my name to a watchful detective. His only reply was: "I have never heard of you," a somewhat disappointing rejoinder which was, however, remedied by a more widely read member of the force. My first view of Mrs. Barney was slightly depressing. She had been described in the Press as "a beautiful member of the so-called smart set", but no doubt partly by reason of the ordeal which she had undergone, and partly in consequence of the life she had been leading, her appearance was not calculated to move the hearts of a jury; indeed she was a melancholy and somewhat depressing figure as she stood in the dock with a wardress upon each side of her.

The proceedings in the Police Court were not unduly prolonged as there was no cross-examination, and the various witnesses told their story as given to the police. There was some additional and rather damaging evidence from Sir Bernard Spilsbury, the eminent pathologist, and Mr. Churchill, an expert in fire-arms, both of whom cast doubts on the likelihood of the prisoner's version of the occurrence. In due course the magisterial enquiry came to an end and Mrs. Barney was committed to take her trial at the Central Criminal Court.

In many ways the defence in a murder trial differs from that in any other case. In the first place, the life of the prisoner may well hang upon almost every question asked; injudicious cross-examination is dangerous at all times, and an unexpected answer frequently brings disaster to an advocate's client; in a civil action the risk may be justifiable, but a capital charge is very different from a civil action, and discretion in a murder trial is of paramount importance. In the next place, witnesses in such a trial always intend to speak the truth. It is indeed rare for a person to enter the witness box determined falsely to swear away the life of an accused person, and it is therefore practically impossible to cross-examine any witness for the Crown with a suggestion that they are lying. Stupid, yes, or perhaps mistaken; even unconsciously exaggerating; but beyond that it is more than dangerous to go. Moreover, it is almost impossible to place complete reliance upon the accuracy of any explanation which the defendant may be prepared to give. Human nature being what it is, it is almost inevitable that a person, feeling him or herself in such an awful position as that of an accused murderer, should clutch at any straw to save themselves, and as a consequence defences are invented which bear no relation to the truth, and which so far from achieving their design very often end in complete disaster. It is for that reason that I have always made an inflexible rule never to see an accused person in his prison, lest I should find myself hampered in the conduct of the defence either by something the defendant may have said or by something he may have thought his counsel may have wished that he would say. I am afraid Mrs. Barney was disappointed at my refusal to see her at any time before her trial.

Of all the witnesses to be called against me, the one I feared most was Sir Bernard Spilsbury, the eminent pathologist. By this time Sir Bernard had become recognised as an almost inevitable witness in a prosecution for murder and I had cross-examined him on many previous occasions. He was an absolutely fair witness and a most knowledgeable and skilful medical man, but unfortunately there had grown up a practice among some prosecuting counsel to treat him almost as an expert on murder. He was invariably permitted to sit in Court throughout the trial and a question of this sort was not infrequently put to him by the prosecution: "Sir Bernard, you have been in Court and you have heard the suggested defence put forward on behalf of the prisoner. In your opinion, is that defence consistent with the results of your examination?" To which Sir Bernard could only reply: "No." In my opinion this was a most unfortunate question. If Sir Bernard was not cross-examined his opinion remained unchallenged; if he was, he would be entitled, and indeed bound, to give the reasons for that opinion, and those reasons given with all the weight of his skill and experience must be most deadly for the defence. I spent much anxious thought in deciding upon the best method of avoiding this particular danger in the case of Mrs. Barney.

The defence had been most ably and carefully prepared by her solicitor, Mr. Coleman. The great point in her favour was apparent. The story she had told to the doctor and to the police had never varied; it was the story she would tell in Court. The main points against her were equally defined. The witness who heard her say: "I will shoot you"; the number of shots fired; the previous attempt to kill—somehow or other they all had to be explained away, and moreover explained without making them appear worse than they were already. The whole scheme of the defence was to bring all the evidence into line with the possibility of an attempted suicide, and above all to meet in advance the evidence of Sir Bernard Spilsbury.

The trial took place before Mr. Justice Humphreys, almost if not quite the best criminal judge I have ever known, and the scene when he entered his

Court must have been as repellent to him as it was to me. Fashionably-dressed men and women were crowded into every corner; eminent authors were employed by the newspapers to write emotional accounts of every happening; the only human element throughout the crowded Court was to be found in the tragic figures of the prisoner's parents, who sat in Court in anxious misery throughout the trial. When she entered the box Mrs. Barney herself created a much better impression than I had feared; she was very quiet alike in her appearance and demeanour and her face showed but little evidence of the life she had led.

Immediately the jury were sworn I rose to make an application; I asked that Sir Bernard Spilsbury should not be allowed to remain in Court during the opening of the case and the calling of the evidence. As far as I am aware, such an application had never been made before—purely medical witnesses are almost invariably permitted to remain in Court, but the judge ruled that I was within my rights in making the application and Sir Bernard left the Court. From that moment it was obvious that everyone in Court anticipated that upon return to give his evidence Sir Bernard would be subjected to a prolonged and rigorous cross-examination.

Sir Percival Clarke conducted the prosecution with his usual courtesy and restraint, but he very properly emphasised the damning features of the case for the Crown; if his witnesses' evidence were true the theory of attempted suicide would seem difficult to establish. The first clash came with the woman who had heard the prisoner scream: "I will shoot you." It was useless to suggest that nothing of the sort had ever happened as the witness was obviously truthful, but a very different complexion might be given to her evidence if the actual words were: "I will shoot." The difference seemed very slight but it was vital, as the latter might be consistent with the prisoner's threat to shoot herself. When the witness left the box it was fairly clear that she was none too certain as to the actual words the prisoner used. The first difficulty had disappeared. The question of the number of shots fired was not so easy, particularly as the police had discovered the mark of a second bullet in the bedroom. But fortunately for the defence the witnesses who alleged that they had heard at least two shots were not wholly satisfactory; they became confused and it did not seem likely that their evidence could be unreservedly accepted as accurate. The real tussle between Sir Percival and myself took place over the incident of the earlier shooting from the prisoner's window. Mrs. Barney's explanation of that incident was that she had once before threatened to commit suicide and that she had fired the revolver not at him but inside her room in order to frighten her lover, and that evidence if accepted would go far to explain the bullet mark found on her bedroom wall. Moreover, we had reason to believe that the young man had referred to the possibility of her committing suicide at the time when the earlier shooting took place, and I applied for leave to put that suggestion to the witness who deposed to the alleged shooting. Sir Percival stoutly objected to the evidence as inadmissable, and he was probably right, but Mr. Justice Humphreys, straining the laws of evidence in favour of the defence, allowed the question, and the witness admitted that the young man had stated to her at the time that he was always afraid that Mrs. Barney might commit suicide. Although the witness adhered to her story that Mrs. Barney had fired at the dead man, undoubtedly we had gone some way to support our theory, particularly as the police had examined every inch of the roadway outside the flat and had been unable to discover any trace of a bullet mark. And then we had a stroke of luck. A vital piece of evidence might be found in the finger-prints, if any, upon the revolver from which the actual shot was fired. If hers alone had been found, her position might have been desperate; if the dead man's were there as well, she might be saved; if at least there were so many prints as to be indecipherable, that again might tend to support the theory of a struggle. On this occasion the police had not acted with their usual acumen. The revolver had been examined for prints but no care had been taken to see that it had not been touched between the time of the alleged crime and the examination, indeed even the police themselves had handled it, and as a result the examination showed many blurred and unidentifiable prints, the only one clearly defined being that of one of the detectives in the case. Upon the whole the defence had no reason to be dissatisfied with the results that had so far been achieved. And then came Sir Bernard Spilsbury. His evidence was purely medical and

MRS. DOLORES ELVIRA BARNEY IN HER EARLIER DAYS
(*Photo: Planet News Ltd.*)

MR. SCOTT STEPHENS WHO WAS FOUND SHOT DEAD IN MRS. BARNEY'S HOUSE, FOR WHICH SHE WAS TRIED AND ACQUITTED

(Photo Topical Press)

MRS. BARNEY AFTER HER ACQUITTAL

(*Photo: Associated Press*)

given with absolute accuracy and firmness, and that evidence was in no way inconsistent with the defence, but, inasmuch as he had so far been out of Court, he had not heard of any theory of suicide, or any other suggested defence, and therefore no question could possibly be asked of him as to his opinion on such a theory; that, no doubt, would come when he was rigorously and severely cross-examined. Possibly to the disappointment of some people, he was not cross-examined at all; no single question was asked of him, and when he left the witness box the last opportunity for the prosecution to offer any expert opinion as to the plausibility of the defence was gone. I never remember to have felt greater pleasure at seeing a witness leave the box. One of our greatest dangers had disappeared. At the conclusion of the case for the prosecution many of our difficulties had been smoothed away or at least ameliorated, and everything must now depend upon the evidence of Mrs. Barney herself. In almost every criminal case the danger point is reached when the defendant goes into the witness box. Many a prosecution which is not too strong becomes immensely strengthened by the cross-examination of the prisoner. Weaknesses in the defence are torn to shreds, improbabilities become glaring in their nakedness, and above all any lying statements that the defendant may have made become accentuated a thousand-fold. The Law which permits a prisoner to give evidence on his behalf is supposed to confer upon him an inestimable benefit, and indeed it is only just and proper that an innocent person should have the right to proclaim his

K

innocence on oath, but to a guilty person, or indeed to one who has something vital to conceal, the privilege is of more than doubtful benefit, and indeed one which many accused persons would infinitely prefer to be without. I confess to having been very anxious when Mrs. Barney entered the witness box upon her trial.

It was the moment for which the morbid onlookers had been waiting; every neck craned forward and every eye was fixed upon her as she left the dock with a wardress at her side to tell the story upon which her life depended. Nobody could help her, her future lay in her own hands and she looked a lonely and a pitiful figure as she took the oath. She looked up and saw her mother and for a moment I thought she was going to break down, but she quickly pulled herself together and began her evidence. It was not a pleasant story, indeed there was little if anything to arouse much sympathy in her somewhat sordid tale; an unhappy marriage was the only possible excuse for the life which she had led, and the most was made of that. Sympathy is a powerful weapon for a defending counsel in any murder trial, but unfortunately or otherwise it is very seldom available. Mrs. Barney's evidence was of necessity limited as far as possible to the actual happenings, and to my intense relief she told her story extremely well. She was much more restrained than I had feared, and though obviously suffering from intense strain her emotions were under control. She said she had been unhappy and on more than one occasion had threatened suicide. Her account of the earlier shooting was a simple denial; she said she merely attempted to frighten her lover and fired the revolver in her own room to make a pretence of taking her own life; the bullet mark found in the room was caused on that occasion. The actual death was an accident. Stephens threatened to leave her and she picked up the revolver, there was a struggle, a shot, and the young man fell to the floor; how it was fired she did not know. There it was. Which story would be believed? Sir Percival Clarke cross-examined her with his usual force and thoroughness but she adhered to her story. It was untrue to suggest that she had tried to shoot her lover in the mews, she had never fired her revolver from the window; she had never said, "I will shoot you," but she might have said, "I will shoot myself." Upon the whole she was not much shaken in her cross-examination, and she returned to the dock a depressed and miserable figure to await the final stages of her trial.

No one will ever know what is the real value of a speech for the defence in a murder case. There was a time when no defending counsel was worth his salt unless he could be relied upon for an exhibition of rhetorical emotion. Those days are past. A City of London jury has seen too many comic advocates upon the films to be greatly impressed by waving arms and streaming eyes. At one time it was thought effective to refer at repeated intervals to the blind Goddess of Justice sitting above the Central Criminal Court, and no advocate of any value was not fully equipped with a heart-breaking and totally irrelevant peroration. I well remember one most distinguished advocate who possessed a soul-stirring passage which he used on all occasions with huge effect; and who was not unnaturally annoyed when an unsympathetic and ungenerous prosecuting opponent replied to him by saying: "I notice, gentlemen, that you were deeply moved by that beautiful peroration to which you have just listened. I am not surrpised. I am also moved, every time I hear it." It was an unkind remark and ought not to have been made, but it perhaps showed the changing of the years. The days of flatulent oratory are gone. A jury has sworn to do its best to give a truthful verdict, and is entitled to be treated with respect for its intelligence. Unless a case is absolutely hopeless, flights of imagination or poetic emotion are best left to the theatre. The only form of final speech which would possibly be of any help to Mrs. Barney was one of pure logic, with a careful examination of the facts which might be thought to tell against her and a reminder of those elements in her story upon which she could properly rely; above all, a total absence of any appeal to false sentiment or emotion which, if put before the jury, the judge would properly instruct them to disregard. The only extraneous circumstance which could legitimately be introduced was an expression of abhorrence of the pleasure-loving crowd of onlookers who had come to gloat over the picture of a woman's torture. One by one the strong points relied upon by the prosecution at the outset were reviewed: the woman who was going to prove the words, "I will shoot you"; on cross-examination they were reduced to, "I will shoot". May they not have meant, "I will shoot myself"? The witness who had heard the words, "Laugh, baby. Laugh for the last time"; she admitted that Stephens had told her he was afraid Mrs. Barney would shoot herself. If Mrs. Barney had really tried on that occasion to kill him, why was there no trace of a bullet mark in the mews? The case against the prisoner was very different from what it had been when it was first opened to the jury. And then the story told by Mrs. Barney herself. If she had ever lied, if she had ever given a different version of the young man's death, the police would know it. But she had not. From the very first moment when the doctor and the police came upon the scene, her story had always been the same. "It was an accident." Everyone had agreed that her condition was hysterical to a degree; that would render it almost impossible for her to invent or prepare some ingenious defence. So why should she not be believed? And last of all: if the police had taken greater care, if the revolver had been examined for the dead man's finger-prints before it was handled, there might have been discovered almost conclusive evidence that her story of the struggle was the truth.

None will ever know what effect, if any, the speech for Mrs. Barney had upon the jury—perhaps it is better that they shouldn't, but at any rate the judge found nothing in it of which he found it necessary to express disapproval. The summing up was, and I knew it would be, absolutely dispassionate and scrupulously fair; there was, however, one passage in it raising a point which the prosecution had not made, but which the judge was bound to place before the jury. Mrs. Barney had stated that she really intended to commit suicide. If in attempting such an act the death of her lover had resulted, it was open to the jury, on her own evidence, to find her guilty of manslaughter. It was upon that note that the jury left the box to consider what verdict they should give.

I have never been able to free myself from the sense of horror which persists during the period in which such a jury is considering its verdict. The prisoner has been taken down into the cells; the door through which the jury have passed is closed; until it opens, no one can ever guess what the result will be. At that moment there is a test which is almost infallible. If the jury look at the prisoner the verdict is NOT GUILTY; if they do not, the sentence is DEATH. When the jury filed back into the Court they looked at Mrs. Barney. She was acquitted.

I only saw her once more in her life. A few days after the trial, term having ended, I was driving my car up the steep hill from Boulogne on the Paris road when a long low car, driven by a woman, dashed round the corner on the wrong side, nearly killing me and my chauffeur who was sitting beside me. As he indignantly picked up his cap he said: "Did you see who was driving that car, sir? It was Mrs. Barney!"

THE CASE OF THE POLISH OFFICER

The Crime Passionelle finds no place in English Courts of Justice. Upon a trial for murder it is idle for counsel, however brilliant, to refer with streaming eyes to the prisoner's love for his mother or his mistress or any other particular woman for whose sake he has committed the crime. Murder is murder, and unless he can put forward some real defence, emotional outbursts by an eloquent advocate are merely a waste of time. That fact may possibly account for the difference between the calm and dignified atmosphere of the Central Criminal Court and the somewhat remarkable exhibitions of mass hysteria which apparently occur from time to time on the other side of the Channel. The trial for murder of Captain X was not an unfair example of the difference in method.

I shall call him Captain X as the tragedy of his life occurred in the not very distant past, and no doubt the last thing he would desire is to have public attention once again drawn to his unhappiness. During the last World War this country was the temporary home of many foreigners, driven from their own country by the German invaders, and amongst them was Captain X. He was a Polish officer of considerable distinction in his own army, not only highly decorated for valour, but a man devoted to his country's cause. Like so many others he had escaped to England and was living in London attached to the headquarters of the Polish Army. His wife had also escaped and she too was living in London, although the relationship between them was far from happy. That he was devoted to his wife was undoubted, but an estrangement had grown up between them owing to the attentions of another Polish officer whom I will call Lieut. Y. Captain X made every effort to prevent a development of this unhappy association, and, according to him, with every expectation of success, but apparently the influence of Lieut. Y was stronger than he had anticipated. While he was with his wife, her old affection seemed to return, but whenever he left her, Lieut. Y once more appeared upon the scene. It is, of course, impossible for an outsider to know anything about the true relations between a husband and a wife, but it became quite clear during the subsequent trial that considerable affection existed between Madame X and Lieut. Y and there were produced some letters of a very loving character. There is only one to which reference need be made, as it assumed considerable importance. It was suggested that the husband had threatened to shoot himself owing to his unhappiness and indeed dishonour, and one of Lieut. Y's letters to the wife contained a phrase more or less to this effect: "Why don't you let him have his revolver and let him shoot himself?"

In this unhappy state of affairs Captain X determined, according to the statement which he subsequently made to the police, to make one last effort to end the association between his wife and Lieut. Y, and with that object invited the lieutenant to come and see him. He was living in rooms in the Victoria district, and accordingly an appointment was made for the visit to take place. The landlord declared that on the fatal morning Captain X left the house and returned shortly afterwards accompanied by Lieut. Y; that the two men went together into the sitting-room, the door of which was closed, and that after a short interval he heard three revolver shots. He described the shooting in a way which, if accurate, was most unfortunate for Captain X. He said the three shots were fired in rapid succession or, as he put it somewhat dramatically, "pouf, pouf, pouf". He immediately entered the sitting-room and found an appalling sight. Lieut. Y was half sitting, half lying in an armchair by the fireplace; he was dead. Captain X was standing with a revolver still in his hand. The police were immediately sent for and upon their arrival Captain X gave his account of the occurrence. He was quite calm and collected and made a statement from which he never varied. He said that he had invited Lieut. Y to his rooms for the purpose of discussing the lieutenant's relations with his wife; that upon getting no satisfactory assurance he had decided to shoot himself, and for that purpose had produced a revolver; that Lieut. Y obtained possession of the weapon and had fired the first shot at him; that thereupon the men had closed and in the subsequent struggle the revolver had been fired and to his surprise Lieut. Y had fallen dead.

It may perhaps tend to throw some light upon the divergent views put forward at the ensuing trial if an explanation is given of the discoveries made by the police on their investigation. Three shots had undoubtedly been fired; two had been fired into the body of the dead man; one had been fired in exactly the opposite direction and the bullet mark was found near the window facing the chair in which the dead man was lying. This was undoubtedly the high water mark in Captain X's favour in support of his contention that Lieut. Y had fired at him. The other two bullet marks were very difficult to reconcile with the account given by Captain X and raised the main difficulty in the defence.

The first had penetrated the heart and had undoubtedly been the cause of death; the second had caused a superficial wound on the dead man's face and had proceeded in a downward direction causing a wound in the body. From the position in which the body was found it would have been quite impossible for that wound to have been caused if the dead man was then sitting in the chair. The theory of the defence being that the two shots were fired during the course of a struggle during which both men were standing up, that difficulty alone was by no means insuperable. But unfortunately the post-mortem examination which was conducted by Sir Bernard Spilsbury raised a question of far more serious import. According to him, and his opinion was quite definite, death had been caused by the heart wound and was instantaneous; the head wound was the result of the second shot. But the real gravity of his evidence arose from the deductions which he made as a result of his examination, namely that the second shot had been fired after the man was dead. He arrived at this conclusion by reason of the fact that he found no trace of blood flowing from the second wound, and according to him that could only be explained by the heart wound having completely stopped the circulation of the blood before the last shot was fired.

To anyone who knew Sir Bernard as well as I did, the deadly nature of this evidence was immediately apparent. I had cross-examined him too often to be under any possible illusion. As a witness he was always strictly impartial and scrupulously fair, but his knowledge was immense, and once he had formed a definite opinion, it was always extremely difficult to shake him in his views. Spilsbury's evidence was the cause of my main anxiety throughout the case.

One other piece of evidence which at one time seemed likely to cause some difficulty was the finding of the prisoner's cigarette-case in the chair in which the dead man was lying, but the importance of that disappeared once it was realised that during their interview the relative positions of the two men may well have changed before any shot was fired.

Having regard to the police discoveries it was inevitable that Captain X should be arrested and charged with murder, and the case was not brought to me until after he had been committed to take his trial at the Central Criminal Court. I have never known a case in which an accused man has more strongly aroused my sympathies. He was a stranger in a foreign land, and at the moment of his tragedy he was practically without friends. It is no part of an advocate's duty to feel sympathy for his client, indeed such a feeling is rather a disadvantage than otherwise. The proper conduct of a defence in a grave and difficult case requires a cold-blooded detachment from any outside influence; the case may change at any moment, vital decisions may have to be made at a second's notice, it is more than unfortunate for a prisoner if his advocate's judgment is to be affected, even in the smallest degree, by any feeling other than the wise and proper conduct of his defence. But in the case of Captain X, some sympathy was unavoidable, and I was only too glad to be able to render him such assistance as I could.

I know nothing of the practice of the Polish Courts of Justice. For all I know, in his own country it might have been sufficient for Captain X to plead: "I am a Polish officer; my honour was involved; the man is dead"; or perhaps again, "I fought a duel, and I was justified"; but whatever is or is not the Polish practice, the law of the Central Criminal Court is very different. To Captain X there was but one defence, namely that there was a struggle and the man was killed by accident.

The fate of many a prisoner has been decided by the decision of his legal advisers before ever he takes his place in Court. The dangerous points against him are well known, and the problem with which they are faced is how to find the best method by which to dispose of them. It is impossible to be rigid in forming a decision. A line of cross-examination which sounds admirable in consultation may be totally destroyed by one unexpected answer, and so every possible line of approach must be thoroughly explored. The two main danger points with which Captain X was faced were obvious. If the evidence of the lodging-house proprietor was accurate and was believed, "pouf, pouf, pouf," it would be extremely difficult to reconcile that evidence with the prisoner's story of a first attempt by the dead man to murder, a subsequent struggle, and an accidental death. Upon the other hand, if the three shots were indeed fired practically instantaneously, it would seem a little difficult to reconcile that evidence with Sir Bernard's theory that the last shot was fired after death. It seemed to me that the plausible and possibly correct explanation might be an interval of time between the first and the last two shots, and the last two alone being fired almost at the same moment. This would be consistent with the defence and possibly destructive of the medical evidence for the prosecution. With regard to Sir Bernard himself, a long experience had taught me the only hopeful line of cross-examination; ask as little as possible for fear of making the case worse than it already was, and trust to the not wholly unreasonable comment: 'doctors are not infallible and are so often wrong.'

There was however to my mind one point which might well produce immense potentialities, if not indeed by way of actual defence, at least sufficient to establish the existence of a real defence, of which the prisoner had been deprived. If the case for the prosecution was correct, the prisoner alone had fired the three shots in question; if Captain X was right, the dead man himself had fired at least one of them. In these days it has become the invariable practice of the police to test the fatal weapon for finger-prints, and the result of their examination is frequently a most important element in the evidence for the prosecution. But it should be, and indeed is, equally available to the defence. The police alone are in a position to make the necessary examination; a prisoner under arrest has neither the opportunity nor the facilities to make such an investigation on his own behalf. If Captain X was to be believed, the finger-prints both of himself and of the dead man should have been found on his revolver; if he was lying, an examination should have discovered his finger-prints alone. The depositions before the magistrate disclosed no evidence of any prints, nor indeed or any attempts at investigation. It was upon this fact that I mainly based my hopes.

When Captain X stood in the dock of the Central Criminal Court, there was apparent none of the atmosphere usually associated with a murder trial. At least there was nothing sordid in the appearance or the history of the prisoner. A tall dignified figure, wearing upon his chest the honours which he had well deserved, he seemed singularly out of place amid his surroundings. As the jury were duly sworn to try the issues joined between "Our Sovereign Lord the King and the Prisoner at the Bar", and to decide whether the prisoner should live or die, I could not help wondering what they thought of him, and what he thought of them. I had never spoken to him, indeed I had never seen him before, but from his appearance, if I had been a juryman, I think the prosecution would have had to work very hard before I should have convicted him. However, I have never been a juryman, and if I had I am sure I should have been a very bad one.

The case for the prosecution was outlined by senior counsel for the Treasury, and in accordance with a tradition which in recent years had become universal in our Criminal Courts, it was presented with absolute fairness; the strong points against the prisoner were properly brought to light, while at the same time the evidence or arguments which might tend to assist him in his defence were placed frankly before the Court. There was nothing either in the opening statement or in the evidence for the prosecution which could possibly have taken the prisoner by surprise. The facts which we had foreseen were placed before the Court neither more nor less forcibly than we had anticipated.

The first important witness was the lodging-house keeper. He adhered stoutly to his story; the shots had followed each other in rapid succession; the "pouf-pouf-pouf" was too firmly in his mind to be removed. But he was not entirely a satisfactory witness. He was a shade too dogmatic in his recollections, and he gave one piece of evidence on cross-examination which I thought at the time did not impress the jury. He was asked what he did after finding the dead man, and sending for the police, and he stated that he went upstairs and continued to make the beds. It may have been accurate and certainly was not very material, but as he said it, it did not sound very convincing, and after all it is the little things which sometimes tend to throw doubt upon a witness's recollection.

Sir Bernard Spilsbury was, of course, a witness of a very different type. He was quite satisfied that the last shot was fired after the man was dead and nothing that I could do would make him alter his conviction. If his view was correct, the last shot could not have been fired during a continuing struggle. His evidence was very difficult, and I was very glad to see him leave the witness box.

The last witness was the police officer in charge of the case, and it was upon his evidence that I largely based my hopes; it is rare indeed for the cross-examination of police evidence to be as vitally important as it was in this case. The question as to whether or not drama is a valuable asset in a defence is largely a matter of opinion and has been the subject of much discussion. The late Sir Edward Marshall Hall would have found little difficulty in framing a reply. Where he conducted a defence the drama commenced upon his first entry into Court and only ceased when he sank exhausted into his seat at the conclusion of a frenzied peroration. To some his drama may have seemed a shade transpontine, but without it there would have been no Marshall Hall, and the Bar would have lost one of its most striking personalities; but whatever may be the wiser view, there can be no doubt that real and legitimate dramatic effect can be obtained both in the voicing and the timing of a question.

The cross-examination was extremely short.

"Immediately upon your arrival at the flat the

prisoner told you, did he not, that there had been a struggle and that it was the dead man who fired the first shot?"

"Yes."

"If his story was true, from the position in which the two men must have been standing, you would have expected to find the mark of a bullet on the window?"

"Yes."

"Was there such a bullet mark on the window?"

"Yes."

"If the prisoner's story is true, the dead man must at some time have held the revolver in his hand?"

"Yes."

"In that case you would have expected to find the dead man's finger-prints upon the revolver?"

"Possibly."

"And if those finger-prints were on the revolver, that must be a vital piece of evidence for the defence?"

By this time the jury had got it; everyone in Court appeared to be leaning forward, waiting for the next question which might decide whether the prisoner had lied or told the truth. It was perhaps legitimate to keep them waiting. It was the crowning point of our defence. At last it came:

"Were the dead man's finger-prints on that revolver?"

"I don't know."

There was no pause now.

"Why not? Is it not the duty of the police to search for finger-prints? Were they ever taken in this case?"

"No."

"Why not? Why not? Has somebody made a grave mistake?"

There was no answer. The police officer was in a most unhappy position. Somebody must have slipped. How it came about I never knew. Why they were never taken I never knew. But this I do know: if the prints had been found on the revolver, the defence would have been triumphant; as the police had never even looked for them, they had deprived us of our strongest piece of evidence and no one in the world would have convicted the prisoner after that.

It has since been suggested that the question went only to prejudice and not to decide any issue in the case, but any such suggestion is wholly without foundation. It was fundamental and I have no doubt loomed largely in the jury's mind when they retired to consider their verdict.

In cases such as this the speeches of counsel are of comparatively small importance. A man's life hangs in the balance, and the jury listen with anxious care to all the evidence, but the issues are too grave for them to be unduly influenced by passionate oratory or forensic ingenuity. The judge's summing-up is very different. Except in the very rare instance of a judge displaying some evidence of partiality with which they disagree, they listen to the careful and measured words with which they are addressed not only with unabated interest but also with the respectful attention which those words deserve. The summing-up of Mr. Justice Humphreys was, as in his case it always was, a masterpiece. I, who knew him so well, fancied that I could read into his words an indication that in his mind there rested an idea that something in the nature of a duel may have taken place in that small room, but whatever he may have thought, his examination of the evidence was careful, accurate and strictly fair.

The jury were absent for a very short time. When the prisoner was brought back into Court to hear their verdict, he stood in the dock so dignified and immovable that he almost resembled a figure carved in stone. I had a strange feeling that even the warders wanted to apologise for standing there beside him. When the jury filed back into Court, every member turned his eyes towards the prisoner. The verdict was NOT GUILTY. The verdict was one I would certainly have given if I had been standing in their place.

THE CASE OF THE HOODED MAN

In the year 1911, at Lewes Assizes, John Williams was tried and convicted of the murder of a policeman at Eastbourne. In due course he was executed. I have no doubt whatever that he was guilty of the crime with which he was charged, but I have equally no doubt that, in Law, his conviction was unjustifiable, and inasmuch as his trial was the first occasion upon which I had appeared for the defence upon a capital charge, the result caused me the gravest anxiety, and indeed disquiet.

The prisoner was certainly the nearest approach to a Raffles in real life that I have ever come across. John Williams was not his name. Whether or not the police ever discovered his true identity, I never found out, but it was not known to me, as he always refused to give any particulars about himself even to his own solicitor.

I was told that he was the son of a clergyman, and that having embarked upon a career of crime he was determined that his father should never hear of the depths to which he had descended. His appearance and demeanour certainly afforded some support to this suggestion. He was a well set-up young man, by no means bad-looking, and his manner of speech gave every evidence of good education and some refinement in his early upbringing. By profession he was a burglar, and was described to me by the police as possessing such remarkable agility that he could scale the wall of a house like a cat. At the time of his trial he was living with a young woman of remarkable beauty, who was on the point of giving birth to a child, which fact formed one of the features of a somewhat unusual trial. His habits were typical of the man himself: when prosperous he was accustomed to live in West End hotels, where he and his companion, faultlessly attired, would dine in luxury; when trade was bad he would return to the more squalid surroundings of the slums. His companions were mainly criminals like himself, of whom the only one who appeared in a prominent position at the subsequent trial was a man named Power. Difficult though it might be to discover any redeeming quality in the character of the prisoner, in the case of Power it would seem to be an impossibility. This man had posed as a close and devoted friend, who shared in many of Williams' criminal activities, while at the same time apparently nourishing a secret passion for the young woman with whom his friend was then living, and it may well be that this suggested passion afforded the explanation of the almost inhuman betrayal of which Power was subsequently guilty.

At the date of the crime there was living in Eastbourne, a lady who was locally known as the Countess. She was a person of both means and position whose house was situated in a road running up from the esplanade, and upon the night in question she was returning from some social visit, when upon approaching her front door she saw what she thought to be the figure of a man trying to conceal himself upon the portico. With considerable courage she entered her house and telephoned to the police, and in response to her call a police officer was sent to investigate her suspicions. The officer himself observed the crouching figure and called upon the man to come down. The only reply was a shot from a revolver and the policeman fell dead.

Inevitably a murder of any kind arouses the keenest investigation at the hands of the police, but when the victim happens to be one of their own body, the hunt becomes if possible even more intense. So it was in this case. Eastbourne was combed for evidence to identify the murderer, but apparently without result, and it can only be a matter of speculation whether or not the author of the crime would ever have been traced had it not been for his subsequent betrayal, a betrayal which took place under singularly revolting circumstances.

A few days after the crime, Power presented himself at the Eastbourne police station, where he stated that he was in a position to identify the murderer. His story was as follows. He said that on the night of the murder, Williams had decided to burgle the Countess's house; that he had started his journey in company with his paramour, whom he had left sitting on a bench upon the Eastbourne front, and that he himself had visited the house, where he had been surprised, first by the return of the Countess, and later by the arrival of the police officer; that he had fired his revolver, whether or not merely to frighten the policeman was not clear, and finding that the man was dead he had rejoined the girl and confessed to what he had done. According to Power both of them became alarmed, and decided to hide the revolver, which they did by burying it in the shingle on the beach. Having no money they communicated with Power, asking for assistance, which he, as their friend, was only too glad to afford, and that he had helped Williams to return to London, where he had made a full confession of the crime.

Upon hearing this story it was at once apparent to the police that the character of Power, quite apart from the revolting nature of his betrayal, was such that no jury would believe his uncorroborated evidence, and in consequence they decided upon a scheme which, while admirable in its ingenuity, was somewhat unpleasant in its execution, although no doubt necessitated by the exigencies of the circumstances. The plan was rendered no more attractive by the fact that Power was of necessity a collaborator, and while the only accurate account of what was arranged was known to the police, that version which reached my ears as being derived from the girl herself, and therefore quite possibly exaggerated, was by no means attractive.

According to her, she received a visit from Power upon a date which must have been immediately after his call upon the police, when he said he had come to save her and Williams from a position of extreme danger. He told her that the police knew the full story of the crime, including the fact that the incriminating revolver had been buried upon the beach, and that they were proposing immediately to retrieve it. Accordingly the only possible way to save Williams from the gallows would be that he,

Power, should accompany her to the spot where the revolver was to be found, that they should together dig it up and remove it to a place where it would be safe from any chance of discovery. The position of the girl was pitiable. She was undoubtedly devoted to her lover, and she was in a condition in which the birth of her child was imminent; moreover she believed Power to be a true, and indeed her only, friend. In consequence she had no alternative except to fall into the trap which had been so cleverly laid for her.

The same night she and Power went down upon the beach. With little difficulty she dug the revolver from the place where it was lying in comparative security, and upon rising to her feet she found herself surrounded by police, when both she and Power were immediately arrested.

What followed next must always remain a matter for speculation, as her story and that of the police did not completely tally. According again to her version, she was told that unless she made a full confession she would be charged with murder, and that her only hope of escape was to incriminate her lover. What, if any, inducement was held out to her it is impossible to say, indeed her condition of health both mental and physical would seem to have rendered little inducement necessary, but the fact remained that she told the full story very much as Power had foreshadowed; and her statement was immediately recorded and signed by her in the presence of the police.

From this moment it became obvious to the

authorities that events must move with extreme rapidity to prevent any possibility of the unfortunate girl retracting the statement she had given. It was accordingly decided to entrust her to the care of a police matron, a course which, while possibly evincing a tender care for her physical welfare, would at the same time prevent any possible communication with outside influence. Williams was immediately arrested and brought before the magistrates, when instead of merely formal evidence of arrest being given, as is the usual practice, the girl's evidence was given at the earliest possible moment. Treasury counsel appeared for the prosecution, and she was taken through her statement line by line, and she was only released from police supervision when her deposition had been formally given and signed.

By this time the case had aroused an enormous amount of public interest. Speculation had been first aroused by the decision of the police that whenever Williams appeared in public on his journeys between the prison and the Police Court, his face should be completely enveloped in a veil. The purpose of this precaution was never quite clear to me, but it resulted in the prisoner being popularly known as The Hooded Man. In addition, the fact that the only substantial evidence in the case was afforded by a girl who was about to become the mother of the prisoner's child, gave rise to an element of romance in an otherwise purely sordid case of murder.

Power's share in the betrayal had been carefully excluded from the evidence, but some suspicion of his complicity must have leaked out, as hints to that effect became apparent.

It has always been a little difficult to understand why the case was brought to me in those early days; the only possible explanation being that the prisoner had no money, and the daily Press had not then developed a practice, which has since become prevalent, of paying large sums for a prisoner's defence in return for his life story if he should survive the trial, or possibly his confession if he should not. Very naturally the case caused me the greatest anxiety. If the girl's story was accepted the result of the trial was a foregone conclusion; there was a suspicion, and no more, that Power had proved himself a Judas, but even if that suspicion should prove to be well founded, it amounted to no more than an element of prejudice. Altogether the period intervening before the trial was by no means a happy one.

My anxiety was increased by the urgent request of the prisoner that I should visit him in prison. The practice of such visits is, in my view, most undesirable. So many ingenious defences have been presented to the Courts which obviously owe their origin to minds far more acute than that possessed by the average murderer, that it is far better that counsel should have nothing whatever to do with them; and, in addition, there is always the grave risk that an accused man in his very natural anxiety may blurt out some statement or even confession that may seriously hamper his advocate in the conduct of his defence. However, on this occasion I yielded to the prisoner's importunities and for the first and only time consented to visit the accused man in his cell.

It was a thoroughly unpleasant experience. To pass through a prison gate, even as a visitor, is a horror. The clang of the iron gates and the jangle of the gaoler's keys are sufficiently depressing, but when followed by a visit to an accused murderer, who in all human probability will never come out alive, the horror becomes a nightmare. It was impossible to see Williams for the first time without some slight feeling of admiration. Whatever his crimes and faults, and they were no doubt many, he was at least possessed of the quality of unflinching courage. He showed not the faintest sign of fear or even anxiety. He said nothing about the facts of the case except to deny explicitly that he knew anything whatever about the murder. About the girl whose evidence against him was so deadly, he spoke with nothing but kindness; the only time he showed any feeling was when Power's name was mentioned, and then he stated with a calmness that was almost startling that if only he could get Power within reach for a couple of minutes there would be no necessity for anyone to defend him on a charge of murder. Before leaving I felt it my duty to warn him that the risk of an unfavourable verdict was very great, and to ask him if he wished me to try for a verdict of manslaughter upon the possible ground that the shot had been fired without any intention to cause death. He brushed the suggestion aside almost with contempt. I have been in prison before, he said, and although I am completely innocent, I would far rather be hanged than go to prison for another twelve months. Altogether I found John Williams a remarkable person.

The trial took place at Lewes Assizes before Mr. Justice Channell, when the Crown was represented by Sir Frederick Low, K.C., and Mr. Cecil Whiteley. The High Street of the old county town was thronged with a crowd of excited onlookers, and throughout the three days of the hearing the interest seemed to increase rather than diminish. Murder can always draw an audience, but when savoured with a dash of mystery and romance, the house is full. Low based his case almost entirely upon the girl's statement. He asked that the greatest possible indulgence should be extended to her owing to her relationship with the prisoner, and more particularly as she was likely to be confined within a few days, but he pointed out that if her evidence was accepted, the result of the case was a foregone conclusion. She was the first witness of any importance to be called. It was the first time that I had seen her, and her appearance created a sensation. Although obviously desperately ill, as was no doubt to be expected under the circumstances, her beauty was unimpaired, even accentuated, by her condition. She took the oath firmly and her first words fell like a bombshell. She could say nothing; she could give no evidence, and she knew nothing whatever about the murder. Low at once asked for and obtained leave from the judge to examine her upon her statement before the magistrates. She was taken line by line through that statement, and while admitting that she had made it, she said that every word was untrue and was only forced from her by the terror of her arrest.

The effect of this retraction gave rise to the real problem in the trial. According to our Law a prisoner is tried upon the evidence given before the jury. It is of course always permissible to cross-examine a witness by confronting him or her with a statement made on a prior occasion, but the effect of such a cross-examination is liable to be misunderstood. As a means of discrediting the witness it may be conclusive, but it does not turn into evidence against the prisoner the contents of the statement the truth of which the witness denies. The result of Low's examination, in my opinion, amounted to no more than this: the jury were entitled to disbelieve the witness when she stated that she knew nothing about the murder, but they were not entitled to treat as evidence the contents of her deposition before the magistrates, in which she had given a detailed account of the occurrence on the fatal night. In other words, her evidence on this part of the case was purely negative.

The examination of Power was even more dramatic. Never in my life have I met a more utterly contemptible human being. The betrayal of his friend was bad enough, but the story of his treatment of the girl, also according to him his dearest friend, must have revolted everyone who heard it. Everything he did to her was in collaboration with the police. When he approached her with protestations of undying friendship, he knew that officers were standing almost within earshot;

knowing that she was unwillingly sending her lover to the gallows, he aided her with a pretence of tender affection in her search for the fatal weapon; when he was arrested with her, he knew that his arrest was nothing but a sham. As the horrible story was dragged out of him, it was scarcely surprising that the warders in the dock closed nearer to the prisoner; few would have doubted what Power's fate would have been if the two men had been allowed to meet. When he left the witness box one thing at least was obvious: no prisoner could ever be convicted if Power's evidence stood alone. After the trial I heard that the police smuggled him out of the country, but whether that was true or not I do not know.

The only other evidence of any importance was that of the prisoner himself. He gave his evidence well and quietly, merely denying that he had any part in or knew anything about the murder. His cross-examination was detailed and prolonged, but did not add very much to the general story, and when the judge summed up, the case remained as it had been throughout: apart from the girl's story before the magistrates there was very little evidence against him.

It was a case in which everything depended on the summing up. I should imagine that few people who sat throughout the trial had any great doubt that in truth it was the prisoner who had fired the fatal shot; they might well think that the girl's story before the magistrates was too circumstantial to be disregarded; but onlookers at a trial are not assumed to know the law. In my view the summing up was most unfortunate. Without going into detail which would be wearisome, it is enough to say that the judge directed the jury that they were entitled to consider the girl's statement as evidence in the case and, if they accepted it, to convict the prisoner. After that the result was a foregone conclusion. The verdict was GUILTY.

There was of course an appeal to the Court of Criminal Appeal, then in its comparatively early stage. Before the hearing the prisoner's child was born. The unhappy mother had no money and no friends, and no hospital would take her in because of her unenviable notoriety, so my wife and I had to provide for her confinement. The hearing in the Appeal Court was unfortunate. The Lord Chief Justice, Lord Alverstone, presided, and although it was the first, and indeed the only, time I ever appeared before him, I was not greatly impressed by his legal acumen. From the outset of the hearing it was apparent that he was satisfied of the prisoner's guilt, and no legal argument seemed to make the least impression upon him. Indeed in his judgment he never referred to it. The prisoner was guilty and that was enough. The appeal was dismissed.

The last thing I heard of Williams came from one of the prison officials. Before his execution he was allowed a visit from the mother and his child. According to the usual custom they were separated by a grille, and he asked to be allowed to hold the baby. The warder in attendance with a not unnatural kindness took the child from its mother and gave it to him. He showed no sign of emotion as he kissed it affectionately, and then pressed a small piece of prison bread into its hand, saying as he did so, "Now nobody can ever say that your father has not ever given you anything." The next day he was hanged.

THE VAQUIER CASE

Jean Pierre Vaquier was the first and only man whom I have prosecuted for murder, and I disliked the case intensely. I was Attorney-General when the crime was committed, and as a law officer almost invariably conducts the prosecution in a case of death by poisoning the task fell upon me. I had no sympathy with the strange little man in the dock, but the trial worried me a great deal, partly because I was quite unable to satisfy myself as to the motive for the murder, and partly because the experience of cross-examining a man to his death was one which I never desire to repeat. The absence of ascertainable motive was undoubtedly the strangest part of the whole case and went far to explain the great public interest which the trial aroused.

Jean Pierre Vaquier was a very odd personality and possessed of a very peculiar appearance. He had thick curly hair, a square-cut black beard, and a flamboyant moustache. Although small in stature he was inordinately vain of his personal appearance and spent immense time on his facial adornments. Undoubtedly his vanity was so pronounced that it controlled all his actions and may very possibly have been the cause of his ultimate downfall. At the time when his career first became the subject of enquiry he was engaged as a wireless expert in the Victoria Hotel at Biarritz, and it was there that he met Mabel Theresa Jones and embarked upon a friendship with her which resulted in the ultimate tragedy.

Mrs. Jones was herself a woman of distinct personality. Although she had been married a good many years she still retained considerable good looks and was evidently a person of character. She was the wife of the licensee of a small hotel at Byfleet, in Surrey, known as the Blue Anchor. Her husband took no part in the drama except as the victim, and very little was known about him. He drank a good deal too much and was possessed of very little, if any, money. Mrs. Jones was a woman of energy and had been engaged on her own account in a business which had resulted in disaster. At the beginning of the year 1924 her own financial position was such that she was on the verge of bankruptcy. Being somewhat affected in health by her financial misfortunes she decided to take a holiday, and early in January she left England and proceeded to the Victoria Hotel at Biarritz. It was a somewhat venturesome journey because she spoke no word of French and had no friends or acquaintances at the Victoria Hotel.

At this hotel sprang up the strange friendship between Vaquier and Mrs. Jones, which developed with remarkable rapidity. It was strange because Vaquier could speak no English, and as she could speak no French all conversation had to take place by means of a dictionary. It was rapid because within a period of days they were living together as man and wife.

At the beginning of February Mr. Jones telegraphed for his wife to return home. On hearing the news Vaquier burst into tears and begged her not to leave him, which would tend to suggest that as far as he was concerned the liaison was based upon some degree of affection. However, Mrs. Jones determined to return and they travelled together as far as Paris, where she left Vaquier and returned to England alone. Before she left she gave him the address of the Russell Hotel in London, so it would seem to be a reasonable supposition that she expected him to follow her.

Mrs. Jones returned to England on the 8th of February and was met at the station by her husband, with whom she returned to the Blue Anchor. The next day Vaquier arrived in London and went to the Hotel Russell, and as far as is known it was his first and only visit to London. During the next few days Mrs. Jones visited him twice in London and intercourse undoubtedly took place between them. On the 14th of February Mrs. Jones was alone at the Blue Anchor Hotel, as her husband was away for a few days, and, according to her, Vaquier arrived unexpectedly and uninvited. He had no luggage, and apparently no money, because he obtained from Mrs. Jones a cheque with which to pay his London hotel bill. From that date he lived continuously at the Blue Anchor until the tragedy occurred. His position in the household was somewhat peculiar. He lived and took his meals apparently in complete amity with both Mr. and Mrs. Jones. He never paid anything for his lodging, and explained his inability to do so by an alleged delay in receiving payment for some invention which he said he had perfected. Upon one occasion during this stay he visited London with Mrs. Jones, which was the only occasion upon which their old relationship was resumed. At the

Blue Anchor itself no impropriety occurred, and according to Mrs. Jones she held out no hope that it might be resumed.

During this somewhat prolonged stay the arrogant little Frenchman was in all probability an object of dislike and derision to the staff and the visitors at the Blue Anchor Hotel. He could still speak no English and was undoubtedly regarded as a nuisance; but there was not the faintest indication that his continued presence would ultimately result in the commission of a detestable crime.

On the 1st of March Vaquier paid his last visit to London. It was that visit which brought him to the scaffold. He called upon a chemist by the name of Bland, from whom he had made sundry purchases while staying at the Hotel Russell. On this occasion his requirements were remarkable. He produced a list of chemicals which he said he required for the purpose of wireless experiments. Amongst other things on his list were 100 grammes of chloroform, 20 grammes of perchloride of mercury, and .12 of a gramme of strychnine. The latter items being deadly poisons, Vaquier had great difficulty in persuading the chemist to supply them, but in the end Bland was over-persuaded, insisting, however, that Vaquier should give his name and address and sign the poison book which a chemist is required by the Law to keep. Vaquier gave his name as "Mr. Wanker" and his address as "Room 60, Hotel Russell", a room which he had never occupied. Vaquier obtained his poisons and with them returned to the Blue Anchor Hotel.

For a month life at the Blue Anchor continued as before, and the relationship between the three principals remained the same. There was no indication that Vaquier had designs against any person nor that he had a deadly weapon ready to his hand. Indeed, up to the last moment he was mainly concerned in an endeavour to persuade both Mr. and Mrs. Jones to abandon the Blue Anchor Hotel and start a restaurant with him in France. It is possible that Vaquier was endeavouring to divert suspicion from himself, or perhaps he was merely awaiting a suitable opportunity.

On the 28th of March, almost exactly a month after Vaquier obtained his poisons, there was some kind of a party in the bar parlour of the Blue Anchor, at which there was a good deal of heavy drinking. After any night of indulgence Mr. Jones made a habit of drinking bromo salts in the morning, the bottle of salts being kept regularly in the bar parlour, where it was at the disposal of Mr. Jones or any of his guests who might require its assistance. It was fairly evident upon the night of the party that both Mr. Jones and possibly some of his guests might visit the bottle of bromo salts the next morning. This was the opportunity for which Vaquier had been waiting.

The next morning he was up very early, and for nearly two hours he sat by himself in the bar parlour. It was bitterly cold as the room was fireless, and he sat huddled up in a great-coat, resisting all invitations or suggestions of the servant that he should remove himself to another room where there was a fire. No one saw him move from his chair, but there he sat, quite alone, in all probability with his eyes glued to the bottle of bromo salts, which remained in its accustomed place on the mantelpiece.

Ultimately his patience was rewarded. After a delay that must have appeared interminable, Jones left his bedroom and came into the parlour. He was obviously suffering from the effects of his previous night's debauch and, as might have been expected, his first visit was to the bottle of bromo salts. Under Vaquier's eye he poured a dose into a glass, added water and drank it.

"My God!" he said, "they are bitter."

Mrs. Jones, who was in the room, tested the contents of the bottle with her finger, and noticed the same result. She put the bottle, which still contained some salts, into the drawer of the dresser. She then gave her husband an emetic of salt and warm water, and he was violently sick, but within a very short time it became apparent that he was desperately ill. A doctor was sent for, who at once perceived that Jones displayed every symptom of strychnine poisoning, and although he did everything possible to effect a cure, Jones died in agony in a very short time.

While the doctor was engaged upon his ministrations, Vaquier's actions were peculiar. He ran into the kitchen shouting, in his broken English:

"Medicine! Doctor. Quick!" and indicating that he wanted to find the bottle of salts. The servant pointed to the drawer in which Mrs. Jones had placed the bottle and Vaquier at once went to the drawer. No one saw him touch the bottle, but the fact remains that, when at a later stage the doctor required to see it, it was found in the drawer to be empty, and showing evident signs of having been recently washed.

The post-mortem examination of Mr. Jones disclosed that his death had been caused by strychnine poisoning. Some few grains which had fallen from the bottle were identified as strychnine, the medicine bottle itself, although recently washed, bore evident traces of strychnine, and the police immediately started their enquiries.

During the next few days the condition of affairs at the Blue Anchor was somewhat chaotic. Everyone in the hotel must have considered themselves to some extent under suspicion. Mrs. Jones must have regarded with the greatest anxiety the possibility, indeed the probability, of her relationship with Vaquier being the subject of enquiry. She suspected Vaquier. Indeed, according to her, Vaquier confessed his guilt as, when she taxed him with the crime, he replied,

"Yes, Mabs, for you."

But it must have been obvious from the outset that the evidence of Mrs. Jones, if uncorroborated, would have been open to severe criticism. Statements were taken from everybody who could possibly throw light upon the affair, and Vaquier himself made a number of voluntary statements to the police, some of which were, to say the least of it, remarkable.

On the 30th of March, he made a long rambling statement, full of inconsistencies, stating among other things that his relations with Mrs. Jones were merely those of a friend and not a lover, and attempting to throw no direct light on the murder.

On the 1st of April, he made a further statement, saying that he loved Mr. Jones like a brother, and that his death was caused by a "coward, jealous of my presence here".

On the 5th of April, he made yet another statement, containing some vague suggestion against the potman, George, in which this remarkable passage occurred:

"I have already said that Mr. Jones had informed me that George, the potman, would never leave the Blue Anchor, even could he make £5 a day elsewhere. I think that the second act of the drama will be the disappearance of the wife of George as mysteriously, and also as tragically as Mr. Jones. George has an incontestable and considerable ascendancy over that unhappy and defenceless woman, Mrs. Jones."

On the 10th of April, he made yet another statement, even more remarkable. In the course of it he gave reasons to prove his innocence, alleging that if he had desired to kill Jones, he could easily have done so without suspicion, inasmuch as upon occasions he carried the deceased to bed dead drunk, and it would have been easy for him to take a bottle of whisky and get him to drink himself to death.

Vaquier was not content to make statements to the police. His vanity was such that he talked freely to newspaper reporters, and even permitted photographs of himself to appear in the papers, where his somewhat remarkable appearance became known throughout the length and breadth of the country. His vanity was his undoing. On the 16th of April, Mr. Bland, the chemist, saw in a daily paper a picture of Mr. Wanker, who had bought strychnine from him for the purpose of making wireless experiments. He then realised that Mr. Wanker was none other than Jean Pierre Vaquier, who happened to be living in the Blue Anchor Hotel upon the day that Mr. Jones died of strychnine poisoning. He immediately communicated with the police, and on the next day Vaquier was arrested. Upon arrest, Vaquier made his last and most important statement. In it he said:

"I will make known to-morrow who administered the poison."

Needless to state he did not do so, and from him the police learned nothing more.

Vaquier was brought up for trial at the County Hall in Guildford on the 2nd of July, 1924. Council for the Crown were myself, the Attorney-General; Sir Edward Marshall Hall, K.C., and Mr. Roome. The prisoner was defended by Sir Henry Curtis-Bennett and Mr. A. B. Lucy. In some ways the trial was a very remarkable one. To begin with, the prisoner was French, and, as he spoke no English at all, the evidence had to be translated. The most curious feature of the trial was the attitude of the prisoner himself. His overweening vanity was self-evident, but his knowledge of criminal procedure came entirely from the French Courts. He expected to be bullied, not only by the prosecuting counsel, but by the judge himself. He expected to be shouted at and called an assassin. The studied courtesy and impartiality with which he was treated appeared not only to take him by surprise but to raise in his mind an entirely erroneous belief as to the course the trial was taking. As nobody shouted at him he thought they liked him; as nobody called him an assassin he seemed to think that nobody thought that he was one. From first to last he appeared to be under the belief that the case was proceeding in an atmosphere of kindness which could only end in a triumphant acquittal.

The first witness called was Mrs. Jones. She was obviously in a somewhat unsympathetic position. Her intrigue with Vaquier as it developed became blatant and indeed contemptible. The picture of a sorrowful wife was somewhat difficult to make convincing, and her evidence upon the whole might seem to require considerable corroboration. The main interest in the trial so far as her evidence was concerned necessarily centred on her cross-examination. The outstanding problem which must have been present to the mind of every counsel concerned in the case was the statement made by Vaquier that he was in a position to identify the murderer, which so far he had not done. It was thought possible that the cross-examination of Mrs. Jones might throw some light upon this suggestion. No one at the Bar was more experienced in defending a prisoner upon trial for murder than Sir Henry Curtis-Bennett. No one could have worked harder in defence of a prisoner than Sir Henry in his efforts for Vaquier. But his cross-examination of Mrs. Jones, although exhaustive and protracted, threw very little light upon the major problem. Apart from the fact that he cross-examined her, there was very little to be learned from the questions that he put to her. There was certainly no possible suggestion against George. There was a vague suggestion that she had a solicitor who was in love with her, and that was all. There the matter remained, and in substance the cross-examination was to the discredit of Mrs. Jones.

Two servants were called, whose evidence was of importance mainly upon the question of Vaquier's actions on the morning of the murder. The main point emerging from their evidence consisted in the peculiarity of Vaquier's determination to sit in the cold and cheerless bar parlour, wrapped in a great-coat, for nearly two hours when he could have been either in the coffee-room or the kitchen before a fire; the prosecution seeking to infer that he was keeping continuous watch upon the bottle of bromo salts. The other material point against him was the fact of his obvious anxiety to secure possession of the bottle from which the salts had been obtained, his opportunity for so doing, and the fact that the bottle showed signs of recent washing.

Medical evidence that Jones had died of strychnine poisoning was conclusive. It was also clearly established that strychnine had been inserted into the bottle of bromo salts. The other testimony against the prisoner, which would be damning if unexplained, was that of the chemist, Mr. Bland. It was proved that no wireless experiments required the assistance of strychnine, chloroform or perchloride of mercury. Why then did Vaquier require them, and why had it been necessary to obtain them by means of a false name?

Upon that note the prosecution closed, and so far there had been little drama in the trial. That was obviously to come. What was the explanation Vaquier had to give of his possession of these poisons, and what was the name of the murderer whom Vaquier was in a position to identify? If his explanation upon both, or indeed upon either, of these points was satisfactory, he might be acquitted; if not, his peril would seem to be very great.

The prisoner was the first and only witness called for the defence. His entry into the witness box was dramatic, even for a Frenchman. If it had not been for the warder who sat behind him, he might well have been an actor on the stage. He was quite self-possessed, almost affable in his demeanour, and his main interest appeared to centre on the effect created by his personal appearance. His examination was conducted at considerable length, and he was most emphatic that he was in no way concerned with the death of Mr. Jones, and denied all the material evidence given against him, including the evidence of Mrs. Jones as to his alleged confession. The interest in Court really developed when he commenced his explanation of the possession of the strychnine. He admitted the purchases from Mr. Bland, with one important exception. He alleged that he had purchased 25 grammes of strychnine and not the amount previously mentioned by the chemist, and he admitted buying 100 grammes of chloroform. He made no reference whatever to the name under which he had bought them. Then came the first dramatic moment. He was asked:

"Why did you buy this strychnine?"

And he replied:

"I was asked to do so by the solicitor of Madame Jones."

He was asked to give the name of the solicitor, but said he did not know it, as he had only seen him twice and spoken to him once. He said that the solicitor had asked him for strychnine in order to poison a dog who had the mange, and had given him £1 with which to make the purchase. I then interposed to say that I would arrange to have Mrs. Jones' solicitor brought into Court, and as far as the examination in chief was concerned there the matter rested. He gave no explanation of his various statements to the police, and in particular gave no other explanation of the person whom he alleged to be the murderer.

As in every other case in which a prisoner is called upon to give an account of matters which would otherwise seem to be gravely suspicious, the chief interest in the crime centres on the prisoner's cross-examination. In many ways the cross-examination of Vaquier was exceptionally dramatic. To begin with, he was a Frenchman and the services of an interpreter were required throughout. It must have been obvious to everyone who heard him that he was under a complete misapprehension as to the peril in which he stood. The extreme courtesy with which the cross-examination was conducted must have increased his feeling of self-confidence. He appeared almost debonair in his manner, and as the questions proceeded he was apparently the only person in the Court who did not feel the horror of the rope being drawn tightly around his neck. At some of his answers a shudder seemed almost to run from the jury box into the gallery, and yet Vaquier appeared more than satisfied with the course of events and even delighted with the effect that he was creating.

It required but little skill to cross-examine Vaquier. The cross-examination was by no means prolonged, but its effect was in its very nature devastating. After a few preliminary questions I went straight to the question of the purchase of the poisons. Quite a few questions and answers were sufficient to make the result of the case a foregone conclusion.

"How old are you?"

"Forty-five years."

"Do you know what strychnine is?"

"I knew it was a deadly poison."

"Has anybody ever asked you before to buy dangerous poisons for them?"

"Nobody."

"Was it only the second time that you had seen the solicitor of Mrs. Jones that he asked you to buy strychnine?"

"Yes."

"So the person who asked you to buy the strychnine

was somebody to whom you had never spoken before?"

"I had never spoken to him before."

"Did you know of any reason why he could not buy the poison for himself?"

"He told me he was very busy and had not time to buy it."

"He gave you a sovereign for the purchase?"

"A pound note."

"Did that strike you as a large sum of money to buy enough strychnine for one dog?"

"Perhaps he had no change."

"Did you ever give him the change that you must have got from buying the strychnine?"

"No, he never asked me."

From that moment the absurdity of the prisoner's suggestion became more and more pronounced. I next directed his attention to the signature upon the poison book, the book itself being handed to the prisoner.

"Is that your usual signature?"

"No."

"What is the name you have written there?"

"Wanker."

"You knew, then, that you were putting a false name to the poison-book? Why did you not put your real name?"

"Because I had been told that when you buy poison you never sign your own name."

"Who told you that?"

"The solicitor."

"Did the gentleman who asked you to buy the poison tell you to sign a false name?"

"Yes."

"Did it strike you as odd that a complete stranger who wanted to poison a dog was telling you to sign a false name?"

"No."

I then left the poison book and went to the purchase of the chloroform.

"What did you want 100 grammes of chloroform for?"

"For my personal use."

"Had you seen Mr. Jones drunk in his hotel at times?"

"I carried him three times to bed."

"Did it ever enter your mind that if anybody wanted to kill Mr. Jones, that would be the most easy time to do it?"

"No."

"At the time when you carried Mr. Jones up to bed would it have been easy to give him chloroform?"

"It was easy to give him anything you like. He was so insensible that he could easily have been suffocated with chloroform—very easy; a child could have killed him."

"What did you do with the chloroform?"

"I inhaled it, to sleep."

From the movement in Court it might have appeared that those answers alone were enough to seal the prisoner's fate.

I put a few more questions to the prisoner dealing with the evidence of the servants and Mrs. Jones, most of which he denied, and then concluded with a

JEAN PIERRE VAQUIER LEAVING THE COURT AT GUILDFORD
DURING HIS TRIAL

(Photo: Central Press Photos Ltd.)

reference to Vaquier's statements to the police.

"Do you desire to put suspicion on somebody else in this case?"

"After what I wrote to the police, that is to be understood."

"What do you mean by this: 'I will make known to-morrow who administered the poison'? Who is the person you intended at that time to name to the police next day?"

"I wish to indicate the solicitor of Mrs. Jones who had asked me to buy the poison."

"Is there anybody else whom you intended to name except the solicitor of Mrs. Jones?"

"I said that the solicitor of Mrs. Jones could not have put the poison in the bottle since he had not been there for eight days."

"What did you mean by your statement in which you say this: 'I think the second act of the drama will be the disappearance of the wife of George'?"

"Because George has not perhaps a clear conscience with regard to Mrs. Jones, because he might know something."

"Did you not mean by that suggestion that the next person to be murdered would be George's wife?"

"Yes, since she wished to go away to France."

"And did you mean by this statement to suggest that the murderer would be George?"

"I cannot indicate anyone."

"You knew that Mr. Jones had been murdered?"

"I knew that he had died from poison."

"You knew that the solicitor of Mrs. Jones had made you buy poison?"

M*

"Yes."

"Have you ever until to-day told the police that this solicitor ordered or asked you to buy strychnine?"

"No."

Although Sir Henry Curtis-Bennett shortly re-examined the prisoner no questions could possibly remove the effect this cross-examination had created. As Vaquier returned to the dock, I rose in my place to make an application to the Court that the solicitor to Mrs. Jones, Mr. Bruce Millar, should be allowed to be called as witness.

Mr. Justice Avory immediately assented. Mr. Bruce Millar was called into the witness box, and in answer to my questions indignantly denied that there was a word of truth in Vaquier's evidence; but by that time it was apparent to everyone that Mr. Millar's denial was really quite unnecessary, as nobody in Court could possibly have believed the prisoner's story.

Being anxious that the prisoner, as a foreigner, should have every possible advantage at his trial, I refused to claim the privilege of a law officer to make the final address to the jury, and allowed Sir Henry Curtis-Bennett to have what is usually thought to be the advantage of the last word. Although Sir Henry did his best for the prisoner it was impossible for him to create very much effect, and indeed the only point of his final speech was based upon the curious fact that the only strychnine traced to the prisoner was the small amount of .12 of a gramme specified by Mr. Bland, whereas Sir Bernard Spilsbury had stated in his evidence that at least two grammes were found in the dead man's body. This point assumed even more importance at a very much later stage of this strange story.

Mr. Justice Avory summed up to the jury with the impartiality and clarity which was typical of that most distinguished judge. Only once did a note of his sardonic disbelief creep into his exposition of the evidence. He was discussing the purchase of the poison and the prisoner's remarkable suggestion about the poisoning of the alleged dog. The learned judge referred to the perchloride of mercury.

"Ask yourselves," he said, "what it was bought for. How is it that there is no explanation forthcoming? How is it that there was not somebody else at the Blue Anchor who asked the prisoner to buy some perchloride of mercury in order to kill a cat?"

The jury retired and upon their return found the prisoner GUILTY.

For the first time Vaquier lost his self-control. He screamed that he was innocent, that his trial had been unfair, and he had to be forcibly removed, shouting and raving, from the dock. But this was not the last act of this strange drama. While Vaquier was in prison awaiting execution, information was conveyed to me of a curious statement which he had made from his cell. He alleged that a few days after the murder he had seen from his window at the Blue Anchor a woman, whom he thought to be either one of the servants or Mrs. Jones, go to a building attached to the hotel and apparently conceal something in the wall; and further that he, Vaquier, being curious as to the purpose of the woman, had subsequently gone to the spot, where he found a loose brick in the wall; that he had removed it and that he had found there concealed the identical bottle of strychnine which he had purchased from Mr. Bland.

I directed the police to go at once to the spot indicated and search for themselves. These instructions were carried out, the loose brick was discovered, and behind it a bottle containing nearly 25 grammes of strychnine, which was the amount which Vaquier alleged that he had purchased. The Attorney-General directed that full information of this matter should be supplied to Sir Henry Curtis-Bennett in order that he might make whatever use he desired at the hearing of Vaquier's appeal in the Court of Criminal Appeal. It was, however, quite useless. The Court of Appeal pointed out that such a quantity of strychnine if purchased by Vaquier would completely dispose of the main point of Sir Henry's argument at the trial, that the amount of strychnine found in the dead man's body was in excess of the total amount ever traced to Vaquier's possession. The appeal was dismissed and Vaquier duly suffered the penalty of his crime.

To anyone who took any part in the trial there could have remained no doubt as to the guilt, but the motive for his crime will always remain a mystery. It was clear that his object was not mercenary, as the prosecution never suggested that either the prisoner or Mrs. Jones could ever benefit by the death of her husband. It may be that Vaquier was obsessed by a passion for the dead man's wife, and had some vague hope that if her husband were removed she might return to him. Upon the other hand it was proved that after Vaquier's appearance at the Blue Anchor Hotel there were no illicit relations between himself and Mrs. Jones, and seemed to be no evidence that she ever held out to him the slightest hope that they might be resumed. Undoubtedly Vaquier's outstanding peculiarity was his immense personal vanity, a vanity alone which seemed to be a comparatively slight incentive to a particularly revolting murder. As the learned judge pointed out to the jury, it is never necessary for the prosecution to establish motive as part of the evidence to convict a criminal; on the other hand, from a psychological point of view the motive is perhaps the most interesting problem in the investigation of criminal action. In the case of Jean Pierre Vaquier the motive must remain in doubt and something of a mystery.

CHAPTER VI

Ave atque Vale

It is finished; my share in the drama of the Law is over and the curtain has been rung down. Never again shall I take my place in the arena and join in the battle. I have fought my last fight. All that remains is the inevitable query, has it all been worth while? Is advocacy merely a glorious way of earning a living, or does it serve some useful purpose? Is the advocate himself of any real value to anyone except himself? Perhaps it is only necessary to watch a litigant in person trying to conduct his own case unaided, floundering through a mass of evidence, quite unable to express the simplest point in such a way that anyone can understand it, in order to realise at once that trained advocacy is an absolute necessity to justice; without the advocate Law as we understand it could not survive.

It is the position of the advocate himself which causes so much misunderstanding. It is a great misfortune to the Bar that the community at large knows so little of the principles by which he is guided. If the public mind were better informed, barristers would no more be harrassed by the perpetual enquiry with which they are now confronted: "How can a self-respecting counsel honestly defend a person whom he knows or believes to be guilty? How can he in honesty represent a client whom he believes to be a liar?" Such a question shows a woeful ignorance of the duties and obligations of the English Bar. In truth these duties are quite simple. Inasmuch as a barrister is the only person who has the right of audience in a Superior Court, that right casts upon him the absolute duty to represent to the best of his ability any client who requires his services and is prepared properly to instruct him. In a criminal trial the prisoner is entitled to be represented whether he be innocent or guilty, and the question of his innocence or guilt is no concern of the advocate who appears for him. Moreover that very question never really comes before the Court at all. The issue which a jury is called upon to decide is not, as is popularly supposed, whether the prisoner is innocent or guilty, but whether the prosecution have succeeded in proving conclusively that he is guilty, which is a very different thing. Many a guilty person has been acquitted merely because his advocate has succeeded in destroying, wholly or in part, the evidence which the Crown is able to produce against him. It is no part of the duty of a barrister to form any opinion as to what verdict a jury should return; his task is to place before the Court, with absolute honesty and to the best of his ability, the defence which the prisoner desires to raise. When he has done that his duty is fulfilled.

In a civil action the position is precisely the same.

It is for the jury or the Court to decide which of the parties is telling the truth. Counsel are not bound to form, nor even justified in forming in advance, an opinion of their own, indeed if they attempt to do so the result may well spell disaster. I learned that lesson many years ago. A client came to see me. He was defendant in a civil action and he wanted to tell me his story himself. He prefaced his remarks by stating that he was quite sure I should not believe a single word he said. He may have been right. He told me a story so incredible that I felt that I was in duty bound to warn him of the risk he might be running if he ventured to repeat that story under oath. But he was adamant in his determination and the case was brought to trial. Never in my experience do I remember a civil action which I approached with more reluctance. I should have been glad indeed if my client had entrusted his defence to some counsel other than myself; the result seemed to me a foregone conclusion from the outset. But I was wrong. Every single word that man had told me was the complete and absolute truth. At first his story had appeared incredible and the evidence given by his opponent in the witness box was so plausible that it seemed to carry conviction in its train, until all of a sudden the witness made one small slip; a chink had appeared in a case that seemed unanswerable, and under a prolonged cross-examination that chink widened; the witness began to flounder and prevaricate; vainly he tried to extricate himself from the position in which he had placed himself, but he failed, and in the end he broke down completely, and his action was dismissed. My own client whom at first I had thought to be a liar was proved to be an absolutely honest man. Never again did I try to form a conclusion in advance.

Unthinking criticism of a great profession is not only foolish but might be intensely irritating to anyone who has been a member of that profession, were it not that such criticism is quite unimportant and very soon forgotten. After all, most things are very soon forgotten; even memories of incidents which seemed to be so important at the time tend to disappear, the reason being that in all probability those incidents were never of much importance even when they happened. To anyone who has spent a long life in an endeavour to achieve some modicum of success, sooner or later there will come a time when he is faced with the same old query, "Has it all been worth while?"

The lawyer has to face the question in a particularly concrete form. He has his memories to confront him. He can look back upon long hours spent in preparation for the coming trial, long days in Court fighting for his clients' interests, and in the end sometimes he has won his case. But can he ever be quite sure that it was he who won it? Can advocacy ever win a case? Was it his unstinted efforts that brought about the much deserved result or did the case simply win itself?

The late Mr. Justice Rigby Swift, a most forceful judge, was once dining at a mess dinner on circuit, when he was greeted triumphantly by the circuit leader: "Well, Judge," he said, "I had a good win before you to-day." Rigby Swift was never one to mince his words. "How dare you say you had a win before me? I sit in Court to see that justice is done. In my Court justice *is* done. No counsel ever wins a case before me." The learned judge was very nearly right. I have known so many advocates, good advocates and very good advocates, bad advocates and very bad advocates, and in the result I am satisfied that at least ninety per cent of all cases win or lose themselves, and that the ultimate result would have been the same whatever counsel the parties had chosen to represent them. But of the remaining ten per cent it is not so easy to speak with any certainty. Undoubtedly a case can be lost by bad advocacy; an indiscreet question may let in evidence otherwise inadmissable; an omission to appreciate an important fact may prevent the Court from ever becoming aware of the existence of the most vital element in the case; there are endless ways in which a bad advocate can do his client irreparable harm. But is the antithesis equally true? Can a brilliant advocate ever win a case which without his brilliant advocacy would have been lost? I know that he can; very seldom is it true, but just on those rare occasions which prove the exception to a general rule. Many years ago a member of the racing fraternity was on his trial for murder; he was defended by a thoroughly competent advocate, but the prosecution was in the hands of the Attorney-General of the day, a man of exceptional brilliance. In those days prosecutions were conducted in a somewhat different method from that to which we are now accustomed, and prosecuting counsel were not unknown to strain every effort and to utilise all the arts of advocacy in order to obtain a conviction. It was so in that particular trial. The case swayed backward and forward as each counsel strove to achieve success; but the Attorney-General had the last word and his eloquence turned the scale; the jury returned a verdict of guilty. The somewhat disappointed prisoner turned dejectedly to his warders: "Blimey," he said, "it was the riding wot did it." The racing gentleman was quite right and his words were well chosen. It was in truth the riding which did it. If the owner of a Derby candidate desires to select a jockey for his horse there are probably a hundred between whom there is nothing to choose, all are competent, in the eyes of most observers perhaps equally competent, but amongst them all there is probably one who is possessed of that touch of genius which enables him at a moment of extreme crisis to pull out a little something by means of which he is able to drive his horse home to win by a short head. The fashionable jockey is an expensive luxury and in most cases the expense will be thrown away, but if the stakes are high enough he will never want for patrons, who will employ him just in case the moment should arrive when his genius would be needed and his presence might make all the difference between success and failure. The position is precisely the same in a Court of Law; cases do occur, so rarely that perhaps they can be counted on the fingers of one hand but without doubt they have occurred, in which an advocate has truly won a case.

It would be impossible to state instances of such happenings because no one could be in a position to speak with certainty, indeed amongst all the onlookers in Court probably not one would ever know how much the successful litigant may have owed to the counsel who represented him; at best it can be to most people a matter of surmise, but to an advocate the certainty that such happenings may occur offers one of the prizes which are perpetually dangling before a young man's eyes.

No one yet has ever known what are the qualities which must be possessed by any advocate if he is to reach the highest rank. Some say it is personality; others that it is an ability to seize the one vital element which is to be found in any case; still more consider that the power to cross-examine is the most important quality of all. Each of these wiseacres is wrong. An advocate, to be really great, must possess all three, one is not enough; and perhaps personality is the greatest of them all. No one who has watched the great figures of the past could fail to realise that from time to time one has appeared who outshone all his rivals; when he entered the Court no one else seemed to exist. It was not that he talked louder than his opponents—shouting is merely a cloak for mediocrity—it was simply that he possessed a personality which seemed to dominate the Court. And that is a gift which cannot be acquired; it either exists or it does not. Probably most ambitious advocates think that they possess it; perhaps it tends to their greater content that they should not realise that they have not got it and that they will never find it.

The ability to pick out the one real point of a case is not by itself enough; it is the courage required to seize upon that point to the exclusion of all others that is of real importance. Painstaking solicitors will place before their counsel perhaps fifty different points, all of them prepared with skill and care; it must indeed cause bitter disappointment to find them disregarded and the whole trial proceeding as though there was only one solitary element that was really worthy of consideration. It requires some courage in an advocate to stake his own opinion perhaps against that of all who are assisting him; it is a great risk. But in a proper case he must be prepared to take it.

Undoubtedly the power to cross-examine is the great, perhaps the final, test of advocacy. Every counsel of experience is able to cross-examine a witness, if by that is meant the asking of leading questions in an emphatic tone of voice at the appropriate moment. He can learn from his instructions the questions which he is required to ask, and there are certain rules which have taught him how those questions can best be formulated, but if that is all that he can do he will never be a cross-examiner at all. The true art of cross-examination cannot be learned by experience or taught by rules, it is a gift from the Gods. Perhaps that is why the list of great advocates will always be extremely small. There is no school of advocacy, in all probability no such school would be of any value even if it could exist, but there might be some alternative; if counsel of long experience who have watched the great men of their day would record some hints derived from all that they have learned, they might confer a lasting benefit upon beginners in their own profession. It is the one drawback to the Bar, perhaps the only one, that a barrister builds up nothing that he can leave behind him; his practice dies with him, even he himself is soon forgotten; but he could at least leave behind the benefit of his experiences. He has seen so much. He should be in a position to know the differences between good and bad, he could give some suggestions, even warnings, before his memories have completely faded. Probably no one would pay much attention to him, but at least the experiment might be worth while.

To attempt a comprehensive definition of anything is difficult, if not impossible, and the word cross-examination is no exception to the rule. The most one can ever hope to do is to formulate in one's own mind the one essential element without which all others are completely useless. For so many years of my life I have cross-examined and watched others cross-examine that I have satisfied myself that no advocate will be of much value unless he possesses the knack, if that is the right word, of assessing accurately and almost instantaneously the personality and the mentality of the witness who is facing him. That is why it is impossible to prepare a cross-examination in advance. How can it be possible to know in advance how to cross-examine a witness you have never seen? Some counsel even prepare notes for their cross-examination. Oh, how I hate those notes! If you can't remember the details of your own case without notes, you must have a very bad memory. Some spend the time during which the witness is being examined in laboriously writing down every word that he is saying, without realising that they are wasting the golden opportunity of studying the witness himself. He may even be a truthful witness, and no one in the world can cross-examine a person who is telling the truth; it may be possible to suggest that he is mistaken, or inaccurate, or even stupid, but any attempt to suggest that he is lying is to court immediate and well-deserved disaster, and the disaster will not be averted by addressing him through the medium of a bundle of carefully prepared notes. It is only by the most careful and meticulous consideration that anyone can decide if the witness be truthful or dishonest, stupid or cunning, intelligent or foolish, and it is not until that decision has been made that it is any use thinking of the questions to be asked or the method of attack. And even that is not enough. It is the first question that really counts. That first question may very well be the turning point in the whole case; it may completely destroy the effect created by the witness; it may change the whole atmosphere in the Court. That is why it is absolute folly for an advocate to decide how to begin his cross-examination until the very last second before he rises to his feet. There must be some weakness in the story he has just heard; he has got to find it and stick to it. A lying witness has been giving the most plausible and convincing evidence; the atmosphere throughout the Court is wholly in his favour; there is a smile of absolute self-confidence upon his face as he completes that evidence and he faces with contemptuous superiority the counsel who rises to cross-examine him. And then—Bang! Out comes the first question. The witness is completely non-plussed. The question is one of which he never dreamed; he was not prepared for it—what can his opponents have found out against him—he wants a little time to think of the best explanation to invent on the spur of the moment. In a flash his self-confidence has gone; the smile disappears from his face and the atmosphere which has hitherto been so encouraging to him begins to change, that strange electric atmosphere coming from the back of the Court which every counsel knows and which tells him with certainty whether or not his questions are having the desired effect: formerly it was friendly to the witness; now it becomes tinged first with doubt and ultimately with hostility. The case which was so overwhelming in its honesty begins to weaken, and all from that first and vital question, selected at the last moment from a host of others. How can such a question be chosen in advance—and above all from notes?

Every member of the Bar knows full well that strange electric atmosphere which permeates a Court of Justice. No one knows exactly from where it springs, but it sweeps backwards and forwards through the Court as though to guide the cross-examiner upon his course. It may be encouraging or hostile, and if it be hostile the wise advocate knows that he has struck a wrong note; he must change the whole conduct of his case, and if possible he must make the change in such a way that nobody must know that it is being made. That electric atmosphere is the only guide that he will ever get and he must always take it. There have been some who have told me that they get all the guidance they require from the faces of the jury. Personally, I don't believe it; but of this I am quite sure: anyone who is insensible to atmosphere will never be any good.

Once launched upon a cross-examination there is one rule that must be rigorously enforced. Never permit assistance from outsiders. Two people cannot possibly cross-examine the same witness at the same time. I have watched enthusiastic juniors assisting their leaders with repeated interruptions. I have seen equally enthusiastic solicitors rising to their feet in order to remind their counsel of some apparently forgotten point. Personally that is not a practice which I encourage; indeed I was once constrained to curb the repeated and indeed perpetual offers of assistance by a particularly irrepressible client by hitting him upon the head with a volume of the *Law Reports* in order to persuade him to resume his seat. That is not a practice I would recommend to a beginner in his profession, as hitting solicitors with law books might well tend to decrease their practice. It is only to be adopted in very extreme cases, as a necessary reminder that the cross-examiner must be left alone. He may be good, bad, or indifferent, but anyhow he will not be improved by interruption.

There is one other question to be selected which

is almost as important as the first, and that is the last. The witness must not be allowed to leave behind too favourable an impression as he quits the box. He may have had time to rehabilitate himself during the course of a cross-examination, which is often much too long, and he may even have partially regained the pedestal from which he had been temporarily displaced; but he must not be allowed to remain upon it; he has been knocked off it once with the first question he was asked; he must go down again with the last. If those two questions have been well chosen the rest of the cross-examination will probably fall into line. The difficulty lies in choosing them.

Inasmuch as I shall never again be called upon to select them for myself, it becomes quite immaterial whether my ideas for cross-examination are good or bad, at any rate I strongly advise everyone to disregard them; advice from others is useless and often harmful. Each must decide his own method for himself and at the end he will remain uncertain as to whether his own method was good or bad. But at least he will be certain of one thing. If he has decided to practice at the English Bar, he will have lived his life amidst glorious surroundings; he will have fought bitter fights with gallant and generous opponents, all of whom will remain his dearest friends. He will have received sympathy in his disasters and ungrudging generosity in his successes; he will have toiled for days and nights at work that has never palled, and at the end he will know beyond any possibility of doubt that his work has been well worth while.

INDEX

Abrahams, Mr., 110, 111, 166–180
Addison, Mr. (afterwards Viscount), 116, 118, 119, 121, 122, 126, 127
Advocate, duty of, x
Alverstone, Lord, 303
American Viscose Co., 196–205
Appropriation Bill (American), 198–202
Assize Courts, 154, 259, 292, 313
Avory, Mr. Justice, 33, 38, 39, 322, 323, 325

Bab Ballads, 101, 105
Bar (English), x, xii. xiv, xv, 38, 326, 327
Barney, Mrs. Elvira Dolores, 245, 263–278
Bedfont Plate Handicap, 74
Bevan, Mr. Stuart, K.C., 139–141, 215, 225
Birkett, Mr. Norman, K.C., 139, 141–143
Bishops Stortford, 56
Bland, Mr. (chemist), 308, 313, 316, 322, 324
Blennerhassett, Mr., 100–106
Blue Anchor, The, Byfleet, 306–325
Bocking (Courtauld factory at), 196
Booth, Frederick Handel, 108, 114–128
Borstal prison, 156
Bournemouth, 56
Braintree (Courtauld factory at), 196
Branson, Mr. Justice, 104, 106
British Broadcasting Corporation, 67, 84, 85, 87, 88, 90, 94–98
British Film Institute, 84–87, 91, 95
British Government, 113, 151, 152, 195–207, 215
British Guiana (diamonds discovery in), 130, 134, 135, 136
Byfleet, Surrey, 306

"Captain X" (Polish officer), 279–291

Carson, Edward, xii
Central Criminal Court, 41, 44, 49, 50, 208–228, 231–235, 245, 247–248, 267–278, 279–291
Chamber of Shipping, 213
Chancellor of the Exchequer, 195, 200, 206
Channell, Mr. Justice, 300
Chapman, Mr. (trainer), 25, 72–83
Charles, Mr. Justice, 188, 194
Chekodieff, Prince (film character), 32, 33, 36, 37
Churchill, Mr. (fire-arms expert), 267
Clarke, Sir Percival, K.C., 270, 271, 275
Cobham (Talking Mongoose case), 90, 91
Coen, Victor, 136–144
Coleman, John (veterinary surgeon), 5
Coleman, Mr. (solicitor), 269
Coleridge, Lord, 123
Conservative Party, 64
Council of Peoples' Commissaries, 150–152
"Countess, The," 293, 294
Court of Appeal, 81, 82, 151, 164, 235
Court of Criminal Appeal, 249, 262, 303, 324
Courtauld, Augustine, 195
Courtauld, George, 195
Courtaulds Ltd., 113, 195–207
Courtauld, Samuel, 195, 196, 200, 201
Crime, 208–209
Curtis-Bennett, Sir Henry, K.C., 313–315, 322, 324
Czar of Russia, 26, 28, 29, 31, 145
Czarevitch of Russia, 28, 31, 145
Czarina of Russia, 28, 31, 145

Daily Sketch, 254
Darling, Sir Malcolm, 67
Day, Mr. (bookmaker), 169
Day, Wentworth, 56, 57, 61
Defence of the Realm Acts, 119
"Deirdre," 181–194
Devilling, 2–3

INDEX

Diamond Syndicate, 110, 129–144
Director of Public Prosecutions, 194
"Doctor X," 157, 159, 160, 163, 164
Don Pat (a racehorse), 73, 75, 76, 77, 81
Doyle (Gambler's Story case), 229, 230, 231
du Maurier, Gerald, xi–xii

Eastbourne (Hooded Man case), 292, 293, 294
Election of Parliament, 1945, 55, 58
Emergency Powers Act, 201
Evening Standard, The, 101, 103, 105
"Evil Eye, The," 87, 91, 92, 93

Financial Times, 100
Finnemore, Mr. Douglas, K.C., 259
Frampton, Mr. Walter, K.C., 266
Fuller, Mr. (Talking Mongoose case), 95

"Gambler, The," 229–235
Gaming Acts, The, 48, 53
George (potman—Vaquier case), 312, 315, 321
Gellygaer, Wales (Blazing Car case), 250, 254, 255, 259, 260
Gill, C. F., K.C., 232, 233
Gruban, John, 108, 114–128
Guildford Assizes, 313
Guildhall (London), 219, 220

Hall, Sir Edward Marshall, 288, 313
Hardingstone, Northampton (Blazing Car case), 249, 254, 260
Harnett, W. S., 100, 155–165
Harvey, W., 169–180
Hastings, Lady, 303
Hastings, Patrick (afterwards Sir), chooses the Law, ix; ponderous oratory, xi; last day in Court, 1–3; devilling, 3; first brief, 4; vans and horses, 4–6; old ladies and omnibuses, 6–13; Lord Chief Justice's Court, 13–21; libel and slander cases, 22–106; tribute to juries, 107–8; junior advocates, 108–110; dislike of breach of promise, 111–112; miscellaneous cases, 114–207; criminal cases, 208–243; murder, 244–325; advocacy and justice, 326; issue before; the jury, 327; cases mainly decide themselves, 330; qualities for successful advocacy, 332; staking own opinion, 333; cross-examination, 333; one drawback, 334; hating cross-examination notes, 334–6; Court atmosphere, 336–7; the first and last question, 338
Hatton Garden, 236–243
Haunting of Cashens' Gap, The, 86
Hemmerde, E. G., K.C., 188, 189
Hereford West, County of, 213
Hinchingbrooke, Lord, 67
Hogg, Mr. Douglas (afterwards Lord Hailsham), 123
Hooded Man, The, 246, 292–304
Horne "Drinking," 41, 46, 47, 50
Horridge, Mr. Justice, 79, 80, 81
Humphreys, Mr. Justice, 269, 272, 278, 290

Imperial Court of Russia, St. Petersburg, 26, 27, 28, 29, 37
Isaacs, Rufus, K.C., 42 (see Lord Reading)
Isolationists (American), 198–200
Ivan the Terrible, 26

"Jeff", a mongoose, 86
Jockey Club, 25, 72–83
Joel, Jack, 41, 43, 44, 50, 51, 52
Joel, Solly, 129, 134, 229, 230, 231
Joel, Woolf, 230, 233
Jones, Mr. (Vaquier case), 306–324
Jones, Mrs. Mabel Theresa, 305–325
Juries (English), 107, 114, 128, 275
Justice (English), x, xi, xiii, 107, 114, 120, 259

"Kathleen," 181–194
Kempton Park Racecourse, 74
King's Bench Division, 104

Kylsant, Lord, 211, 213-228

Labour Party, 55, 67, 70
Ladbroke, Messrs., 170
Lambert, Mr. (editor), 24, 84-99
Laski, Harold, 24, 55-71
Law, xi, xii, xiii, 25, 79, 81, 82, 107, 112, 153, 273, 292, 301
Law reports, xii, xiii, 337
Lawrence, Mr. Justice, 174
Lend-Lease Bill, 198-200, 207
Levita, Lady, 84-86
Levita, Sir Cecil, 24, 84-99
Lewes Assizes, 292, 300
Libel and Slander, 22-106
Lichtenberg (diamonds discovery at), 134
"Lieut. Y" (Polish officer), 280, 281, 282
Listener, The, 84
Lloyd George, David, 114, 115
Lloyds Underwriters, 236
London Chamber of Commerce, 213
London Council for Physical Research, 85, 86, 89
London County Council, 85
London Stock Exchange, 100, 103, 104, 105
Lord Chief Justice's Court, 1-3, 13-21, 26-39, 44-54, 55-71
Lost Pearls, The, 212, 236-243
Low, Sir Frederick, K.C., 300, 301
Lucy, A. B., K.C., 313
Lunacy Acts, 157, 159, 160, 163
Lunacy, Commissioner of, 158, 159, 160, 161, 163, 164
Lush, Mr. Justice, 160, 164
Lusitania, S.S., 108, 123

MacKinnon, Mr. Justice, 148, 153
"Madame X," 280
Man, Isle of (Talking Mongoose case), 85, 86
Marconi Scandals, 114
Mathew, Theobald, K.C., xv
Matthews, J. B., K.C., 17, 18, 160
McCardie, Mr. Justice, 139, 142, 143
McClintock, Sir William, 219
McNulty, Mr., 101, 106
Maher, Danny, 229, 230
Melbourne Club, 48

Metro-Goldwyn-Mayer Pictures Corporation, 26, 31, 32
Meyer, Max, 236
Middle Temple, x
Millar, Mr. Bruce, 322
Mills, Mr. (Sievier case), 42, 49, 50, 51, 52
Moika Palace, St. Petersburg, 26, 27, 30, 35, 38
Monte Carlo, 41, 46, 47
Moreland, Harold, 211, 213-228
Munitions, Ministry of, 117, 118, 121, 126, 127
Murder cases, 244-247
Murray, Gladstone, 24, 85, 87, 88, 90, 92, 93, 94

Neale, Sir Phené, 219, 220, 225
Newark (Laski case), 24, 56, 60, 61, 62, 69
Newark Advertiser, 56-59
Newmarket Heath, 25, 72, 75, 76
Norman, Mr. (of B.B.C.), 87, 90, 92, 94
Nottingham Guardian, 58, 61

Oppenheimer, Otto, 110, 131-144

Paley Palace, 145, 147, 150, 151, 153
Paley, Princess Olga, 110, 145-153
Pari-Mutuel Ltd., 169
Parliamentary Commission, 84, 98
Paul of Russia, Grand Duke, 145, 146
Pennsylvania (American Viscose Co.), 196, 197
Perez, Mr. (Diamond Syndicate case), 131, 132, 137
Pimm's Restaurant, 102, 104, 105
Plender, Lord, 220-225
Power (Hooded Man case), 293, 294, 295, 297, 298, 299, 301, 302
Press, xii, 78, 80, 112, 185, 186, 262, 266, 298, 313
Price & Gibbs, 236
Price, Harry, 85, 86, 87, 91
Price, Mr. (of Price & Gibbs), 236-243
Psychology of murderers, 249

INDEX

Racing Calendar, 72, 76, 77, 80, 81, 82
Racing Rules, 75, 76, 77, 80
Rasputin, Grigory E. (Russian monk), 26–39
Rasputin the Mad Monk, film, 32, 33, 37, 38
Rayon industry, 196
Reading, Lord, 42, 44, 49
Reflections on the Revolution of our Times, 59
Reforms, period of, xi
Rhodes, Cecil, 129
Richmond and Gordon, Duke of, 78
"Robinson, Mr.," 181–194
"Robinson, Mrs.," 182
Roome, Mr. H. D., K.C., 313
Roosevelt, F. D. (President, U.S.A.), 198, 200
Rouse, Alfred Arthur, 248, 249–262
Royal Courts of Justice, xii, 22–39, 44–54, 77, 104–106, 111, 145–153, 188–194
Royal Mail Steamship Co., 213–228
Russell Hotel, London, 307, 308
Russell, on Crimes, 60
Russian Government, 146, 147, 153
Russian Law, 147, 150, 151, 152
Russian Revolution, 26, 31, 110, 145, 146, 148, 152

St. Petersburg, 110, 145, 146, 150
Sandown Park Race Course, 5
Sankey, Mr. Justice, 120
Sceptre (a racehorse), 40
Sievier, Punch, 48
Sievier, Robert Standish, 23, 40–54
Simon, Sir John, K.C., 215, 222, 225, 226
Simonds, Mr. Justice, 204
Singleton, J. E., K.C., 215
South Africa (diamond mines), 129
Soviet Republic, 148, 151, 152, 153
Spilsbury, Sir Bernard, 267, 268, 269, 270, 272, 282, 283, 285, 288, 322

"Spitting Joe," xiv, xv
Stephens, Scott (Mrs. Barney case), 263, 264, 265, 275, 277
Submit (a racehorse), 5
"Susan," 181–194
Swift, Mr. Rigby, K.C. (afterwards Mr. Justice Swift), 90, 123, 124, 127, 329, 330
Synot, Mr. (solicitor), 121, 122

Talbot, Mr. Justice, 259, 261
Talking Mongoose, The, 24, 87, 91, 99
Tallents, Sir Stephen, 90, 95, 96, 97
Tally Ho Corner, Barnet (Blazing Car case), 253, 260
Times, The, 76, 77, 81, 82
Topping, Mr., 42, 52, 53
Treasury, The, 202, 204, 214, 215
Tsarskoe, Seloe, 145, 150
Twain, Mark, 105

United Diamond Fields of British Guiana Ltd., 129–144

van Antwerpen, Mr., 138, 141, 142
Vaquier, Jean Pierre, 246, 305–325
Victoria Hotel, Biarritz (Vaquier case), 305, 306
Virginia (American Viscose Co.), 197

Waldorf Hotel, 189, 191
Walton Heath (golf course), 105
Weatherby, Messrs., 81, 82
Weisz, Mr., 146, 147, 148
Whiteley, Mr. Cecil, K.C., 300
Williams, John, 292–304
Winning Post, The, 41
Wootten, Frank, 42
Wootten, Richard, 42–54
Wootten, Stanley, 42
World War II, 198
Wright, Mr. Justice, 221, 227

Younger, Mr. Justice, 120
Youssupoff, Prince Felix, 26–39
Youssupoff, Princess Irena Alexandrovna, 23, 26–39
Yo-Yo (a game), 25, 100–106